QUENTIN

QUENTIN CRISP

The Profession of Being.
A Biography

Nigel Kelly

Foreword by Guy Kettelhack

McFarland & Company, Inc., Publishers
Jefferson, North Carolina, and London

LIBRARY OF CONGRESS CATALOGUING-IN-PUBLICATION DATA

Kelly, Nigel, 1963–
    Quentin Crisp : the profession of being. A biography /
Nigel Kelly ; foreword by Guy Kettelhack.
        p.   cm.
    Includes bibliographical references and index.

    ISBN 978-0-7864-6475-3 ∞
    softcover : 50# alkaline paper

    1. Crisp, Quentin.   2. Gay men — Great Britain —
Biography   3. Gay men — United States — Biography.
4. Authors, English — 20th century — Biography.   I. Title.
HQ75.8.C74K45 2011
306.76'62092 — dc23
[B]   2011038946

BRITISH LIBRARY CATALOGUING DATA ARE AVAILABLE

On the cover: Quentin Crisp portrait by Maurice Heerdink
(www.mauriceheerdink.com)

Manufactured in the United States of America

McFarland & Company, Inc., Publishers
  Box 611, Jefferson, North Carolina 28640
    www.mcfarlandpub.com

To my wife Karen and sister Heather
for all their love, support and
encouragement down the years

Table of Contents

Acknowledgments

When I think about how many people have helped me with this book I realize just how much of a collaborative effort it has been. Without them all it would be so much less, and I know how much I owe them.

So here they are:

Performance artist Penny Arcade knew Quentin for the last eighteen years of his life and was a constant support to him, especially during the last years. In 1992 he named her his "anima figure." Penny created *The Last Will and Testament of Quentin Crisp*, which they performed together for many years until his death. They also appeared together in *An Evening with Quentin Crisp and Penny Arcade*. Penny is a significant figure in the biographical film about Quentin, *An Englishman in New York*.

Guy Kettelhack was a friend of Quentin's throughout his time in America. Guy's book *The Wit and Wisdom of Quentin Crisp* is a wonderful compendium of all things Crispian and he became known as a "Crisp expert." Guy was an influential figure during Quentin's years in America both professionally and as a friend. He was also Quentin's executor for many years. I owe him a huge thank you for his wonderful foreword.

Phillip Ward knew Quentin during the last fourteen years of his life, and particularly during the last years was a constant practical and emotional support. I also owe him thanks for allowing me to use extracts from Quentin's last as yet unpublished book, "The Dusty Answers," and material from the *Quentin Crisp Archives*, and for giving me his permission to use the many quotes from Quentin which appear throughout the book. Phillip is Quentin's executor and runs the *Quentin Crisp Archives* on the Internet.

Tom Steele first met Quentin shortly after his move to America and the two remained close friends until Quentin's death. Tom was associate publisher and editor of *Theatre Week*, *Christopher Street* (for which Quentin wrote film reviews), *Opera Monthly*, and the *New York Native* (for which Quentin wrote a weekly diary). Tom was also one of Quentin's most frequent cinema companions during his years in America. Tom is a major figure in the new film *An Englishman in New York*, in which, for dramatic reasons, his character is amalgamated with

Phillip Ward (Quentin's executor). Tom gave me some invaluable advice about publishing.

Richard Gollner knew Quentin for thirty years, from the late 1960s until his death. Richard was Quentin's agent and later manager, and accompanied Quentin on his first visits to the United States and elsewhere. Richard worked with Quentin on creating his one-man show, *An Evening with Quentin Crisp*, in 1975, which he produced and directed. At this writing Richard works as a literary agent in London.

David Leddick, during an amazing life, has not only been a naval officer but a dancer at the New York Metropolitan Opera, worldwide creative director for Revlon and international creative director for L'Oreal, a novelist and biographer, an actor and cabaret entertainer. He knew Quentin for the last twenty years of his life and created *Quentin and I: A Mini-Musical* as a tribute to his late friend. He deserves thanks for allowing me to use material from his show *Quentin and I.*

Louis Colaianni knew Quentin for many years and ran a Web site called the *Quentin Crisp Museum*. He is a prominent voice and text coach in the professional theatre. He is an adjunct associate professor at Vassar College; teaches at The Actors Studio; and was associate professor at the University of Missouri–Kansas City.

I am also indebted to the late film producer June Lang. June was one of the first of Quentin's friends to make contact with me after I launched a Web site dedicated to him, *Quentin Crips Info* (www.quentincrisp.info). She was so supportive and encouraging. We remained in regular contact after that, talking about Quentin and her latest projects. She produced the short film *My Lunch with Quentin Crisp* as her tribute to her friend. Quentin also featured in her documentary *Farewell to the Deuce*. Sadly, she passed away in August 2008 from cancer. I am sorry she did not get to see the book in print; she would have been so pleased.

John W. Mills first met Quentin in 1947 and formed a friendship with him which would last for decades. I think you will find some of his memories very interesting.

My thanks to Quentin's nieces, Denise Pratt-Renner, Elaine Pratt-Goycoolea and Frances Ramsay, his great-niece Michèle Elaine Goycoolea Crawford and his great-nephew filmmaker Adrian Goycoolea for helping me fill out their family tree. Thanks also to Adrian for giving me a copy of his film about Quentin, *Uncle Denis*; more on this at the end of the book.

Writer, actor and producer David-Elijah Nahmod produced the film *Red Ribbons*, which starred Quentin, and wrote and starred in the short film *Aunt Fannie*, in which Quentin played the title character. Writer and director Neil Ira Needleman produced the films *Aunt Fannie*, *Red Ribbons* and wrote and directed the film *Famous Again* in which Quentin also appeared. Georgina Spelvin starred with Quentin in the films *Red Ribbons* and *Famous Again*. Georgina has written the first volume of her autobiography, *The Devil Made Me Do It*, and is currently working on volume two. Sara Moore wrote and directed *Homo Heights*, in which Quentin gave his last feature-length acting performance.

David Hartnell has had a highly successful career as a makeup artist and has worked with many legends of the film world from Mae West to Joan Collins. In 1978 he was in New Zealand and did Quentin's makeup for his tour, as well as helping out during the stage performances. I owe David a big thank you for his advance publicity for my book.

My gratitude is extended to the following people for their generous contributions to this work. Film actor and stage performer Stephen Sorrentino, who co-starred with Quentin in the film *Homo, aka Happy Heights*, gave me permission to retell his story of how Quentin got his name. Morgan Fisher told me about his experiences interviewing Quentin in London in 1980 and allowed me to use his photographs.

Michael Andersen-Andrade (Connie Clausen's son) allowed me to use the photos of his mother. Character actor Richard Louis James allowed me to use a photo from his one-man show *Tea 'N' Crisp*, in which he brings Quentin back to life in the format of *An Evening with Quentin Crisp*, updated for the twenty-first century. My thanks also to the photographer, John D. Kysela. Screen and stage actor Leon Acord permitted me to use the photo of him as Quentin in Jeffrey Hartgraves's play *Carved in Stone*. Leon reprised his role in Los Angeles in the spring of 2009. My thanks go also to the photographer, Peter Solari, for giving me permission to use it.

Tim Fountain, author of the play *Resident Alien: Quentin Crisp Explains it All*. Tim is also the author of the biographical book *Quentin Crisp* and made the television documentary *The Significant Death of Quentin Crisp*. Actor John Watson provided the photo of him as Quentin in the New Zealand production of *Resident Alien*. I would also like to thank John for putting me in touch with David Hartnell. Also, my thanks to the photographer Maxwell John Osborne.

Photographer David Whitworth shared his experience of meeting Quentin in New York on New Year's Day 1997 and permitted me to use his photographs. Designer Miguel Adrover talked to me about knowing Quentin in New York and his Quentin Crisp mattress overcoat creation (it will all make sense when you've read the book). I also owe a thank you to Miguel's assistant Lluis Corujo.

Thank you to Richard Laxton (director of *An Englishman in New York*), to James Burstall, who is CEO of Leopard Films, and to actor John Hurt for giving me their permission to use a photograph from the film. Thanks to Joanna Nicholas, James Burstall's personal assistant, and to Jessica Sykes and Jennie Miller, assistants to Richard Laxton.

Maurice Heerdink allowed me to use his beautiful portrait of Quentin on the front cover of this book. Maurice is a dedicated admirer of Quentin and shared with me his wealth of knowledge.

To L. Brandon Krall, my thanks for sharing her experiences of meeting and filming Quentin during his 90th birthday run of *An Evening with Quentin Crisp* at the Intar Theatre.

Victory Van-Dyke Chase for all her efforts in getting me material for the book.

My gratitude to Raymond Luczak for letting me use his photograph of Quentin Crisp and Tom Steele doing their rat-face.

So many people were, throughout, wonderfully supportive and encouraging. They took time out of their busy schedules to respond to my contacts, answer my questions and supply so much material and help. Penny, Guy, Phillip and Tom all read my manuscript. Phillip once said to me, "I want your book to be the best it can be." I suspect there were times when I became a nuisance but they never once complained or refused a request. I do not now remember which of them it was who told me years ago that they would have done anything for Quentin while he was alive and still would. When I finally told them I had found a publisher, they were so delighted. Louis Colaianni said, "If Quentin is watching, he is smiling." It is a testament not just to each of them, but also I think to the person Quentin was, that they so wholeheartedly participated in the creation of this book. It has been a privilege to have made contact with them and in a small way to have gotten to know them.

My sincerest thanks and admiration to you all.

A special thank you is extended to the following.

My sister Heather Kelly, who proofread my manuscript so many times, corrected my spelling and grammar and spotted those split infinitives. Heather quoted Quentin in her master's dissertation and was a valuable sounding board for ideas.

My wife Karen Curlett Kelly, who as always was totally supportive, encouraging and understanding throughout, and without whom nothing would be possible. She drew up the family tree at the end of the book, helped with images and so much more.

I would also like to thank artist Tommy Barr for putting the idea of writing a book in my mind, though neither he nor I realized it at the time. He was my first "public" reader.

Lastly but by no means least, there is of course Quentin Crisp himself. So many times I found myself floundering, not knowing how to proceed, how to phrase something. At these times I would remind myself of Quentin's advice about writing: "All you have to ask yourself is, have you said what you meant to say." It always got me moving again.

Thanks, Quentin.

Foreword by Guy Kettelhack

I can think to offer no higher praise of Nigel Kelly's warm, straightforward, detailed account of Quentin Crisp's life than to say that its abiding effects are conversational. Mr. Kelly provides as simple and direct an extended answer as can be imagined to the question, "Who was Quentin Crisp?" As if over coffee at Quentin's favorite East Village diner in Manhattan, most readers will, I think, enjoy a sense of "settling in" with Nigel Kelly to hear a full report of a very rich life — full of incident, art, writing, theatre, travel, family, friendship, losses and gains: indeed, a much more "normal" life than one might have expected from the P.R. (which Quentin Crisp, of course, did nothing to discourage), promoting the persona of a sort of lost waif — an ill-equipped creature cast upon the waters of "fate" who initiated no choice beyond that which resulted in his remarkable appearance. "What else could I do?" is a *quint*essentially Crispian (and maybe not rhetorical) question.

Of course the question of who Quentin Crisp was remains, and surely will always remain, a conundrum. But one of the challenges — perhaps obstacles — to gaining entry to the Realm of Crisp through the writings of others, is that nearly every writer who's opined about him — myself included — has largely not been able to keep from appropriating Crisp for his or her own uses. I was introduced to Quentin Crisp in 1982, shortly after I signed on as his agent Connie Clausen's assistant. It was the beginning of an extraordinary friendship which, because it was involved with business (that is, the sacred object of getting Quentin money), became quite powerful, I'd like to think, in both our lives.

A word about Connie Clausen, which, simply because I'm one of the few still here to report on her friendship with Quentin, I seem all too singularly able to provide. She and Quentin adored each other — so comment is called for. Connie was a brilliant, beautiful, exasperating force of life — blonde and Wisconsin-raised — as American as Quentin was not. She'd had a stormy life full of dramatic rises and falls, which saw her going from being a pink tutued girl on the back of an elephant in the Barnum and Bailey circus (about which she later wrote a vibrant memoir), to working at MGM publicity during the heyday of Rooney and Garland, to acting on Broadway and television, to discovering *Jonathan Livingston Seagull* and *Watership Down* at Macmillan (which instantly made her a vice-president), to starting her own literary agency on the proceeds of a settlement she'd received from New York City for having fallen down an open manhole — well, that gives you the barest sense of the wild ride. She'd seen Quentin perform in 1981, I believe, and was instantly smitten: decided right then and there that she had to represent him. Quentin (surely reiterating his eternal "I want what you want") happily agreed. Thus began an extraordinary bond — which I was privileged to observe from the front row — which consisted for me, often enough, of sitting at their knees during scotch-and-spaghetti dinners to which Quentin would bus uptown weekly. Hollywood, to both Quentin and Connie, was Olympus — or anyway, had been during its heyday. I was privy to a charmed love — Connie with her good-natured cursing, Quentin with his incisive very funny "politesse." It was the first clue of many — many more provided by Nigel Kelly in this biography — that Quentin Crisp was, despite many rumors to the contrary, a very happy man.

Talk to anyone who knew Quentin in as particular a way, and you'll receive a flood of anecdotes. It's my contention that you could get to know the essential Quentin Crisp merely by having lunch with him at his favorite diner — you could, anyway, if you were paying attention. He gave himself unstintingly to anyone who asked. Of course what you made of what he gave you wasn't his business. And indeed, a lot has been written and said about him which always says more about the observer than about Crisp.

Not that Quentin minded this — or would mind now. He expected it, and applauded it. (It was publicity, which he craved!) Like two of the icons he most revered, Greta Garbo and Andy Warhol, he wanted only to provide a "blank canvas" onto which others might feel free to paint their own pictures — which virtually always became self-portraits. We are, as Quentin believed, not trapped but liberated by our own points of view. We may be all we have, but oh — the wonders that embracing our idiosyncrasies can bring to life — and to engaging with each other! The shows we can put on! (Like the Connie-and-Quentin show.)

So, we have a not inconsiderable body of articles (academic and otherwise), plays, biographies, memoirs, films and one-man/woman-shows created either by those who "knew Quentin when" or who for some ideological or personal or mercantile reason felt that he represented something crucial which required expression — but which, whatever their merits or failings, can't allow us to see the unadorned Crisp.

Nigel Kelly has come closest to anyone I've read to doing just that: not only by providing a clear narrative of Crisp's life — but by regularly punctuating it with Crisp's own words. I don't think I've ever heard Quentin Crisp emerge more strikingly, in a context provided by someone other than himself, than in this book. Crisp's sharpness, acuity, wit, intelligence all gleam herein — not least because of the marvelously unobtrusive frame Nigel Kelly provides.

The only fault I can find in Nigel Kelly's modesty is that he says virtually nothing about himself. He will, I hope, forgive me for telling what I know about him. I had the pleasure of meeting Nigel and his wife, Karen, on a very wet Thanksgiving night in London in 2009. He and Karen hadn't been to London for some years — they live in a town in Northern Ireland — so I had the welcome sense that this was as much a special trip for them as it was for me. Circumstantially, things couldn't have gone worse. Not only was it raining hard, but the Chelsea pub (one I had thought from the outside would be civilized and quiet enough for conversation; it also wasn't far from the Chelsea Arts Club which figures in Quentin's past) and the South Kensington restaurant to which I dragged the long-suffering Kellys were rowdy and noisy and we had, virtually, to shout at each other to be heard. But what amiable shouting it turned out to be. Following Quentin's example, we soldiered on — wet, deafened and bedraggled. We had a great and gratifying time.

Nigel Kelly told me he was a boy in his early teens when he first saw *The Naked Civil Servant* on television. He lived in a then still very war-torn part of Northern Ireland, collectively a society in which revealing "who you were" had great and often fatal consequences. Nigel was riveted by Crisp's courage: by this tale of a man who clearly didn't feel he could be anything other than "who he was." He began what has turned into a lifelong fascination with Quentin Crisp, whom he regarded then, and regards now, quite simply as a hero. Chance, luck, interest and receptivity alerted him to various opportunities which have led him to a worldwide correspondence with Crisp's friends, Crispian "experts" and other aficionados via a Web site he constructed for the purpose, which have led him to the writing of this book.

Nigel will, I hope, forgive me for outing him as a heterosexual — which I do here only to underscore that "sexuality" or a "gay" identification with Quentin Crisp, isn't, as it has been for so many others, what's drawn him to Crisp. Nigel seems to me to have "gotten" Quentin Crisp in a very rare way: he sees the man without defensiveness. I'm not sure one can say that about very many other Crisp observers. His interest here is, I believe, in teasing out the particulars of whatever gave rise to the phenomenon of a man who so evidently, heroically (and for so long) was able to "be himself." This degree of self-realization took something extraordinary — something which will always deserve our attention and curiosity. Nigel Kelly does his considerable unpretentious best to offer us, if not explanation, then at least a better sense of the context and details of Crisp's life which underlie this "achievement of self" than we've had from anyone else.

Do please sit down now with Mr. Kelly's story of Mr. Crisp, and find this out for yourself. You'll enjoy the conversation. Then, as I think you will want to do, return to the extraordinary words of Quentin Crisp himself— words to which this book provides a wonderfully welcome and useful introduction.

Guy Kettelhack is the editor and compiler of The Wit and Wisdom of Quentin Crisp *and, with Connie Clausen, Crisp's former New York agent.*

Preface

When Quentin first started doing his one-man shows in the mid 1970s, he would introduce them as "a straight talk from a bent speaker!"[1] When someone objected to this phrase he introduced his next show thus: "I have been forbidden to introduce this evening as a straight talk from a bent speaker!"[2] I think I would introduce this book as "A straight talk about a bent speaker."

Like most people of my generation I first became aware of Mr. Crisp with the televising of his autobiography *The Naked Civil Servant*. I was still in high school at the time but I do not think any other film has had such impact on my life. Here was one of the most extraordinary human beings I had ever seen. He was a man of such integrity, intelligence, courage and humanity that he became for me a representative of the best a human being could be, a true life hero. Over the succeeding decades, as I followed his life and read as many of his books as I could (though it would be many years before some of his other books would be available to me), I started to realize that his greatest attribute was his philosophy, which was profound and unique. His was a "real-life" philosophy, and he actually lived by it. It is his greatest legacy to the world. His philosophy has become known as *Crisperanto*, a term Quentin himself first used in the American edition of his second autobiography, *How to Become a Virgin*.

When at the end of 1999 I heard of his death I was shocked and saddened, even though he was almost ninety-one years old. After the initial shock, I felt I wanted to try to keep his memory and legacy alive, and try to enlighten those who might not know about him. I am a Web developer and was aware that only a few Web sites existed about Mr. Crisp. So I decided to develop one. I called it www.quentincrisp.info because I wished it to be first and foremost an information resource about Quentin. The site was launched in early 2000, and since then I have been contacted by many people who have told me how much they have learned about Quentin from it. I have also been con-

5

tacted by students who have used the site as a resource for their work. Over the years I have made contact with many of his friends, who have given their own time and support, and many have contributed to the site and now to this book.

This book is a physical extension of my efforts to keep Quentin's memory alive and to try to bring the man and his philosophy to more people. In some ways I could say I have been researching it for most of my life, but really the bulk of it was done in the eight years after his death. I began seriously working on it and put the first words on paper in the summer of 2007. Over the next year and a half I re-read his own books and those books written about him; I watched as many of his film performances as I could get my hands on; documentaries made about him, of which there are many; interviews with him, of which again there are many; met with his friends and generally immersed myself in all things Quentin. The result of all this time, effort is the book you are holding in your hands right now.

No book could possibly tell you everything about this extraordinary man; rather it will, I hope, engage your interest and make you want to learn more. It is for you to judge if I have succeeded in doing so and if it has all been worthwhile. For me it has been an enriching and rewarding experience and has reinforced for me how Quentin's philosophy can have such a positive influence on someone's life.

I did not know when I started writing that by the time my book would be finished a second film biography of Quentin (titled *An Englishman in New York*), with John Hurt starring again as Quentin, would be finished and have its world premiere at the Berlin International Film Festival on 7 February 2009. Since that date it has premiered at many film festivals throughout the world. It had its American television debut on October 18, 2009, and on British television at the end of December 2009. By then John Hurt had already won the first of what I am sure will be many best actor awards for his performance. For those who want to know more about Quentin, the film is a must-see.

Lastly, if you are feeling altruistic you can pass this book on to someone else. You might just be giving them something special.

1

Childhood

"The trouble with children is that they are not returnable." — Quentin Crisp, *The Naked Civil Servant*

In 1908 one of the largest meteorites ever to hit the earth missed its mark and landed in Siberia. Quentin Crisp was born on Christmas Day in England. That is how he describes his birth in his first autobiography, *The Naked Civil Servant*. Listening to Quentin and reading his books, it is clear that he felt he was not supposed to be born. "As soon as I stepped out of my mother's womb on to dry land, I realized that I had made a mistake.... I felt that the invitation had really been intended for someone else."[1]

You can easily understand why he felt this way. Born into pre–World War I middle-class England was hardly a match made in heaven. Quentin would have a long and hard road to travel before the world would accept him for who he was. It would take sixty-seven years. The early years would find him collapsing in the street from hunger or waking up in the gutter, having been beaten unconscious by a gang of gay-bashers. Of those years Quentin said that the most surprising thing was that he was never killed. But he never once tried to disguise who he was. He said that the greatest fear many people have of homosexuals is that they might be among them. So he made sure everyone knew what he was; from a mile away they knew.

Within a few days of his birth he developed pneumonia. While he was ill his mother devoted her total care and attention to him. However, once he had recovered she returned to balancing out her love between all her children. Quentin felt that he never fully recovered from this loss of total love and devotion. "A fair share of anything is starvation diet to an egomaniac."[2] He was to spend the rest of his childhood trying to regain it.

Although he would occasionally manage for brief spells to drag his brother Lewis into his childhood games, he preferred to play with girls. Boys wanted to wrestle, climb trees and kick footballs, activities which he loathed and at which he would have lost and gotten hurt. The games he played with his "little friends"³ were always the same — they involved dressing in women's clothes and pretending that he was a beautiful woman. At the beginning of the twentieth century most English houses still had the traditional trunk of old clothes in their attics and to Quentin these must have seemed like a treasure trove. He certainly made the most use of them. Dialogue for these games would be along the lines of, "This wheelbarrow is my carriage, I gather up my train as I get in. Get in the other side, you fool. I nod to the servants as I leave. No. I ignore them. I am very proud and very beautiful."⁴ He could keep this going for the entire evening. On one occasion while engaged in his fantasy game with one of his little friends he was completely disoriented when his friend's cousin suggested that he play the part of her lover. He was rescued by his friend who, without missing a beat, replied, "Oh Denis (as my name was before I dyed it) never plays the part of a man."⁵ As he grew up the gulf between this fantasy and the reality of his life would never narrow.

His other source of amusement came from the servants. For these he would dance and recite poetry which he made up as he went along. Although they applauded his efforts, he himself admitted that it is more probable they simply found this entertainment a slightly more preferable option to doing their chores.

I have already mentioned Denis's brother Lewis, who was thirteen months older, and he had a sister Phyllis eight years older and another brother Gerald, seven years older. In his autobiography Quentin states, "Before any of us were born there were bailiffs in my parents' house in Carshalton."⁶ Although his sister Phyllis would dispute this statement, their father was declared bankrupt on 3 November 1902. This did not stop him from continuing to work as a solicitor, however, and he was soon setting up in new offices, which does show a certain drive and determination on his part. By the time Quentin was born his parents had already moved house four times. To his parents, maintaining the family's middle class lifestyle was apparently a full time occupation, but it was not until he lived alone many years later that Quentin realized "how much cheaper it was to drag the Joneses down to my level."⁷

Quentin's father, Spencer Charles Pratt, seems to have had at least sporadic success in his efforts to keep up with the Joneses, and by the time Quentin was born their situation seems to have improved dramatically. During Quentin's early childhood the family was living in a house with the rather grand title of Wolverton which was situated in Egmont Road, Sutton. The family also took regular holidays by the seaside, where they rented a cottage. In later life Quentin would often repeat that he disliked the sea: "The ocean is not my friend. Why does it keep banging away at the helpless shore and making all that noise? What does it want?"[8] But he had learned to swim and would squeak with delight on seeing the waves only because his siblings acted like this and he thought that the same was expected of him.

Quentin's name at the time was Denis Charles Pratt. The family also had a live-in governess called Miss Birmingham to look after the children, though most of her energy was probably spent on keeping young Denis in hand.

In early childhood Denis was physically frail and constantly sick, but was also an incorrigible show off; remember the dancing and poetry, with an unquenchable lust for attention. If he could not get sufficient attention by performing his dancing or reciting his poetry he would resort to threatening destruction of some household item. Anyone visiting the house could be sure of being made fully aware of Denis's presence. In later life his sister Phyllis told him, "You were a terrible child!"[9] And in later life Quentin himself would say, "In fairness to my family, I must admit that I was a most objectionable child."[10]

Denis's mother, Frances, known as Baba to her friends, had worked as a governess before marrying his father. She was a sociable woman who had many friends with whom she would maintain contact throughout her life. She was also very well read, intelligent, with fashionable ideas and social aspirations. Perhaps she thought that her marriage to a solicitor would allow her to realize these. She had a regular stream of visitors, both friends and relatives calling, but would be annoyed when visitors had the bad manners to arrive exactly on time. As the years passed she become increasingly unhappy and disenchanted with her marriage and would spend periods in nursing homes. Quentin would later describe her as being very beautiful. He also asserted that she could from a distance tell the difference between real and fake diamonds.

Baba seems to have been accepting of the feminine aspects of her son's personality and at times even to have encouraged them. Certainly Denis very much enjoyed her company. They both enjoyed talking and she gave him the impression that dressing up in women's clothes and pretending to be of high birth was "a taste we shared."[11] Perhaps in her youngest son she found a form of companionship which was missing from her marriage.

Denis had two aunts, May and Kay. May's husband, John Washbourne, had died young, leaving her alone with a son, Morris, to bring up. Denis's mother urged him and his brother Lewis to be kind to their only cousin when he came around to play, but the two brothers decided instead to make his time with them as miserable as possible. This anecdote does show that there was a level of cooperation and interplay between the two brothers, and we shall meet Morris' descendants later.

In later life Lewis kept a close connection with Denis (his family would always call him Denis even to the end of his life) even though Lewis would by then be living in South America. Lewis even named one of his daughters after him (Denise). Indeed it seems that of his three siblings, Quentin had perhaps the closest relationship with Lewis, who also was perhaps the most like Quentin in personality. Lewis was highly intelligent with a well-developed, deadpan sense of humor. He would start letters to Quentin with "Dear Sir or Madam. Please delete whichever is inappropriate." His daughters remember how Lewis would say the funniest things with a completely straight face, while those around him would fall about laughing.

Baba does seem to have indulged her youngest child. She brought Denis a pair of blocked ballet shoes presumably in the hope he might become a dancer. He also remembered once begging her to wear gold shoes to a wedding. On another occasion she allowed him to appear, wearing a dress, as a fairy in a production of *A Midsummer Night's Dream*. His sister, Phyllis, also had a small part in this production, but apart from Denis there was no one else on stage in drag. Denis danced himself into a frenzy but it was not until he fought with another fairy for a better position on stage that his performance elicited any reaction from the audience, who laughed and applauded his antics. A "resting" actor had been employed to direct this production in an effort to give it a more professional gloss. During rehearsals Denis had sat on his knee, where he showed Denis photos of himself naked except for a strategically placed bunch of grapes. The actor pronounced Denis to be his favorite. The day after the production this actor was arrested for inappropriate behavior with one of the other boys. Evidently Denis was not his favorite after all. In *The Naked Civil Servant* Quentin expresses his regret that "the greatest scandal in Sutton during my childhood came and went without my being able to convert it to my own use."[12]

Baba was an avid reader and introduced her son to literature by reading to him from works such as *The Lady of the Lake* by Sir Walter Scott and *Idylls of the King* by Lord Alfred Tennyson. According to Quentin she had a very good poetry reading voice. When he was deemed ready to read for himself he was given fairy stories and from these quickly graduated to the books of Rider Haggard of whose work the family had the complete collection. Sir Henry Rider Haggard, was famous for his "boys' own" adventure stories. His books included *King Solomon's Mines*, *She* and *Allan Quartermain*. Denis's mother also introduced him to the theatre and to the movies. He developed a lifelong love with what he called the "forgetting chamber."[13] One of his books would be titled *How to Go to the Movies*. But he could hardly have imagined in his wildest dreams that he would eventually appear in over thirty films.

Despite her indulgences of her youngest son, it was Baba who tried to prepare him for the outer world, while his father merely threatened him with it. Unfortunately, neither of them ever said, "You're mad but, when you go out into the world, you will doubtless meet people as mad as you are and I can only hope that you get on all right with them."[14] It might perhaps have been the best piece of advice they could have given him; however, they did not know there were other people as mad as he was.

Of his relationship with his father, Quentin wrote: "My father did not like me.... In later years I had to supply various subsidiary kinds of fuel for the furnaces of his hatred. In infancy my existence was enough."[15] Spencer Charles Pratt's personality seems to have been the opposite of his wife's. He certainly did have the same social aspirations; he would eat a banana with a knife and fork. But according to Quentin he was actually an unsociable man who was not a conversationalist. His evenings consisted of falling asleep in his chair after dinner, and his only interest was the second-hand cars at which he would tinker. They were the only things he ever displayed affection for. He always purchased second hand cars so that he could escape his family during the weekends by spending his time in the garage. Quentin would later say his father was a good mechanic but not a genius. Indeed, these cars seem to have only seldom left the garage and only very occasionally would the family be treated to a weekend drive, and these would be accompanied by his father's repeated question, "Can you hear a rattling?"[16]

To his father Denis seems to have been at worst an unwelcome and unpleasant addition to the family, an irritation; at best it is most likely that Mr. Pratt simply had no idea how to interact or deal with a son who behaved as though he was a beautiful princess and spent his days walking around the house in an exotic swoon. So he decided to go on "as though nothing unpleasant had happened."[17] On Quentin's part, perhaps his relationship with and attitude towards his father can best be summed up with his comment, "One wished he wasn't there."[18]

In later years Quentin would say, "If anyone shaped my character, I suppose it was my parents, particularly my mother, and regretfully because of them I am invincibly middle class,"[19] but he would also throughout his life insist that parents were a mistake. One of his most quoted bons mots was, "If one is not going to take the necessary precautions to avoid having parents, one must undertake to bring them up."[20] This might seem a bit harsh given his mother's efforts on his behalf, but when pressed to explain further he would say that really it is the relationship between parent and child which is the mistake. He would often express his view that one day all children would be born in a little glass dish in a laboratory and looked after by a man wearing a white coat and glasses, who will never say, "and after all I've done for you!"[21]

As was normal for this time Baba had no money of her own or any kind of bank account and relied totally on her husband's income. Quentin remembered her often asking her husband for money to pay whatever tradesman or deliveryman was calling that day. Yet she would tell her son that money was never to be spoken of. Quentin said his parents were miserable and only stayed together because they shared the same social aspirations.

At home Denis was taught how to play the piano, though he would profess a lifelong dislike of music and called it "the most noise conveying the least information."[22] Among the card and board games was chess, a game he enjoyed for the rest of his life. Was this tuition delivered by his mother or his siblings? It certainly would not have been by his father. In his first autobiography he also makes fleeting mention of being exposed to art. "The first paintings that I consciously looked at were Lord Leighton's classical mock-ups."[23] Lord Leighton was a highly successful and critically acclaimed Victorian painter and sculptor, the first English painter to be given a peerage. Denis also had a natural gift for drawing, which he would continue and develop for the rest of his life. With piano lessons, chess, art, literature, ballet slippers and probably dance lessons, trips to the cinema and ballet, it could be said that young Denis was being given a cultured upbringing.

Despite all of this activity, his mother's indulgence of him and having her almost continuous company during his early childhood, in later life Quentin would say that his childhood was very unhappy. He felt that as the youngest child he was the butt of his siblings' jokes and scorn from the word go. Considering how in-built cruelty and insensitivity can be among siblings, this is probably to an extent true. Certainly his extreme effeminacy, both in his behavior and physicality, would have made him an easy target for them. He would actually say that his father was the only member of the family who did not make fun of him, but this is perhaps more because the two rarely spoke or interacted in any way. Many years later when his friend Andrew Barrow asked him if he was suicidal during this period, he replied, "All the time. I wished I was dead."[24]

There was one day on which he truly managed to get the full attention of everyone in the family and the whole street. The family's governess had decided to take the two youngest boys for a walk, but on telling Denis this, he started to apply his usual techniques of being as difficult and uncooperative as he could, holding his arms rigid so that she could not get his coat on. She really earned her money! On this occasion her patience broke and she took Lewis and hid. Baba, unaware of what was happening, when asked by Denis where they had gone, told him he could go only as far as the gate in his search. Denis went through the gate and walked off down the road. Considering that "then as now I didn't hold with the outer world,"[25] this can only have been another attempt to garner attention. On this occasion it went wrong; or perhaps it went better than he had planned. It depends on your perspective.

As Denis walked along he was met by what in his autobiography he called a "rag and bone man"[26] who gave him a lift in his cart. Meantime, not only the whole family but the whole neighborhood had been alerted that Denis was missing. His mother had even called the police. Denis was eventually found two hours later in Sutton Downs, two or three miles from home, by a friend of his mother's. On his return Denis was examined by a doctor, who advised his mother never to question him about what had happened. Can we assume from this statement that the doctor had discovered that something unpleasant had indeed happened to Denis during his adventure and felt that the best way to deal with this and for young Denis to "get over it" was to try to forget all about it? Quentin would later say that he regretted this because he could not remember anything that had happened to him while he was with the rag and bone man. Quentin had an exceptional memory. Could he really not remember, or had whatever happened caused him subconsciously to block it out? In his autobiography Quentin is typically dismissive of the event. "Perhaps one should regard the kidnapping as just the first instance of my being picked up by a strange man at a street corner."[27]

Denis was only five when the First World War started, but he remembered soldiers being billeted with the local families. To his neighbors they were simply an inconvenience, but he found them "emotionally disturbing."[28] He also remembered the local girls waving them goodbye as they marched off to Flanders. He found the scene "wistful and romantic."[29]

In the same year the Pratt family moved again, this time to a house called Cotlands in Cornwall Road, which was just minutes' walk from their previous abode. It was from here that Denis was first sent to school, despite his protests that while his brothers wanted to be beacons of manliness such as fire-fighters and train drivers, he wanted to be a chronic invalid. He felt he had a certain natural flair. However, his parents pointed out that the family could not afford to support such a career, hence school was required. This was a private school in Belmont where his brothers were already installed, which does show that there must still have been some financial buoyancy left in the family. The piano lessons must have held him in good stead because when asked by a teacher how he felt he had done in a music exam, Denis replied that he thought he had passed, as the exam was quite easy. It was only when the rest of his classmates burst into laughter that he realized he should have said the exam was hard. In later life Quentin professed that he was miserable at school, where his unusual mannerisms and behavior meant he quickly became the centre point for the amused attention of everyone, fellow pupils and teachers, who after realizing that he was an easy and vulnerable target would score points off him. What form this took he does not tell us.

For the first half of the war the Pratt family continued to live its middle class lifestyle. They were still having their seaside family holidays presumably with Denis still feigning his delight at the waves. In September 1916 their oldest son, Gerald, was sent to Bloxham's private school, where his father had also studied. At this time financial constraints, presumably exacerbated by Bloxham's fees, caused Mr. Pratt to move his family again. This move was an even physically shorter one than the last, just to the other side of the road, but in terms of social standing it was a much greater distance — downwards. The house called Pemberth was much smaller and had no room for live-in servants. Denis had lost his captive audience. However, it was here that Baba started to expand her son's social education; she started taking him to the cinema and to the ballet. Although as I have mentioned Quentin developed a lifelong love for the cinema, at this time he preferred the ballet, though he said that his fascination with it then came from the tantalizing prospect that one of the dancers might break his neck. (He would make this observation to Rudolf Nureyev when they met decades later.) In later life Quentin would say that when he looked back on this he was not sure if he really loved the ballet or just loved being in love with it. It was also while in Pemberth house that he again became aware of his emotional reaction to men. Some workmen were digging up the road in front of the house and he would spend hours watching them to the point where one of them told him to clear off.

After the end of the war Mr. Pratt's financial situation must have improved. He acquired new offices and in 1919 was able to move his family again. This would have been the Pratts' seventh move; to a much larger house in Epsom with the rather unusual name of Wanganni. I do not know where this name originated from other than that there is a town in New Zealand by that name. In the past, the end of the nineteenth century, the town also had a newspaper called *The Wanganni Herald*. But whatever its name, it was a significant step back up the social ladder for the Pratts. This house had enough rooms for live-in servants so that young Denis had a new captive audience and he quickly resumed his performances. The house had large grounds and a tennis court at which Denis did his best to play, but as with other physical activities he lacked coordination and strength.

The family was now doing pretty well at least from the outside, but Baba's mental state had started to decline. We can only speculate as to the cause. Was it the strain of keeping up with the Joneses, was she becoming disenchanted with her marriage, was it the strain of having such an unusual and emotionally demanding child as Denis? Maybe all three? For whatever the reason, she would be in and out of nursing homes for the next few years. In her absence her daughter Phyllis, who was now in her late teens, ran the household.

The following year, 1920, Denis, now age eleven, was moved to another school called Kingswood House in Epsom. In keeping with the Pratt family's social aspirations, this school prided itself that it did not take in children from working class families. Here he found that despite his increased years his coordination and physical strength had not improved and he was still bad at any form of physical games. However, somewhere within his fail frame he must have found a vestige of physical ability, because he managed to become a Boy Scout and attend a scout camp in the Isle of Wight.

His lust for attention had not abated. At school he found that the way to get this attention was to excel academically, though he would later say that in those times academic excellence was mostly a matter of having a good memory. In his autobiography Quentin only makes the most fleeting mention of this establishment, which he describes as a preparatory school. He does say that here he also received mistreatment similar to that at his previous school. His academic efforts to gain attention must have paid off, for he also says that from here he won a "very poor scholarship"[30] to a public school.

-2

The Teenage Years

"I was half-starved half-frozen and humiliated in a number of ways." —
Quentin Crisp, *The Naked Civil Servant.*

Having won his scholarship, he was sent to Denstone, a private boarding
school for boys. Why his family sent him there and not Bloxham, where his
oldest brother Gerald had been school captain and where Lewis would also
become school captain, as had their father before them, is not known. Was
it a financial decision? The "very poor scholarship"[1] only knocked a quarter
off the yearly school fees; was the family that hard up financially? Did the
family not wish to besmirch the good reputation that they had built-up at
Bloxham by introducing them to Denis? As his mother took him for his first
day at Denstone he had his usual fit of weeping. She warned him that this
kind of behavior would not be acceptable here. He did not cry again.

Quentin described the school as "a cross between a prison and a church,
and it was."[2] It was built on top of a hill so that "God could see everything
that went on."[3] It was built in the Gothic style, sparse and devoid of any kind
of ornamentation or decoration. It must have seemed very foreboding to any
small boy. He was "half-starved half-frozen and humiliated in a number of
ways."[4]

His efforts during his first year there were concentrated on simply surviving, which he achieved by "lying low under fire and laying the blame on
others."[5] It was not until his second year that he started to realize this school
was even more emotionally charged than his previous one. He became deeply
interested in the sex lives of the prefects. The prefects were forbidden by
school policy to speak to the younger boys. This gave rise to the occupation
of go-between, a post filled by the middle year boys who ferried the love
letters between the prefects and the smaller boys and through whom Denis
could keep up to date with what was going on. It was the result of one of
these liaisons which found Denis witnessing his only public school flogging.

16

The boy had been caught making a daring raid on a younger boy the night before. The entire school was, according to Quentin, deeply shocked and disgusted by the scene, and on his part, "Before that day I had disliked the head; afterwards I hated him."[6]

During his years at Denstone, Denis came to the interesting observation that true homosexual boys are among those who least engage in sexual acts with other boys. His argument for this was that for most heterosexual boys the act itself is merely a release of built-up sexual tension; they are really fantasizing about girls, which for the homosexual defeats the purpose.

Denis himself longed to have a school romance, but his unusual appearance and lack of any physically appealing attributes acted as a "formidable natural chastity belt."[7] Personality was more important to him, so he found himself naturally drawn to his masters. He still had a lust for attention and here he continued with his efforts to attain this by attempting to please the masters through academic achievement. He swotted like mad, entering the exam room with his head bursting with facts and leaving with it completely empty. At one point a teacher declared Denis to be the cleverest boy in the school. This drew the hatred of the other boys and for the rest of his life he carried a scar on his wrist where some of them vented their hatred by sawing through the skin with a jagged ruler. It will perhaps surprise many that he also became an officer cadet with the rank of lance corporal and commanded cadet squads. We can only speculate that this was an extension of his efforts to please his masters. All of this effort managed to get him into sixth form when only fifteen.

Denis was in boarding school for four years; however, he tells us that after only two he found he had reached the limits of his educability. It was at this point that he realized that the masters were now starting to hate him as well. He started to find reasons to excuse himself from his various subjects until he was able to spend most of his time sitting alone reading books. Later Quentin described himself as having a crossword puzzle mentality; he could memorize but not analyze. Perhaps he gave up on his classes, not because of any perceived lack of mental ability but because he now realized that his efforts to please his masters had come to nothing.

The crossword had around this time winged its way across the Atlantic from America and the Pratt family had become addicts. Quentin would become a voracious crossword solver and continued to do them throughout his life. When he moved to America he would sometimes be spotted searching his neighbors' bins to try to find discarded newspaper crosswords, and his friends back in England would collect and post him crosswords from the British newspapers. "I mustn't claim that they are better than those devised by other nations, but they are different in that solving them requires only ingenuity. American puzzles demand general knowledge which, as I barely live in the real world, I lack. I don't know the name of the capitals of obscure African countries; I don't know the first names of long-dead baseball players."[8] Despite this comment, Quentin did put his general knowledge to use on American crosswords. When Phillip Ward and his partner, Charles Barron, were sorting out Quentin's room after his death they found a stack of completed New York Times crossword books. It seems Quentin had been given a New York Times crossword puzzle subscription and would complete a puzzle almost every day. He once described crosswords as the aerobics of the soul and stated that he became jittery if he did not do at least two a day.

But whatever he may have learned in school, the one overriding lesson he received was that he had a natural gift for being unpopular. He hated school so much that he once went to bed with a handkerchief stuffed into his mouth in the hope that he would suffocate during his sleep. It was also here that he learned to bear injustice and to become accustomed to the negative attitude displayed towards him by almost everyone. This was a valuable lesson, because it gave him a foretaste of what he could expect when he eventually faced the world outside. It was during these years that he started to develop his armor and he admitted many years later that had he not gone to Denstone, he doubted if he would have survived the treatment he would receive when he lived in London.

He did manage to get into bed once with another boy. This boy, an Indian, was more liberated than the rest, and Quentin tells us that he boasted that during the school holidays he went with prostitutes. His one night of lust was spent at the end of a term, but he does not tell us which term or which year. Somewhat strangely, he says that he did not expect, nor was there any pleasure involved, it was merely enough for it to be known that he had done it.

In the interim years the Pratts had continued their wandering ways and it was during a spell in a lodging house that Denis would discover the full pleasures of bath time. When he had been deemed old enough to bathe himself, he had started staying in longer and longer, "until my body had passed from lobster-pink to scum-grey."[9] It was during one of these marathon bath sessions that he discovered masturbation and had his first orgasm. When he awoke the next day he was frightened that he might either die or contract some horrible disease. As the days passed and neither of these fears was realized, tranquility returned and a new routine set in. It would become the only fact of life he would ever fully understand. "Masturbation is not only an expression of self-regard: it is also the natural emotional outlet of those who, before anything has reared its ugly head, have already accepted as inevitable the wide gulf between their real futures and the expectations of their fantasies."[10] Many years later he would also assert that sex was a poor substitute for masturbation.

From the gate lodge the family moved in 1924 to an apartment in Clarence Gate. The following year they were on the move again, this time to Battersea Park. It was also in this year that his sister, Phyllis, married a clergyman called John Payne. Denis was allowed out of Denstone for the day to attend the wedding.

Towards the end of his time at Denstone his father sent a letter to the school asking for any advice as to what Denis could possibly do on leaving. Considering that Quentin states that his father never took any interest in him, was this letter actually dictated by his mother? Given the social climate at the time, it would probably have been considered inappropriate for a mother to write such a letter. The masters, at a loss as to what else to advise, suggested he had literary ability and might take up journalism.

3

Leaving School

"I stumbled on the very truth that was just what the doctor had ordered.
I learned that I was not alone." — Quentin Crisp, *The Naked Civil Servant.*

As Denis left Denstone College in July 1926, now seventeen years old,
he must have been extremely apprehensive about his future and what he was
going to do. How despairing he was might be gleaned from his reaction on
hearing the Indian boy talk about male prostitutes: "I wonder if I could do
that?"[1]

However, his mother, as she would do so many times in the following
years, came to his rescue. Taking on board the comments from Denstone,
Baba now sent her son to King's College London to do a course in journalism.
In his autobiography Quentin makes almost no mention of anything that
happened at King's College during his time there, except that he left without
his diploma. He says that even by this time the word homosexual had no
meaning for him. He did not yet fully understand who and what he was.
During this period he seems to have spent most of his free time either at the
theatre or the cinema and it was then that he developed his true love for films
and also started, through them, to dream of America. Most of the films he
watched then and in which he would become completely absorbed were American, with stars such as Greta Garbo, over whom he swooned, not with passion
for the person, but for "the accoutrements of her beauty, the sumptuous set-
tings, the huge fur coats, the heavy diamond jewellery."[2]

At this time homosexuality was still "thought to be Greek in origin,
smaller than socialism but more deadly — especially to children."[3] When the
lesbian novel *The Well of Loneliness* was published in 1928 there was a huge
public outcry and condemnation. Through his family's strict middle class
upbringing he had been made painfully aware of the sin of homosexuality.

At this time Denis, as he was still known, made the acquaintance of one of his mother's friends, Mrs. Longhurst, a stewardess and portrait model. He describes her as a "wonderful woman."[4] They became friends and he would visit her often to play card games and talk. In later years he would say with regret that he wasted an opportunity. Mrs. Longhurst and his mother were the only people he ever heard at that time discussing lesbianism or homosexuality. We must wonder if Baba did not at this point and even earlier have some inkling of her youngest son's true nature. He was sure that if he had told Mrs. Longhurst the truth about himself she would have listened and not condemned. "This would have been at least a thin rope flung from my tiny island towards the mainland."[5]

Denis was now eighteen and had become so listless that his mother, thinking he must be ill, sought a medical opinion. The doctor said that all he needed was a "lesson in life,"[6] a remark which Denis met with "blank incomprehension."[7] Based on this remark it is difficult to know what the doctor really thought of Denis. Did the doctor know or suspect that he was homosexual and thought that a "lesson in life,"[8] by which we can only assume he meant intercourse with members of the opposite sex, would be enough to sort him out; an attitude which prevails among many heterosexuals towards both homosexuals and lesbians, even today? Despite this prognosis Quentin would keep him as his doctor even into the 1970s, presumably until he either retired — or died, so he must have had some confidence in him. His father was not happy at having to pay a doctor's bill for "these few glib words."[9] Quentin would later remark that it was fortunate that psychology had not then filtered into the middle classes or his father would have had to pay a great deal more for even less.

To try to alleviate his boredom, and perhaps to try to get out from under his mother's feet, he took to wandering the streets of the West End, and there "I stumbled on the very truth that was just what the doctor had ordered. I learned that I was not alone."[10] On the street corners of Piccadilly and Shaftsbury Avenue he encountered young men who made no effort to hide themselves, indeed they advertised themselves in such a way that "a passer-by would have to be very innocent indeed not to catch the meaning of the mannequin walk and the stance in which the hip was only prevented from total dislocation by the hand placed upon it."[11] And who when approached by him, would say something like, "Isn't it terrible tonight, dear? No men about. The Dilly's not what it used to be."[12] As I mentioned earlier Denis had heard about male prostitutes while in school, but he never thought he would actually meet any. It was one of these young men who would introduce him to their local gathering place, a café in Old Compton Street which was known locally as The Black Cat. Here he found people who were in the same sexual dilemma as he was. Until then he had thought that "sexually I was quite unlike anyone else in the world."[13] Here they congregated day after day and spent the hours exchanging makeup advice and talk about their predicament. In no time Denis had learned by heart all the arguments against the persecution of homosexuals.

Of course they could not just sit at the tables chatting, so to try to justify their presence they would buy each other cups of tea, they could not afford anything else, which they would try to make last as long as a four course meal by taking tiny sips from their cups, much to the annoyance of the manager, who would occasionally throw them all out.

This man would later be charged with murder. In the 1930s Brighton became infamous for what were called the Brighton Trunk Murders. The first was in 1927 when a dismembered woman's body was found in separate trunks at Charing Cross Station. The woman's name was Minnie Bonati. John Robinson was found guilty of her murder and hanged in Pentonville Prison on 12 August 1927. The second happened in 1934 when a pregnant woman's torso was found in a trunk at King's Cross Railway Station. Her legs were found in a trunk at Brighton Railway Station. Her head was never found and the woman's identity would never be uncovered. In the coming weeks during a house-to-house search the police discovered another woman's body in a trunk in Kemp Street Brighton. This woman, Violet Kaye, a prostitute, had with her lover, Tony Mancini (former manager of The Black Cat) moved to Brighton from London in 1933. Mancini claimed to police that he had found his lover already dead and in a panic hid her body in the trunk. At his trial Mancini's lawyer argued that Violet Kaye had been a heavy drinker and a morphine addict and that these may have caused her death. Despite overwhelming evidence against him, Mancini was found not guilty. Journalists present commented that not only did the judge seem surprised by this verdict, but so did Mancini himself. As no evidence could be produced to link him to the murder of the second unnamed victim, he was set free. However, in 1976, at the age of sixty-eight, in an article in the British newspaper *The News of the World*, Mancini confessed to Violet's murder. Despite his written confession, the director of public prosecutions ruled that he could not be tried a second time for the same murder.

In his autobiography Quentin states that, if they had known then how volatile Mancini was, he and his friends would have provoked him with much greater vehemence. But in his dealings with Denis and his friends this man showed great tolerance and he always allowed them back in after he had cooled off.

Some of the local working class men also frequented The Black Cat and seem to have found Denis and his friends fascinating. With their heavy makeup, hair and mannerisms they were more exotic than any woman. These men would chat them up and ask for cups of tea. In the film version of *The Naked Civil Servant* this relationship is shown as a negative, even abusive one, but Quentin would later say, "We saw in them someone who saw in us what we were"[14] and that their arrival had "a strong erotic flavor."[15] Indeed, one cannot help but wonder if in a strange kind of way their visits were welcomed by Denis and his friends.

From their base in The Black Cat Denis and his new friends would set off on expeditions into the neighborhood streets in search of love, money or both, returning to apply more lipstick, drink more tea and argue over who was the most beautiful of the Hollywood screen goddesses and presumably continue to get on the nerves of the manager.

While on the streets sometimes one of them would scream as they ran by, "They're coming!"[16] They treated the police as one might treat a wild animal. As they passed the police they did not run, but if the police started to run, they spread out so that only one of their herd would fall prey.

For the young men who frequented The Black Cat, being a prostitute was not something they felt ashamed of; it was their day jobs they felt they had to live down. Before long Denis, too, would be "on the game," though this would last for only six months during the winter of 1928–29. During this period he did not actively solicit or stand at street corners as many of the others did, rather he found that he would be approached merely walking along a street. These encounters usually ended in a doorway or in a taxi and seldom involved anything more than undoing the required number of fly buttons. There was always the possibility of the man having to make a quick get away.

He developed a typically Crispian philosophy about all this. Accepting payment for sex absolved him of the sin of enjoying it for its own sake; he could claim that he only did it for the money. His other argument went like this — a woman accepts the possibility of being loved by a man as a natural part of her life, so when told by a man that he loves her, she will immediately believe him; but for a homosexual, "Love and admiration have to be won against heavy odds. Any declaration of affection requires proof.... A ten shilling note shows incontrovertibly just how mad about you a man is."[17] The cash was also a small compensation for the insults which he endured daily from every direction as well as being irrefutable proof that he was desired by someone.

Denis had now started seriously to experiment with makeup, assisted by his new friends. But he could not allow his parents to have any glimpse of this new persona, so on leaving home he would go to the nearest public toilet which he deemed safe enough and apply his new look. Although this new look was a far cry from that which he would finally adapt, it was still enough to draw attention from people in the street, and once while out walking he was passed by his brother Lewis and his girlfriend, who turned to Lewis and asked, "Did you see that? [to which he replied] Yes. Matter of fact, I've seen it before!"[18]

After leaving King's College without his diploma in July 1928, now age nineteen, Denis did not find work, but the Denstone's masters' insight would prove prophetic. In a writing career which spanned 1936 to 1996 he would write sixteen books, numerous poems, stage and radio plays and more. Quentin was once asked if he had any advice for budding authors and his reply was "Never read."[19] Or, more specifically, "No one who intends to take up writing as a career should read any work that lies in the category in which his own efforts would be placed. If he disobeys this rule, he will almost certainly feel that he must write literature instead of trying to say what he means."[20]

Baba now decided that art might be the means by which her son could earn a living. This hope of his mother's must have had some basis in his ability to draw, and indeed, his artistic abilities would gain him his only periods of employment during the coming years. Thus in September 1928, Denis, now approaching his twentieth birthday, was enrolled in an art course at Battersea Polytechnic. He spent a year there, but like his previous schooling, he says in his autobiography very little about anything he did during this year, but does tell us about a girl he met there who would become one of his closest friends for the next few decades. He actually uses the word "friend"[21] when talking about her and in a rare expression of affection even once described her as "infinitely appealing."[22] Her name was Pat and she had been crippled by polio as a child so that one leg was encased in a metal frame. Because of her handicap she was particularly sympathetic and probably drawn towards anyone who was in any way handicapped or deemed an outsider or inferior, so a strong friendship blossomed between them. Quentin would state that she was the only good thing to come out of Battersea Polytechnic.

During this year Denis had continued his curious double life. When not either at home or at school he spent his time with his friends at The Black Cat. However, this double life was soon to come to an abrupt end.

4

High Wycombe

"My starved eyes would see mirages of the London Pavilion and Marble Arch and I would stumble towards them with little cries." — Quentin Crisp, *The Naked Civil Servant*

In the summer of 1929 Quentin's mother finally succeeded in getting her husband to move from their Battersea flat, which she hated, to a house near High Wycombe. Both his brothers had by now left home. Gerald had gone to India and according to family lore he would later marry a Russian princess, though apparently this marriage would later fail and Gerald would return to England just before the Second World War to take a job with the Ministry of Agriculture. Lewis had gone to South America where he would do well. Lewis and Quentin seem to have gotten on better as they grew up and on Lewis's returns to England the two would get together. So at this time only Denis remained at home. Having no job and no money, he had no choice but to go with them. This house, called Hillcrest, was much more spacious than their Battersea flat, with enough room inside and out for both a live-in maid and a gardener. Perhaps by now Denis had grown out of his need for constant attention and this new captive audience were left alone to do their chores.

Spencer Charles Pratt must have still had considerable financial resources or at least been able to find new sources for getting into debt. He still maintained an office in the city and commuted every day. At least their life now appeared to be one of luxury, but for Denis it seemed that his father had now lost all his senses completely. His greatest distress at this new move was that it severed him from the West End and his life there with his friends at The Black Cat. He became very depressed and despondent. "My starved eyes would see mirages of the London Pavilion or the Marble Arch and I would stumble towards them with little cries,"[1] he would write later.

His main pastime during his two years at High Wycombe seems to have been walking his mother's dogs, which he hated doing. He would later say, "A dog is a terrible thing to happen to anyone."[2] Perhaps this contributed to his lifelong dislike of dogs and disdain for keeping pets in general; "We've got enough dumb friends without them."[3] It was here that a friend of his sister, Phyllis, once, with extraordinary foresight and courage asked, "I wonder what you would have been like if you'd been a woman."[4]

Baba was still intent on art as a possible career for her son and at the beginning of 1929 he was sent to an art college in High Wycombe. He was older by a few years than any of the other pupils and by his own admission behaved as though he was a genius. Perhaps his already unusual appearance and feminine behavior encouraged the teachers to think that he had some natural artistic abilities and he was left to a large extent to do what he wished, though he did do technical drawing and especially enjoyed life drawings, but found the models uninspiring. It was this experience which encouraged him to adopt such dramatic poses when many, many years later he himself became a model.

It was during this period that Denis took his second tentative step onto the stage (the first was his fairy in *A Midsummer Night's Dream*), on this occasion acting the part of a mad man in a play put on by the local amateur theatrical company. Unfortunately I know nothing more about this production, but it does show that from an early age Quentin had aspirations in this direction.

In 1930 his mother left the family for a short while. We can only assume this was another trip to a nursing home. In his autobiography Quentin postulates, "Perhaps she left in self defence?"[5] To his amazement he and his father actually interacted with each other, though not very well. During one exchange his father stated, "The trouble is you look like a male whore!"[6] and this was towards Denis when he was in his greatly toned down "home" version of himself. One can only imagine how Mr. Pratt would have reacted had he had a glimpse of his son during one of Denis's walks around the West End. According to Quentin, "The remark was the first acknowledgement that he had ever made of any part of my problem."[7] To show his appreciation of this, he promised his father that when he next went to London he would endeavor not to come back.

5

Leaving Home

"I was excited, exhausted and worried by these crowds but, because I had never been savaged by them, I was not frightened. Because I still believed that I could educate them, I was happy." — Quentin Crisp, *The Naked Civil Servant*.

On Christmas Day 1930 at age 22, with a red handkerchief full of cosmetics over his shoulder, Denis took a trip to London. There he fulfilled his promise to his father never to return home, and indeed, as his father would die just a few months later, perhaps they never saw each other again.

He shared a flat with a man he had met at The Black Cat whom he called Thumbnails. Apparently this nickname had come about after the young man had paid a visit to Quentin's home. According to Quentin's account of this, his mother was repulsed by his thumbnails, which were wider than they were long. Whatever Quentin's source for the name, it is clearly intended to be derogatory and shows Quentin's distaste for him. Thumbnails had literary aspirations and raised some eyebrows at The Black Cat by exclaiming that he was not on the game, though as Quentin would describe him as being the most unpleasant of them all, perhaps his services in this area were not sought after.

Denis and he got to know each other quite well.

Thumbnails paid Quentin visits at Hillcrest often, staying for the evening meal. Thumbnails was the only one of his own age Denis knew who also lived in his own flat in London. During his time at High Wycombe, when he had enough money, Denis would travel into London and spend weekends at Thumbnail's flat, presumably working up towards the time when he would move in permanently. They were not lovers and soon not even friends. That Denis moved in with Thumbnails, who was then living in Baron's Court, is a measure of how desperately he wished to leave home and return to London.

One must also wonder why Thumbnails allowed Denis to share his flat.

Denis was not working and had by now given up on sex as "the last refuge of the miserable."[1] Soon he had no money. In *The Naked Civil Servant*, Quentin suggests that Thumbnails had social aspirations and associated with him because of his middle class background. There must have been some form of connection between the two, but however flimsy it may have been, it would soon be whittled away even more. One of the great tenets of Quentin's domestic philosophy was, "You only need to do the dishes after you've passed the fish barrier. It works like this — You taste your plate and it says egg so you think 'I could have some bacon.' Next morning your plate says bacon so you think 'I could have some fish.' But after the fish you have to do the dishes."[2] This and his other domestic philosophies did not make his relationship with Thumbnails any easier.

Although Thumbnails had intermittent work, they were so poor that they had to resort to subterfuge just to be able to eat. One of their tricks went like this. They would separately enter a café during the rush hour and ask for separate bills, but sit at the same table. Whoever left first would ask the cashier for change of a sixpence so they could make a phone call. Thus the manager would see him going to the till as though to pay. He would then quietly leave. If stopped on the way out he would say that his friend was paying. The person now left behind had a number of gambits to try. As it was the rush hour, he could try to sneak out with a crowd; he could also ask for change at the cash register; he could claim his friend had already paid for both meals. If these failed he could pay for his own meal or as a last resort pay for both. According to Quentin this last option was almost never called for. They usually managed to get one free meal a day.

It was in January 1931 during his stay at Baron's Court with Thumbnails that his father finally lost his battle with the Joneses; he died of cancer at the age of fifty-nine. On hearing this news Quentin said he only felt irritation at having to go home to attend the funeral. Baba quickly sold the house and moved in with her daughter and son-in-law in Exmoor.

It was while at Baron's Court that Denis made his only public appearance in drag. In *The Naked Civil Servant* he does not tell us why he did this, presumably it was simply an experiment to see what happened, or maybe he was making one last attempt to act out his lifelong internal fantasy that he was in fact a woman. The experiment was a failure; no one took any notice. He traveled on the Underground to Piccadilly Circus wearing a black silk dress with a velvet cape. Thumbnails wore a dinner jacket. He returned home totally deflated. He had discovered that while his "normal" attire made him appear very feminine, wearing actual woman's clothing exaggerated the masculine aspects of his character, thus totally defeating the purpose. This scene would be reproduced for the film version of *The Naked Civil Servant*. He would never wear drag again, except much later in life for film or stage roles.

After only a few months at Baron's Court they moved to a double room near King's Cross Station. Denis much preferred this location. It was "loud with the noise of steam trains and lousy with tea shops."[3] Thumbnails must have had some connection with the literary world, as the following story of how Denis stepped onto a stage for the third time will show. Thumbnails had interviewed a dancer and told her that if she was able to repeat a certain dance step a specified number of times it would be some sort of record and would be worth an article in the newspaper. The dancer failed in her efforts but the article appeared nevertheless, presumably written by Thumbnails. (I wish I could give his real name but his true identity remains a mystery to this day.) As a result she was invited to dance at a charity event, but in order to complete her desired program she needed a stage assistant. Denis stepped in to fill the breach. We have only his own account of this event, and according to this, his performance was so inept that the audience laughed and applauded uproariously. Presumably they thought it was all a planned part of the show. What the dancer thought of all this, he does not say.

Shortly after this event his mother's network of social contacts would come to his rescue. Through one of her friends Baba managed to get her son his first job as a tracer for an electrical engineering firm. He seems to have toned down his appearance for starting this job, as he tells us that until he had worked long enough to be eligible for the dole, he barely drew breath, but once this milestone had been reached he relaxed and his hair and fingernails slowly returned to their original length.

Although this job must have been a very important step for Denis, by far its most significant impact was that he could now live alone and escape Thumbnails. In *The Naked Civil Servant*, Quentin describes his "ecstasy"[4] at being able to live alone. While other people would tell him of the pleasure they felt at finding someone to live with, "the heightened perception of the world around them, the inability to refrain from taking little skips as they walked,"[5] this was how he felt on realizing he might never have to live with another person again. Indeed, for the rest of his life he would never again live with anyone for any length of time, except for one notable exception, which will be discussed later.

He found a room in Pimlico. Here, alone for the first time, he started pursuing his literary ambitions and wrote plays, poems and libretti. Unfortunately, although Denis must have worn down a lot of shoe leather visiting publishers, none of his efforts would make it into print. He even tried to advance his future job prospects by trying to enroll in an art course in a local school but was turned down on the basis that he was already employed. But he did manage to get into an evening drawing class at a polytechnic.

Quentin says that at work he never knew what he was doing; when given plans to copy he would simply reproduce them exactly, mistakes and all, so that engineers would phone the office to find out why their plans were telling them to erect a pylon in someone's back garden. Looking back, he wondered how many pylons and transformers might today still be in the wrong place. But he was happy!

He was now becoming truer to himself and his appearance was becoming even more effeminate. This combined with his natural exhibitionist nature meant he soon became "blind with mascara and dumb with lipstick."[6] As he walked along the streets of Pimlico people would sometimes start to follow him; at times this following would grow into a crowd so large that a policeman would be required to disperse it. "I was excited, exhausted and worried by these crowds but, because I had never been savaged by them, I was not frightened. Because I still believed that I could educate them, I was happy."[7]

Although Quentin said that during this time his friends were few, there did seem to be a steady stream of callers at his room. He himself had great difficulty in visiting his friends, as many had relatives or landladies to whom his presence would have been unwelcome. He could not even meet many of them in public due to the embarrassment this would cause them. His crippled student friend Pat was a regular visitor who was also occasionally accompanied by her cousin. On one occasion he was alone in his room with this cousin when she fell to the floor in front of him. There she proclaimed her love while stating that she was unworthy of him. "This was true but I never understood why she brought the subject up."[8] It was here also that he was first introduced to the "Czech gentleman with an unspellable name"[9] who would have a recurring part in *The Naked Civil Servant*, both the book and film versions.

His most frequent visitors were an Irish boy and a deserter from the Seaford Highlanders. Along with them came a woman who acted as go-between for the two men. Why she was necessary or involved in this triangle Quentin does not say. The Irishman had an apparently inexhaustible supply of hard luck stories which usually ended with him getting money from Denis. This friendship lasted for several years and we must wonder what was really going on here. In *The Naked Civil Servant*, Quentin seems to tell us that he gained some pleasure in knowing someone who was even poorer than he was. But can this really be the full reason? He also states that if at that time anyone had asked him what the word "con" meant, "I would say that it was something done by impecunious Irishmen to English queers."[10] It does seem to imply a certain resentment or disdain at this situation.

6

Becoming Quentin Crisp

"As soon as I had put on my new uniform my life solidified around me like a plaster cast." — Quentin Crisp, *The Naked Civil Servant.*

It was during these years of the early 1930s that Denis started to look seriously at who he was. He was now not just becoming fully aware, but also fully accepting of the truth of his sexuality. He decided that he would no longer make any attempts to hide it, but rather to make it clear. He would make homosexuality his cause. From childhood he had certain characteristics, such as his expressive hand gestures which gave rise to ridicule, but which could be excused. What he wanted now was to adopt an appearance, a set of characteristics which could not be ignored, could not be excused as anything other than homosexual. At a time when men were attempting to remove any vestiges of femininity as if exterminating lice, Quentin was wearing makeup, using henna to dye his hair red and wearing long red fingernails. Years later when actress Malya Woolf first met him, she asked if his long fingernails got in the way, to which he replied, "I can't do a thing."[1] A lifelong friendship had started.

From this point on he also realized that sex was a thing of the past. If he allowed himself to be picked up by strange men it could be argued that his exaggeratedly feminine appearance had been adapted to that end, which would have defeated the purpose. However, he found that men now gave him a wide berth. Due to his appearance, any man seen walking beside him would immediately have given his intentions away. But even this was not enough; he needed to make it clear that his appearance had not been adopted for the purpose of trying to pick up men, and so he also adopted a manner of walking everywhere at breakneck speed and never looking left or right. Friends told him he now seemed aloof and arrogant, but in truth his posture was born out of fear. He knew that if he was to stop and look around all he would see were expressions of hatred and disgust.

By the time he had completed his new "uniform" he had transformed himself from the frail, sickly plainness of his youth into what Philip O'Connor described as "one of London's works of art."[2] The finishing touches to the creation of his masterpiece were put in place with his decision to change his name and Denis Pratt became Quentin Crisp. It is a name which works on many levels. It gives the impression of a middle or even upper class background; it has an arty or literate tone and is also quite feminine.

For many years I have wondered how Quentin came to be his new name. I have so far found three different versions of how this happened.

In his 2002 book *Quentin and Philip*, Andrew Barrow tells us, "This took place gradually, bit by bit, during these years ... for a while he was known as Denis Crisp ... and eventually it was a "committee" of unknown friends who decided on Quentin Crisp."[3]

I heard the following version in 2008. This story was related to me by American character actor Richard Louis James. Richard was having dinner with Stephen Sorrentino, who starred with Quentin in the film *Homo Heights*,

Richard Louis James as Quentin Crisp in *Tea 'N Crisp* in 2008 (photograph by John D. Kysela).

and Sara Moore, who directed the same film. During dinner Stephen told the following story. Quentin had told Stephen that when he was a young man he had gone back to his room with a friend. During the friend's stay Quentin was talking on the phone and the caller asked if he was with anyone. Denis, as he was then still known, noticed a bag of crisps which were called Quentin's Crisps, so he replied that he was with a wonderful man called Quentin Crisp and that was where he got the inspiration for his new name. Stephen would later verify this story to me personally.

The third version is from Guy Kettelhack and is similar to that of Andrew Barrow's story. Guy says that both of Quentin Crisp's names were actually given to him. "His surname by chance

... something to do with having at short notice to pretend to be a 'Mr. Crisp' at one of his Soho coffee bars; his first name conferred on him by the collective decision of friends."[4]

He now found that where previously his appearance had drawn groups of presumably just curious followers, it now engendered anger which at first manifested itself through a daily barrage of insults and derisive comments shouted at him as he walked by, but quickly escalated into violence. People would slap his face or stomp on his toes. This physical abuse also escalated into outright assaults which left him bloodied and sometimes unconscious. He must have been terrified every day of his life and would later state that he was in no doubt that were he beaten to death, there would have be nothing but the most perfunctory investigation, doubtless resulting in no conviction. But his internal journey continued unabated. In later life he would simply say that he had no choice but to be who he was. For Quentin to have been less than totally true to himself would have been the greatest form of deception. Anyone who would have known and befriended him would have really been doing so with someone of the same name but who was an impostor.

He found that there was relative safety in daylight, apart from the occasional slap in the face or broken toe. It was at night as he tried to make his way back to his room that he had to run the gauntlet. Sometimes he would offer his pursuers what pennies he had and they would take them; others would slap them from his hand and the beating would be more severe. He picked himself out of the gutter, counted his teeth and staggered home, to reconstruct himself for the next day. Some, however, would be more severe, requiring hospitalization.

He also now found himself being refused entrance to many cafés and other public places. Even The Black Cat turned him out. In contrast, there were some pleasant responses to his new appearance, possibly the most notable coming from the doorman of a hotel that he walked past regularly who would give him a fresh flower each time.

The job with the engineering firm lasted eighteen months until the owner came to his senses. Although he now found himself worse off than when he had first come to London, in some respects it was easier. As he now lived alone he could apportion what little money he had to suit himself and he could claim the dole. However, in order to get this money, he found himself having to run another kind of gauntlet. As he queued in the line at the labor exchange he would be mercilessly harassed by other men who would try to grope him. It was a relief when he was able to press his genitals against the counter to allow him to free one of his hands so he could sign the book. He tells us that only the presence of two policemen prevented an all out physical confrontation. Were these policemen required on other days? He endured this abuse for several weeks until on one occasion he was ushered into the manager's office. Quentin described this gentleman as "truly enlightened";[5] their exchange was cordial and even sympathetic. He allowed Quentin to leave via the staff entrance and, placing his hand on his shoulder, told him that if it became too much he should come back to see him and he would try to do something.

He could no longer afford his room in Pimlico but found one even cheaper in Clerkenwell. The room was in the attic of the house and was so small that he could not stand up in it. At night he would crawl through the tiny window and sleep on the ledge which went around the house. He hoped that one night he might fall off and achieve a cheap death. On week days he could eat at a diner near Euston Station. If he arrived just after the rush hour the owner would give him the food which her previous customers had left on their plates, while it was still hot. When the weekend came he brought a loaf of bread, a pint of milk and a piece of chocolate. These he managed to get to sustain him until Monday by lying on his bed and not moving unless necessary so as to use as little energy as possible. On one occasion when he fainted in an Express Dairy the manager took him downstairs and fed him from her own hands. Through these and other kindnesses he managed to survive, just.

Quentin was only able to get unemployment benefits for six months but rescue came once again from his mother. Through the husband of a friend she had managed to get him a job in the art department of a printing company. For the first three months there he was not paid, as he was deemed to have been on trial. At this point in his life Quentin was so desperate to maintain employment that he would sometimes work throughout the night to try to ensure the art department paid its way. He seems to have done better at this job than his previous one, although initially his boss had him into his office to say, "Fact of the matter is we don't particularly like employing people with plucked eyebrows and pointed fingernails."[6] To appease his boss Quentin allowed them to return to relative normality. After a while Quentin was assigned a female assistant. This was the only time in his life when he was anyone's boss and he tried to make up for what he saw as an inappropriate situation by being as polite and as tactful as he could possibly be. On the only occasion in which he ever criticized her work, she responded, "Thank God, you've said what you really mean at last."[7]

While employment allowed him to find a better room and food to eat, he did not view work as first and foremost a way of making money; rather, "What I wanted to wrest from regular employment was something with which to bargain with the heterosexual world for acceptance as a homosexual."[8] So what happened next must have come as a devastating blow. Most homosexuals "camped"[9] in private but "watched their step in public."[10] Quentin by his very existence threatened this deception. The homosexual community started to turn him from their doors. "Finding that homosexuals didn't like me was harder to bear than the hostility of normal people... The coldness with which I was received ... was wounding in the extreme."[11]

How well he did at the job with the printing firm can be gauged by the fact that he was there for four years, during the last earning three pounds a week. Unfortunately the firm was then sold and Quentin got the feeling that the new owners did not take as liberated a view of him, so they parted company. It was during his last year with this firm that he published his first book. This was a collaborative effort with Albert Frederick Stuart. It was called *Lettering for Brush and Pen* and is a serious study of typography. The introduction states, "The object of this book is to present a series of alphabets of practical value to both craftsmen and amateur, rather than to deal with lettering in general terms; to give definite examples of styles, not vague instructions and a few odd samples which leave the rest of the alphabet to the student's imagination."[12]

The book must have had some merit because it was still in print over thirty years later.

It was also during his last year with this firm that Quentin took his now famous trip to Portsmouth. Then Portsmouth was known as the homosexual capital of England and Quentin's visit was in "a spirit of hilarious research."[13] The visit was made possible by an actress friend who wished to put on a series of Shakespeare's plays in the Isle of Wight, where her mother ran a boarding house. Quentin had assisted her efforts by lending her £10, which was a great deal of money then — equivalent to many hundreds of pounds today. Part of this scheme involved Quentin also traveling to the Isle of Wight. Why? Was he to be further involved financially? Were his acting skills to be used? Or was he simply being allowed to tag along because of his donation? He doesn't tell us. What he does say is that this trip compelled him to pass through Portsmouth. There he stayed at a hotel (more expense) and having arrived in his suite, fell asleep. When he awoke it was night time. As soon as he stepped out of the hotel's front door he was approached by a number of sailors. Stating that he would like to walk along the sea front, he found himself being escorted by his own personal navy. This swelled in number as they made their way to the beach. The interaction remained entirely verbal; the sailors were flirtatious, relaxed and friendly. The chat never fell below the level of the risqué, and as it became clear that nothing else was going to happen, they started to drift casually away until only two older men were left. By now the hotel was shut, but his companions managed to get them into a kind of tea room where they sat chatting until morning.

The next day he left Portsmouth. In *The Naked Civil Servant* he describes this adventure as "the first, last and only time that I ever sat in a crowd of people whose attention I really desired without once feeling that I was in danger."[14] When this scene was re-enacted for the film it was done as a dream-like sequence in the studio and later would be voted by British viewers as one of the top one hundred favorite television moments of all time.

During the years of the early to mid 1930s, Quentin changed his address so often that his mother complained that he was filling up her address book. Most of the rooms he rented during this time were either in such bad locations or of such poor quality, or both, that the owners would not have dared ask for money for them from anyone else. I shall not mention them all, only those of note. From the attic room he moved to Maiden Vale, where he shared a room with an out-of-work actor who slept on the only bed while Quentin slept on the sofa. However this man's active sex life forced Quentin to move on to a room on Lynhope Street.

It was here that Quentin received his first visit from the police. I have already mentioned the Irishman, the Scotsman and their female friend. Apparently the Irishman had now disappeared, but the other two were still around. It was in their effort to find the Scotsman's address that the police had visited Quentin. The Scotsman had not reported to his probation officer. Quentin did not give them his address. The police warned him that he could be charged with harboring undesirables, to which Quentin replied that if the Scotsman had been undesirable he would not have bothered. They left.

Quentin quickly moved into a two room flat which he shared with his art student friend Pat.

Around this time Pat started an affair with the Czech with the unspellable name, and they shortly after ran off together. The Czech man's wife, who had up to then been an artists' model, decided she had had enough and became a nightclub hostess. She moved to a two-room flat near Oxford Street and Quentin moved into the second room. At Quentin's suggestion she also took in another lodger, the daughter of a clergyman known to Quentin's sister, Phyllis. She was a drama student and introduced Quentin to various actors; it was through her that he had met the actress who would initiate his trip to Portsmouth, and through her he was able to get free theatre tickets. However, she eventually proved to be more trouble than she was worth, and according to Quentin's autobiography, "stole whatever money was left in the house."[15]

The Czech man's wife eventually divorced her husband and married an ex-serviceman who had lived in the same house where she and Quentin shared her two-room flat. She and her new husband moved out of London.

Quentin was now living in a room in a new boarding house in Chelsea. By now he had moved eleven times. It was in this boarding house that Quentin states that he felt at home for the first time. "It was run by actors and soon filled up with stock characters — an actress (tempestuous), a fashion artist (brittle), an American girl in search of experience (bewildered) — and we all ran in and out of each other's rooms making tea and talking about our futures."[16] Considering that his average stay in a room during these years was four months, he stayed in the Chelsea boarding house a long time — a whole year. It was the first place he had lived, ever, that felt like home. "Any real people who did succeed in crawling past the screening devices merely murmured to themselves, if they met me in the hall, 'That illusion again,' and went upstairs to take two aspirin."[17]

Unfortunately, as he was in the process of moving out, his future memory of his year there was besmirched by an accusation from another lodger that Quentin had stolen money from him. This turned up safe and sound but then he was accused of having replaced it. This accusation Quentin received with even greater indignation, as it showed that his enemies considered him capable of remorse. To Quentin an apology for harm done was only appropriate if the act had not been intended. If it had, apologizing to the victim merely placed them in the position of having to feign acceptance of an apology from someone who had wronged them deliberately and thus merely inflicted even greater cruelty on them.

7

Freelancing

"I cannot claim that from this moment I was always happy but, from the age of twenty-eight, I never did for long anything that I didn't want to — except grow old." — Quentin Crisp, *The Naked Civil Servant.*

By the time Quentin left the printing firm it was 1937. He decided that the solution to finding himself repeatedly out of work was to give up looking for employment. Instead he decided to try his hand as a freelance graphic artist and found that he could make enough money that he did not starve to death.

This decision presented a new problem. Whereas a job interview requires the one face-to-face meeting, being a freelance worker required these to take place every week as he went around the agencies trying to persuade them to use his services.

He found it necessary to develop a routine. When he first ventured into a new agency he had to appear not to notice the reactions. Anyone with eyesight would rush off to tell their colleagues about who or what had just come in. Then he needed to find something to do while waiting to talk to the manager so that he again would be able to feign not to notice as each employee would file past his seat for a better look. Finally, when introduced to the manager, he had to engage in some form of business, such as checking his portfolio, which allowed him to look away while his prospective employer had a good look at him and become accustomed to his appearance. By the time Quentin had gotten through all of this and the manager had realized that he was neither an apparition nor dangerous, the manager would sometimes give him the work simply out of relief.

In his autobiography he states that from this point on he never did anything for any length of time which he did not want to do except grow old. He also states that he ceased to care what other people thought of him, yet makes the apparently contradictory statement that he tried continuously to make himself more appealing to others.

Original watercolor by Quentin Crisp, 1938, created as an artist's proof for his book *Colour in Display*.

He was now renting a room above a ballet studio in Belgravia. The ballet teacher, Hilda Lumley, would become one of his dearest, closest, long-term friends. It was she who, when someone said, "Well, Quentin has a problem adjusting himself to society," replied, "I don't agree." Quentin does exactly as he pleases. The rest of us have to adapt ourselves to him."[1] She even bought him furniture for his room. Quentin seems to have had an exceptionally close friendship with the ballet teacher; certainly she was very good to him and he would later christen her "Miss Lumley who can do no wrong."[2]

He was still maintaining a close relationship with his mother and his sister, Phyllis; both his brothers were long ago dispatched to foreign fields. During 1938 he accompanied his sister's family on a holiday to Norfolk. As a point of curiosity, on the door outside he had three names written: Quentin Crisp, Denis Pratt and Lawrence Arkell. Why did he use all these names? Quentin Crisp and Denis Pratt are at least understandable, but where did Lawrence Arkell come from? To the best of my knowledge Quentin never mentioned this name either in interview or in print.

His new room above the ballet studio had only one window which was so high that even the bottom was above Quentin's head, so due to the physical effort involved he never drew the curtains. This brought about his second visit from the police. On this occasion they came in a pair, a detective inspector who did the talking and a younger version who blocked the door to prevent his escape. From the inspector's discourse it was revealed that some of Quentin's neighbors could see through this high window directly onto his bed. They did not like what they saw. After advising him that he could get seven years for what his neighbors had seen, Quentin promised to be more careful and the two policemen left. Quentin would later surmise that the only reason he was not arrested there and then was that none of these neighbors were willing to testify about what they had seen. When the police had left, Quentin telephoned all those who would not wish to visit his room, knowing it was now being observed by the police.

Quentin had always made it clear that he did not expect anything from anyone who knew him. Indeed, "Anyone who allowed himself to become my friend was doing me a favor. I always tried to make it clear that I was aware of at least some of the penalties that went with knowing me."[3] For example, he made it clear that if any of his friends met him in the street they did not have to acknowledge him in any way.

He had recently broken seven years of happy celibacy by starting an affair with a civil servant. In *The Naked Civil Servant*, Quentin only refers to him as "the man from the ministry."[4] All we know of him is that he was middle aged and apparently rather a drab and unassuming individual. The affair seems to have been a rather limited one — limited only to sex. The man from the ministry only visited Quentin in his room and they never went out anywhere. I think we can safely assume that it would not have done his career any good had he been spotted with Quentin. However, he did continue to visit Quentin even after the police visit.

During this period Quentin supplemented his income by giving tap dance lessons while the ballet studio was not being used. His students were probably unaware that Quentin was always only one step ahead of them. He also did regular design work for a company called Blanford Press, which, in 1938, commissioned his second book, *Colour in Display*. This book was about window dressing, the main theme that maximum interest lay at the point of maximum contrast.

The preface states "A book about colour in display is definitely dangerous unless the function of colour is well understood; for of all the attributes of display, the one that it is least suitable to consider separately, the one that can never be all-important is colour ... colour is like style. It is only when it is good that one does not notice it. It is precisely the discordant use of colour that makes prospective customers colour conscious, that distracts their attention, in other words, from the goods that it fondly hoped that they will buy."[5]

War was just around the corner, so it took several years to sell out its only edition. It is now very rare and much sought after by collectors. He earned £60, (£600 in today's money) for this effort, which was a tidy sum in those days considering how little he lived on. The rare copy which comes up for sale today goes for £600 to £800. According to Quentin, the fact that his book sold out its edition "only proves once more that people will pay to read what they already know."[6]

8

The Early War Years

"I noticed at once that, though some of the buildings had been ruined, most of the people had been improved. Everyone talked to everyone — even to me. The golden age had temporarily arrived." — Quentin Crisp, *The Naked Civil Servant.*

When war was declared in September 1939, Quentin went out and purchased two pounds of henna and a stockpile of cosmetics; he did not know how long it might last. Apart from this he decided to ignore the war and never bought a newspaper for fear people might think he approved of what was going on in the world.

During the war years he found that his lifetime habit of walking everywhere at breakneck speed while trying either to dodge or ignore the looks of hatred, obscenities and flying stones which were directed at him came in handy. He simply applied this technique to the new dangers which filled the streets.

The war years would be significant and eventful ones for Quentin. The first consequence was that work dried up overnight. Within months he was starving. Hope came in the form of a letter requesting his attendance at a medical board as the first step to call-up for the army. In an effort to try to improve his chances of getting through, he toned down his appearance (he had also knocked five years off his age) to the point where anyone who knew him then would have thought some great calamity had befallen him. It was not enough. After considerable physical examinations, questions about his private life, and much discussion between the various doctors who had now appeared, he was given an exemption on the grounds that he was suffering from a sexual perversion. One of his friends, a woman named Marshall, objected to the use of this phrase. "Shouldn't it be 'glorifying in'?"[1]

He also received a letter from the labor exchange to the same effect. These documents would prove useful in the next few years, as there came into existence a new group of hooligans in the areas Quentin frequented: draft dodgers and deserters. These men could not leave whatever dark cellar they had crawled into. But if they could endure the disgrace of being known as Quentin Crisp better than the prospect of jail and possibly a firing squad, the use of his exemption papers would allow them to walk in the daylight for a few hours.

Quentin found that with the advent of war everything reached new extremes. People seemed to lose all restraint and while on the one hand he was kissed passionately on the lips by a total stranger, on the other he was left unconscious on the pavement after a particularly savage beating outside Holborn Station.

Around Christmas 1939 Quentin was stopped in his tracks by a tall bearded stranger. Angus McBean was a theatrical photographer and took the now famous black and white portraits of Quentin, one of which is in the National Portrait Gallery. "Mr. McBean longed to take photographs as fervently as I desired to be photographed."[2] The two quickly formed a strong friendship, spending quite a lot of time together with Quentin regularly appearing as background characters in McBean's photos. They would remain friends until Angus's death.

McBean was another of those great English eccentrics. His hobby seems to have been buying houses and totally redecorating or rebuilding them so that they became a form of art. A door might be painted so that it looked as though it was open and you could see the next room through it. A wall might have a window painted in the middle showing an apparently beautiful country scene. A ceiling might be painted to look like it had vines growing on it. Later in the war he purchased a house outside London and had allowed a number of young men to escape the blitz by living there. When the authorities found out about this he was arrested, charged with the perversion of minors and sentenced to four years in prison, even though some were there with their parents' knowledge and in some cases even at their parents' request.

During Angus' incarceration Quentin's mother was staying in a hotel in Somerset when a phone call came from Angus McBean for his mother, who was also staying there. Baba, observing the woman's embarrassment, said, "You have nothing to fear because I am Quentin Crisp's mother!"[3] The two women pooled their disgrace and became lifelong friends; Baba sometimes staying with Mrs. McBean.

Things did start to improve, however. The ballet teacher, Hilda Lumley, had to move her studio, and in an act of great friendship and generosity gave Quentin all the furniture from his room for a minimum payment. He could now rent cheaper unfurnished rooms and after an intermediate stop-off in

Fulham landed in Beaufort Street, where he would stay for the next forty-one years. "I had thought once before that I had reached home. Now I really had."[4]

For the first time ever he had life on his terms. Growing up he had watched his mother as she spent hours cleaning her house. Once as she was dusting the books in a bookcase Denis exclaimed that he would never do that, to which she replied, "I know you wouldn't. That's why I must."[5] He decided that he would never be a slave to the daily rituals of domesticity, and it was here that he developed the next great tenet of his domestic philoso-phy — "Never clean the place where you live, because after the first four years the dust doesn't get any worse. It's just a question of not losing your nerve."[6] At night he would slip into his bed as gently as possible and lie ramrod straight throughout the night so as not to disturb the sheets. In the morning he would slide out from under them so that it almost looked like no one had slept in the bed at all. His only concession to cleanliness was to take his bedding to the local launderette once a week. He realized that if he left it for longer they might not accept them.

This house was owned by Violet Vereker, a devoted libertarian, and Quentin would often say that it was the only boarding house left in London which was run for the benefit of the lodgers. Quentin called her "the patron saint of hooligans."[7] Just how liberal Miss Vi was can be gleaned by the fol-lowing story. Once while the front door was open a tramp had sneaked in and hidden in the cupboard under the stairs. When Vi discovered this she started to give him a regular supply of food and told him to stay as long as he wanted, even suggesting that some of the other residents might give him a blanket.

At this point it might be worth mentioning another resident of Beaufort Street: the actor Gordon Richardson. Richardson was then engaged primarily in repertoire but would later, during the 1960s, 70s and 80s, establish himself as a reliable bit-part actor in films and television, usually playing doctors. He appeared in a number of episodes of *Dr. Finlay's Casebook,* an episode of *Dr. Who,* and in the cinema he was in *Carry on Loving* and *The Go-between.* He would occupy the ground floor front room for many years, like Quentin becoming one of the fixtures. Gordon seems to have had an independent income of some sort and would once or twice a year hold a party to which he would invite everyone he knew. Like Quentin he was also gay and highly eccentric. Beaufort Street seems to have attracted eccentrics and Gordon would often say that Quentin was the only sane person there. Gordon had a glass eye and as a prank would take it out and polish it, usually while someone was eating. He is especially worth mentioning in the context of Quentin's life story, as it was often through Gordon that Quentin would meet other people who would become long term friends and have influence in his life.

It was at Beaufort Street that Quentin acquired his first telephone, through which he found a new way of getting in touch with the outside world. The flip side of this was that those who abused him in public now had a means of reaching him in his private sanctuary. Often as someone was trying to convince him, in the sexist voice they could muster, that they knew him from some previous intimate encounter, he could hear the muffled laughs and sniggers of those who were listening in from behind; presumably they found this to be a form of entertainment. Some would be insistent that they must see him in person. These he invited to visit at a time when he would already be at home, so as not to inconvenience him if they did not turn up. Surprisingly, none of these encounters turned out to be dangerous. On one occasion when asked why he had come the man simply replied that he had been dared to by others. As the years passed these calls and visits would diminish but never completely stop.

Why did Quentin permit these calls and visits? Why not just hang up the phone as soon as he realized the true nature of the call? Quentin's approach tells us a lot about his relationship with the outside world, the resolve of his character and his profound understanding of the human mind. If he were to slam the phone down, the caller would have known that he had achieved his goal of annoying and irritating Quentin. The result would have been that the caller, renewed in his efforts by his previous success, would have repeatedly called back. But if Quentin simply allowed the caller to talk until they had exhausted all they had to say, which wasn't much, without him showing any signs of annoyance or irritation, they would eventually hang up feeling deflated and invariably not call again. In much the same way, a child who throws a stone at a stranger's window, will, if the owner ignores them, go on to the next house, and try to find better entertainment there. To the requests for visits he applied the same technique.

A convenient death having been denied him by the army board, he now needed to find some way to survive, and so he ventured back into the world of commercial art. The new telephone proved invaluable, as he could now get in touch with possible employers without having to endure the ordeal of making a personal appearance. Most of the work which came his way was designing covers for paperback books. He developed an approach to these which involved the least effort and time. If the book was aimed at women the cover would be in pastel shades with a dark haired heroine with small breasts; if it was aimed at men it would be dark with a red-haired heroine with large breasts; if for children it would have bright colors and a heroine with no cleavage, and if it was a documentary it required no illustration.

In 1940 a few months after his encounter with Angus McBean, his unusual appearance brought him to the attention of the painter Clifford Hall, who telephoned him to ask if he could paint his portrait. After reluctantly agreeing to pay Quentin for his time a deal was made. Hall, another of the area's "characters," would, during the next year, paint three portraits of him. Quentin was flattered by Hall's interest in him and he may have been able to persuade Quentin to sit for one of the paintings as a nude. Very regrettably, the whereabouts of these are now unknown.

Towards the end of 1940 Quentin's writing aspirations were given a fresh lease on life by an old acquaintance. The actress Estelle Murison, who would later marry writer and designer Paul Holt, had shared a boarding house with Quentin four years earlier. She was now the director of The Threshold Theatre in Nottinghill. Needing some new material, she approached him to write a revue. Unfortunately, neither this nor two other plays he wrote — an "anti-Pirandello" play and another set in the Trojan Wars called *A Man with a Sword* — would ever be presented to the public. Murison described his work as "wholly brilliant and playable,"[8] though she may have been a touch biased. If they were so brilliant why didn't she put any of them on? As we shall discover much later in this story, the writing of fiction does not seem to have been one of Quentin's fortes.

Despite these disappointments he was a regular member of the audience at The Threshold Theatre. It was during one of his visits that he first saw the young Peter Ustinov in a play called *Fishing for Shadows*. Ustinov had also translated the play from French to English. It was during one of these performances that he first made the acquaintance of the writer and actor Peter Noble, with whom he seems to have particularly enjoyed talking. In later years Peter would also add the titles of producer and historian to his already packed curriculum vitae.

Shortly after this, life got better still when his art skills came into demand in the fledgling documentary film industry. One of his fellow lodgers in Beaufort Street was secretary to a film producer and through her he managed to get employment doing the titles for a number of documentaries. The producer must have been pleased with Quentin's work, as he passed his name on to his colleges and for a time Quentin had so much work he could barely keep up with it. At one point he acquired the post of artistic director for one film, with full responsibility for all images and graphics. This was the first time in his life he had found work which he actually wanted to do and for a time abandoned his philosophy of inaction, throwing himself into it with enthusiasm. His efforts would eventually land him a full time job for a company called Studio Film Laboratories which lasted nine months.

During this period Quentin was still making regular visits to his crippled student friend Pat, who was still living with the Czech with the unspellable name. This man had always been eccentric, but in the company of Quentin and his friends this had not seemed remarkable; however, as the war progressed he began to show signs of increasing mental instability. One day Pat phoned Quentin to ask him to visit, as she feared the Czech was having a nervous breakdown. On arriving Quentin found him standing with his back against the wall, terrified and refusing to move in case "they should come in."[9] Shortly after this he was institutionalized. This was by no means the last Quentin would see of him, as we shall find out much later.

9

Becoming a Model

"I twisted and turned, climbed up the walls of the life room, morning, nude and night." — Quentin Crisp, *The Naked Civil Servant.*

Perhaps the most significant event in his wartime life occurred in 1942 towards the end of his period with Studio Film Laboratories. An artists' model friend whom he had known since she lived in a room in one of his former boarding houses phoned him in desperation. She was unable to attend a posing session she was booked into for the next day and had already exhausted her other acquaintances, all of whom were busy. "You're always saying it must be nice to be a model. Now's your chance."[1] So dressed in an old pair of boxer shorts converted into a posing pouch, he did his first session as an artists' model at Toynbee Town Hall the following evening.

The instructor asked him if he could hold a crucifixion pose, to which Quentin replied that he had died after three hours the first time. When four hours later he was still on his feet, he realized that he had discovered a new way of earning a living. In many ways this might seem to have been the perfect occupation for Quentin; his unusual and highly colorful appearance, his exhibitionism, desire for attention and flamboyant gestures could not have fitted the post better. Indeed, it would become the only job he ever did which he fully understood and for many, many years would represent total fulfillment.

He found a level of comradeship among the models, some of whom would recommend him to other schools. Also by this stage in the war there were not many physically intact and able bodied men still in England. As it became known that he was reliable, the teachers also started to take him with them as they traveled between schools. This at least assured them that when they reached their destination they would have a model for their class. Indeed, those teachers who worked with him then remembered him not just for his eccentricities but for his level of professionalism and reliability.

Remembering his time at the Art College in High Wycombe, where he was frustrated by the uninspiring posing of the models, he decided "to force upon the students the qualities that I felt life drawing should possess."[2] "I twisted and turned, climbed up the walls of the life rooms and rolled on their paint-daubed floors morning, nude and night."[3] His reputation, due to his elaborate and eccentric poses, spread quickly. On one occasion a frustrated art teacher exclaimed, "All you have to do is stand as though you were waiting for a bus."[4] Which was no help to Quentin; when he was standing waiting for a bus he looked like he was posing for a painting. Another teacher let him loose on his pupils with the comment, "Now draw that. Wings optional."[5] All of this effort had an effect he had not anticipated. Quentin had initially hoped that he would get on well with the pupils, but his exotic poses stretched their skills often to breaking point; they hated him!

His new career did bring on him one form of attention which on occasions reached an unwelcome level. Throughout his life Quentin had found that there was a particular type of woman who was attracted to homosexual men. For these women such a relationship provides "an opportunity to lavish emotion upon a pseudo-man without paying the price that in heterosexual circumstances would be inevitable."[6] He found that among the art pupils were a significant number of these women. Mostly their attentions did not progress further than chats over cups of tea brought to him on the dais during his standard 10 minute breaks in each hour. But on one occasion while waiting in a college corridor to be paid, one of these women who had brought him tea during the session took his hand and kissed him before running away. A number of weeks later she wrote to him requesting a meeting. Foolishly, as he later realized, he agreed. Their time together had gone well until Quentin took her to the bus station for her trip home. Here she flung herself at him imploring that he kiss her. Shortly after this he received a letter from a friend of hers begging him to see her again, with the implication that she was in such a state of distress that her friend feared she might resort to suicide. Quentin replied that, as it was clear that this lady was seeking something more than mere friendship, any further contact would be pointless. It would take several more such literary exchanges to bring this episode to a close.

One evening while posing at St. Martin's School, the very same one to which he had been denied access to as a student ten years earlier, he was told that a model who was working in the next room wanted to meet him. This man's name was Peter Fisk and after they had finished their duties for the evening he invited Quentin to accompany him to one of the cafés in Charlotte Street which he frequented. This would prove to be one of the most significant events in Quentin's life and the opening of a whole new world for him. These cafés formed the nightlife of Fitzrovia and could have only been found by someone who already knew of their existence. Due to the blackout conditions which were then necessary, they looked totally indistinguishable from the other buildings.

Here for the first time in his life Quentin found himself totally welcome; his homosexuality and appearance were of no significance whatsoever; indeed he was warmly welcomed. Here among the "bookies and burglars, actresses and artisans, poets and prostitutes,"[7] he was accepted purely for who he was. Also among this clientele was found a new group: deserters and draft dodgers, for whom, as I have mentioned earlier, Quentin's exemption papers were to prove to be of particular value. In some of these cafés he was even given meals on credit and would on occasions act as go-between, purchasing goods on the black market which the other customers and staff would sell in the cafés.

It was in this café life that Quentin started to develop a whole new layer to add to his personality. In his youth the driving force for his social interactions had been to inform and reform, but here there was no need, the reformation had already happened; so now in middle age he wanted to entertain. "I began a whirlwind courtship of the whole district."[8] One of his standard phrases when meeting someone new became "tell me the story of your life."[9] Quentin always said that while he loved his friends, he was simply mad about strangers. He certainly seems to have become very popular and well liked. "Compared to Quentin other homosexuals were pale shadows"[10] was a typical comment from those who knew him then.

During this period Quentin much preferred the cafés to pubs; in these he found people who would willingly sit for hours listening to him; however, in the pubs, within an hour of opening time alcohol had already begun to deaden the senses of those imbibing. "Conversation did not flow with the drink; it drowned in it."[11]

During this period he made many new friends, some of whom he would keep for life. Joan Rhodes became a celebrity with her strong woman act *The Mighty Mannequin* and throughout the years would regularly have Quentin over for sumptuous dinners. There was Maria Gabriele Steiner, who had moved to England from Vienna in 1937 and in 1943 rented a room in Fitzrovia. Quentin described her as "the most beautiful woman in the world."[12] They became good friends; Quentin showed her the best and cheapest places to eat. She would later say, "I used to feel proud to be with him. I was actually quite in love with him."[13] For his part, Quentin had actually thought her to be a lesbian.

It was also around this time that he met Philip O'Connor, who was then also one of the district's eccentrics. Quentin often gave Philip money during the coming years, generosity Philip would repay in his own way many years later in an act which would play an important, perhaps even seminal, part in Quentin's life. A couple of years later Philip would start an affair with Maria Steiner, much to Quentin's dismay, and over the next few years fathered two children by her.

In later years Maria would use Quentin as a babysitter. Quentin's social and domestic abilities were always much more highly developed than he liked to admit. On one occasion he went to visit a friend who had recently had a baby and found her in hysterics. Quentin packed her off to the bedroom to compose herself while he changed the baby's nappy.

Philip O'Connor would later achieve his own level of fame with the publication of his autobiography, *Memoirs of a Public Baby*.

This same year introduced another unanticipated but wholly welcome aspect to Quentin's life; the Americans landed. Labeled "With love from Uncle Sam,"[14] they walked beside him, not behind, and even those who had mistaken him for a woman, remained friendly.

> American: "Can I walk you home, ma'am?"
> Me: "You think I'm a woman, don't you."
> American: "You waggle your fanny like a woman."
> Me: "Oh, I should ignore that."
> American: "I'm trying to but it's not easy."
> Conversations like this told me I was by nature American.[15]

Even rejection they accepted good-naturedly. "Never in the history of sex was so much offered to so many by so few."[16] It was the openness and directness of their natures which appealed to Quentin above all. "At the first gesture of acceptance from a stranger, words of love began to ooze from their lips, sexuality from their bodies and pound notes from their jackets like juice from a peeled peach."[17]

To the British happiness was not to be directly sought, but rather achieved by the attainment of some higher, noble goal, such as helping the poor, or finding a cure for some terrible disease. The Americans believed they had the right to pursue happiness for its own sake. It was at this time that he started to dream about living in America.

Quentin initially played the field until he met a soldier from Seattle who had a magnificent physique and an Italian name; they settled into an eighteen month affair. "Never before had a physical relationship been presented to me so completely without stint and without overtones."[18] In *The Naked Civil Servant*, he makes a point of stating that he was not in love with his American and that he would not have put him before one of his own friends, and the American would not have expected him to do so. When this man ceased to call he took it calmly and would never know what happened to him. "I had no idea whether he had gone to heaven or New York — but, then, to me they were the same place."[19]

One of the publishers for whom Quentin did design work — Ivan Nicholson and Watson — evidently impressed by his abilities, suggested that he write a book. So in 1943 his third book, *All This and Bevin Too*, was published. The entire of this unusual book is in the form of a limerick telling what happened to a kangaroo who answers an ad placed by the local zoo. By persuading him that the book was already guaranteed publication, Quentin managed to get his friend and fellow habitué of Fitzrovian Café life, Mervyn Peake, to illustrate it. Peake had just been invalided out of the army and was then already regarded as the most fashionable illustrator in England. With Mervyn Peake on board Quentin managed to finalize the book's publication. It is a damning indictment of the Ministry of Labour, and is now a much sought after collectors' piece. Quentin, in his typical dismissive way, would state that when he went to the booksellers' on the day it was released, he could see only one man looking at it, and that was Mervyn Peake.

The publishers must have been pleased enough with his efforts, because they paid him to do another book. *Between the Devil and the BBC*, though written, was never published and seems now to be lost.

In 1943 Marguerite Evans, then an art student, painted his portrait, which now hangs in the National Portrait Gallery in London.

Shortly after this he acquired his next full time job. He became friendly with a Scotsman called MacQueen, who on hearing of Quentin's design abilities, offered him a job in his firm. However, this company did not actually exist at that moment. Quentin seems to have played an important part in helping MacQueen set up his new company, even helping him acquire other staff; thus he found himself interviewing art students who had drawn him in college. This firm designed exhibition stands and other types of displays, and Quentin would stay there for a number of years, even after the end of the war. During these years he continued posing in his spare time. And of course there was the steady stream of American servicemen to keep him occupied. His life must have been very busy indeed.

The following year, 1944, saw what his friends had been telling him would happen for years; he was arrested. Quentin had been walking the streets looking for a shoe shop which stocked shoes small enough for him when he was approached by two policemen "disguised as human beings"[20] who asked to see his exemption papers. "When my inquisitors had retrieved their eyebrows from the roots of their hair, they gave me back this by now rather grubby document and I moved on."[21] Unknown to Quentin they then proceeded to follow him around for the next half hour. During this period Quentin had met a number of friends with whom he had exchanged pleasantries. The two policemen then reacquainted themselves and stated they were arresting him on the charge of soliciting. He was marched to the police station, where the duty sergeant took his fingerprints. In *The Naked Civil Servant*, Quentin muses that there are to this day a set of fingerprints on file at New Scotland Yard which must cause wonder to anyone who looks at them because of the little squiggles above each print, left there by his long fingernails which the desk sergeant could not keep out of the ink. When he finally got out of his police cell late that night he rushed home and contacted as many friends as he could to appear for him in court the next day, including some of those he had been talking to that day. He also phoned his employer, Mr. MacQueen, to advise him that he would not be in work the next day, or indeed for some time to come if things went badly.

Quentin realized this was his big moment, but also that if he was to get through it, he must summon up all of his capacity for survival. He was pleased with the magistrate who patiently explained to him the proper court procedures, but dismayed by the unpleasant bitchiness of his clerk, who played to the gallery with such comments as, "You are a male person I presume."[22] When the police had given their evidence, the magistrate offered Quentin the option of speaking from where he was or taking the witness stand, where he would have to be sworn on oath. He choose the witness box because there he would be raised above those in the court and would be facing his audience. Conducting his own defense and knowing that he must never accuse the police of lying, he argued that they, already knowing he was homosexual, had misinterpreted his encounters of the previous day. He followed this by trying to explain that, as someone who dressed and behaved openly as a homosexual, his appearance set him apart from the rest of society, making it difficult for him to make friendships; that he had learned many years ago that for his own safety, as he walked down a street, he did not interact with anyone unless he already knew them. How could he hope to solicit anyone in broad daylight in a crowded London street looking as he did?

After listening to numerous character witnesses and being presented with a letter from Quentin's employer, Mr. MacQueen, who expressed his total confidence in Quentin, the magistrate declared that he had no case to answer (which was judicial speak for "the policemen are lying"). Quentin was triumphant; he had shown in a court of law that he was both "homosexual and as stainless as Sheffield steel."[23] This court appearance would play an important and defining central scene in the film version of *The Naked Civil Servant*. Quentin's victory was quickly whittled down by the police, who took their defeat badly and began a campaign of getting him barred from the public houses of Fitzrovia. When one of his friends complained to one of the landlords, he replied that it had been pointed out to him that he could not retain his license and Quentin. This was a great blow to Quentin and must certainly have impacted the quality of his social life for the next years.

He did not lose his friends, however, and would visit them when he could. It was while at a party in the house of a writer called Meadmore, whom Quentin had met while posing for Mr. Hall, that he would meet a man with whom he would become close friends — George Melly, who was on leave from the Navy. At these parties Melly sang and danced with such exuberance and abandonment that Quentin became concerned for his physical wellbeing. According to Quentin, Melly's discourse was risqué to the point that "Mr. Melly had to be obscene to be believed."[24]

George's own account of their first meeting actually takes place in a restaurant where he was introduced to Quentin by a mutual friend. George described him as "quite beautiful."[25] What they do agree on is that they became friends. On one occasion when they were traveling by bus to Chelsea to see the film *Gilda* a woman passenger shouted at George, "Can't you get yourself a girl then, sailor?"[26]

10

Peace Breaks Out

"Death-made-easy vanished over night and soon love-made-easy, personified by the American soldier, also disappeared!" — Quentin Crisp, *The Naked Civil Servant.*

On the day peace was declared Quentin bumped into Thumbnails again for the first time in fourteen years. All Thumbnails could say was, "You look terrible."[1] And of course the Americans went home. "The horrors of peace were many!"[2] Quentin was still working for MacQueen's display firm. It was here that Ann Valery, future actress, writer (co-author of the series *Tenko*) and BBC personality, who had found employment with MacQueen, first met him. She describes their first meeting thus: "I was confronted by a bird of paradise perched at the drawing board — hair the colour of rubies; midnight-blue jacket, topped with scarf and anchored with a brooch, and, best of all, not a mitten in sight, but rings and fingernails pink with polish.... 'My name is Mr. Quentin Crisp. I am the art department, and you may approach' ... I thought he was wonderful and from that moment on he became my mentor in matters of makeup."[3] They would become friends and would occasionally meet after work in the evenings and weekends. Years in the future Quentin would become her fiancé! This will be explained later.

But on the street he found that attitudes towards him had now changed. The expansiveness and open mindedness which the prospect of instant death had brought to the residents of wartime London had now faded and people were starting to regret their past behavior. "I, who had once been a landmark more cheerful looking and more bomb-proof than St. Paul's Cathedral, had ceased to be a talisman. I had become a loathsome reminder of the unfairness of fate. I was still living while the young, the brave and the beautiful were dead."[4] Also at this time the ban on him in Fitzrovia which had been imposed by the police after their failed attempt to prosecute him in 1944 was still in effect. He found new haunts in places like Kings Road, Charlotte Street and Old Compton Street. There he made a new set of friends.

For his new audience he would endeavor to put on an improved performance. His journeys to and from posing classes allowed him the opportunity to practice his routines, which would also include impersonations of the female stars such as Bette Davis and Barbara Stanwyck. From then on he would continually polish his skits to the point where each new acquaintance would be met with "a complete cabaret turn."[5] The writer Bernard Kops described him thus: "He spoke very beautifully ... and always said to any stranger, 'Tell me the story of your life.' What's more he listened."[6] The general consensus among those who knew him then was that he was very, very nice and exceptionally intelligent.

At this time he met a friend who would perhaps have the greatest impact on his life. John Haggarty was an ex Royal Air Force man, 6' 3" and very handsome. The two got on very well from the start and clearly both men admired each other. Haggarty was strictly heterosexual but secure enough in his own sexuality that he had no problem in being seen walking along the street with Quentin or in admiring Quentin's abilities with makeup. They must have made an odd looking couple; Haggarty tall and broad, conservatively dressed, Quentin so much shorter and slight, dressed-well, like Quentin. Haggarty said of Quentin, "I never imagined that such a person existed. He was a great original ... a remarkable man.... I didn't see him as a wee poofter."[7] They would meet regularly over the next three years frequenting the area's cafés, though neither would visit the other's home. Haggarty would later describe them as being "Like a couple of birds in Trafalgar Square, strutting around together for a while and then flying off in different directions."[8] Quentin makes no mention in any way of Haggarty in *The Naked Civil Servant*, though many people have since postulated that Haggarty was Quentin's original unobtainable great dark man; if so would writing about him have then been too painful for Quentin? Quentin would, however, make up for this omission in his second autobiography, *How to Become a Virgin*. By the late 1940s Haggarty had established himself as a script writer and filmmaker. But it would be many years before the significance of this would become apparent.

In 1946 Quentin's artistic abilities got him the job of illustrating the book *Og and Other Ogres* by Reginald Reynolds, and his literary efforts continued with some success also. He had a number of articles published in the then new intellectual magazine *Facet*. In the first of these, *The Genius of Mervyn Peake,* published in October 1946, he discusses the talents of Peake, admitting that in some instances he displays such a level of genius as to render even

Quentin speechless. In February of the next year his article *Patronage in the Age of Negation* appeared in the same magazine, in which he discusses the history of art and argues that it is "an elaborate striptease act."[9] In the summer of 1947 the magazine also published his poem *Spring*, also planned to appear in his last book, *The Dusty Answers*, yet unpublished. Quentin makes no mention of any of this in his autobiography, nor does he mention anything about his family. He still maintained his strong relationship with his mother, often sending her money, and around Easter 1946 he had his first meeting with his niece Frances, then in her teens, who would over the succeeding decades become one of his closest relatives.

Quentin had by now been posing for a few years and his reputation and fame had become set in stone throughout the art school community. Although he often said how the pupils disliked him for his eccentric poses, this was by no means always the case. John W. Mills, who would go on to have a highly successful career as artist and sculptor, first met Quentin in 1947 when John was a pupil at Hammersmith School of Art. John told me, "As a new student brought up in South London, my first impression of the colourful blue rinsed Quentin Crisp was one of surprise and fascination, but this was quickly followed by a high regard for Quentin's professional attitude to his work as a model, no matter what pose we asked him to adopt he did with the utmost concentration and seriousness, he might occasionally ask 'are you sure?' This was typical of him during all the following years that we worked together as teaching artist and model."[10] John recalls that Quentin was actually concerned about and responsive to the students, whom he called "the young things."[11] He addressed the teachers as "sir." John told me, "He was stimulating and kind and his responses to student fears and forebodings based on years of listening in on student conversations and teaching altercations yielded a rich harvest of advice and genuine concern."[12]

John would continue to work with Quentin on a regular basis for the next three decades. In later years when John had become an art teacher and used Quentin as his model, Quentin would address him as "sir." "I asked him when we first encountered each other as teacher and model why he now called me Sir after all those years of treating me as just one of the students, 'Sir you are now in a position to hire and fire,' he said."[13]

In the years following the end of the war Quentin began escaping real life as often as he could by going to the cinema. However, he needed a companion. His explanation of this being that if God discovered him in the cinema and asked what he was doing there, he could not just say that he was enjoying himself, instead he could point to the person beside him with the excuse that he was only there to accompany his friend. This must be taken as very tongue

in cheek. Did Quentin simply prefer to share the experience? After all, one
of the pleasures of watching a film is in being able to discuss it afterwards
with someone who has also seen it. By now most of Quentin's friends — his
fellow Soho hooligans — had left, some got married and even worse had children, making his search for a film companion more arduous. One friend who
did accompany him regularly was a woman named Beeson who lived on the
same floor as he at Beaufort Street. Her insatiable sexual appetite would often
wake her neighbors during the night as she returned home with her latest
conquest. They went every Wednesday for several years. Sometime later Miss
Beeson got religion and would lecture Quentin and Gordon on their sinful
lives, causing Quentin to tell her he liked her better when she was a nympho-
maniac. Another regular cinema companion in the coming years would be
Barbara Markham, a dressmaker who had a shop in Covent Garden. She got
quite a lot of business from Quentin tailoring his second-hand clothes so that
they fit his small frame. Quentin's need for someone to fill this post when
friends were not available was so great that he often paid for their ticket as
well as his own, yet another example of his financial solvency. During these
years he managed to watch at least one film a week, sometimes as many as
three. He preferred American films as opposed to British and European, which
were as boring as being alive. For Quentin the cinema should be a "forgetting
chamber"[14] where you go to escape real life.

This period of dedicated cinema going would last for the next twenty
years, during which he would acquire a vast knowledge of the film world. He
was still most interested in the female stars, but as time passed the greats such
as Greta Garbo and Marlene Dietrich were replaced by the likes of Marilyn
Monroe; much to his dismay. For Quentin the stars of the Golden Age of
Hollywood represented romance; an unattainable hopeless love which had to
be won against great odds and with effort and dedication. By the middle of
the twentieth century men no longer expected or wanted to have to win love,
and so "someone had to invent espresso sex and to serve each cup of this taste-
less beverage there had to be a mechanical doll whose only recommendation
was her infinite availability."[15] This was what the new stars such as Monroe
and Brigette Bardot represented for him. Of Monroe he observed, "Her direc-
tors persuaded her to flaunt her astonishing sexual equipment before us with
the touching defencelessness of a retarded child. She was what the modern
young man most desires in life — a mistress who could be won without being
wooed."[16] However, he continued his dedication to the "forgetting chamber"[17]
on the basis that any film, no matter how bad, was at least better than real
life. With the absence of stars he concentrated on the storylines, and as these
became for him more disturbing; "Over and over again I saw heroines for-

given — even praised — for the most dubious behaviour if they could claim that their object had been sexual fulfilment. To me this seemed not merely a flimsy excuse but a circumstance that only increased the crime."[18]

He started to concentrate on the techniques of filmmaking. During these years life became for Quentin "a series of those jarring moments when the screen goes blinding white, the jagged edge of a torn strip of film flicks one's eye-ball and there is a flash of incomprehensible numerals lying on their side (like a message from Hades) before the dream begins again."[19] This vast wealth of accumulated knowledge would be put to good use years later when he emigrated to America and got a job as a film reviewer, culminating in his book *How to Go to the Movies.*

11

Becoming the Stately Homo

"I had changed from the festive season to Lent." — Quentin Crisp, in
Quentin and Philip: A Double Portrait.

One of the most significant events of his life happened in 1948: he turned
forty. People started to accuse him of dying his hair red to make himself look
younger. Deception of any kind was abhorrent to Quentin, so he started phas-
ing red out and blue in. This would show that while he still dyed his hair, he
now accepted that he was growing old. He would embrace his decline. This
process started with him cutting his hair short, well short by Quentin's standards, two inches, followed by six months of slowly forcing red out and blue
in. Some of his friends were not so sure about this transformation; John Haggarty remembers, "This piece of lavender came walking towards me...."[1]; and
another commented, "What the fuck have you done to your hair?"[2] He now
found that attitudes towards him in the street were less severe. "Without my
scarlet hair I was like a Westerner without a gun."[3]

Another even more unfortunate event happened at this time; he developed eczema. His friends told him this was the result of an allergy and indeed
there have been cases showing a link between eczema and henna, which
Quentin had been using to dye his hair for the previous twenty years. He
would suffer from this condition with increasing severity for the rest of his
life.

By now Quentin had become an established part of London life. As an
example of just how much, consider that in the novel *Scamp*, Roland Camberton based the character of Douglas Vanner on Quentin Crisp. If you doubt
this, then consider the following excerpt: "The finest, the purest, the most
beautiful flower of unnatural truth is Douglas Vanner. He may be man, he
may be a woman. He has a blue chin and long waved ginger hair. His clothes
are neither this nor that. His eyes shine and his smile is delicate, poised and
more than civilized. His wit glitters perfectly and artificially, from the first

greeting 'Tell me the story of your life.' — to the last farewell —'But I expect to suffer!'"[4]

The following story also shows that his fame had even reached across the Atlantic to New York. A friend of his had been in New York and, feeling homesick, had noticed someone whom he thought by their clothes might be British. He started a conversation with this man, and when he told him he came from London the stranger asked him if he knew someone called Quentin Crisp. When he acknowledged that he did indeed, the stranger replied, "I thought somehow you really didn't want to know the way to Grand Central Station!"[5]

In 1949 his literary output again met with some success, and he had two plays broadcast on BBC radio. *Letting a Flat* is about the life of a number of robots, including a policeman and a housemaid. *The Black Thing* is about a man who is pursued by a mysterious black object which eventually drives him insane, and he murders his wife.

It was in 1949 also that Quentin first tried his hand at some autobiographical writing. In a book titled *Little Reviews Anthology* edited by Denys Val Baker, he had an essay published called "The Declining Nude." In this he discusses his experiences as an artists' model in government schools. Other authors published in the same volume included Sir John Betjeman and Dylan Thomas. That Quentin's work was then deemed of good enough quality to be included with these other authors is perhaps a foretaste of what was to come many years later. The author James Kirkup has described "The Declining Nude" as "an autobiographical essay of unbelievable brilliance."[6] Indeed, there are some wonderful Crispian pieces here. "It comes to this. You can either take easy poses and die of boredom or difficult poses and die of an enlarged heart. To each is given what defeat he will."[7] Of the changes in the art school environment in the years since the war, he tells us, "Because of the grants that the government is distributing like confetti among demobilized art students ... now, on the first day of the session, a howling mob of would-be students waving their Government grants above their heads clamours at the doors of every art school in the country. When at ten o'clock the doors are open the crowd rushes in and up the stairs and sits down wherever it can. And if you happen to sit down in the lavatory that is what you study for that term."[8]

These minor successes were however, not enough to cause any real change in his life, and so in his effort to get out of modeling Quentin now took a job in the art department of a publishing house. In *The Naked Civil Servant* he tells us that this was the only job he got though answering an ad in a newspaper and describes it as an "organization run like a rest home for retired gentlefolk."[9] Harrap and Co. was actually a highly respected company, having been formed in 1867 by George Godfrey Harrap. In 1932 its new offices at

182 High Holborn were opened by none other than Winston Churchill. It also seems to have been very amiable employer and the atmosphere there was very relaxed. He was always treated with respect and courtesy; doors were held open for him and he was always addressed as Mister. Perhaps the best description of this company was his observation that if someone had turned up for work drunk they would have been sent home in a taxi and listed as absent due to illness.

By this stage in his life Quentin was starting to feel that he had reached the limits of his own personality and so tried to involve himself with his new acquaintances. But, "it wasn't easy."[10] The art editor of Harrap and Co. once asked him, "What do you hold with — apart from yourself?"[11] Quentin racked his brains but couldn't think of anything. Although he says he took this job to get away from posing, he nevertheless continued to do the occasional evening. It would seem that he was not yet ready to give up being a model, or was it rather that he assumed that like all previous jobs, Harrap and Co. would not last, and by keeping his hand in with the posing racket he could still earn a living when it did end?

By the start of the 1950s he was still working for Harrap and Co. but would soon leave them after a publisher he knew had suggested that he write a novel, and because he had by now, thanks to his habit of never spending more than half his wage, accumulated enough savings to live for a year. Despite his immediate boss's response to his resignation, "You swine,"[12] he received a present from his colleges, and the manager invited him into his office to tell him, "I just wanted to say how tolerant I think you've been."[13] Quentin had been there for two and a half years, a long time by previous standards; during this time he had clearly become an established, respected and much liked member of the staff.

Six months later he delivered the manuscript for *Love Made Easy* to the publishers' office. His book was based on real-life people and incidents he had personally known and witnessed, and according to Quentin every line in it was true, in that it had actually been uttered by someone. Only the narrative was fictional. The publisher did not like it, commenting that it was "satire without anger."[14] His ballet teacher friend, Hilda Lumley, after reading it, commented, "I wish you hadn't made every line funny. It's so depressing."[15] After months of trying he failed to find a publisher and gave up. Of this experience he said he had learned that "if you describe things as better than they are, you are considered to be romantic; if you describe things as worse than they are, you will be called a realist; and if you describe things exactly as they are, you will be thought of as a satirist."[16] He pushed the manuscript under his bed and forgot about it for the next twenty-five years.

12

A Midlife Crisis

"Whatever I could hope to do or say or be, I had done and said and been." — Quentin Crisp, *The Naked Civil Servant*.

For the next few years Quentin went through what today would be called a midlife crisis. He was becoming increasingly disenchanted with posing. It seemed to him that he had done every pose possible and now his age made them harder to hold long enough for a student to finish their work. With regard to the things he enjoyed and actually wanted to do, he felt he had failed. He had failed to stay in the film industry and his efforts at writing, despite having had three books, numerous magazine articles and poems published and even two of his plays broadcast by the BBC, none of this had brought him wealth, success or fame. He felt that he had reached the summit of his life and what lay ahead was downhill. "I would not yet describe myself as miserable but I was deflated. I realized that the future was past."[1]

Until he reached his forties he had not considered his own mortality. Once during a conversation with his crippled friend Pat he stated, "I can never get it into my head that I shall one day die." She replied, "Neither can I, but I practice like mad."[2] By now the Czech was in a mental home. "What we both needed was some way of filling in the time between now and the grave."[3] Pat would take up religion and become a nun. Quentin took up sex. However, he soon found that, "one cannot for long put off the monotony of sex for sex's sake."[4] He also found it exhausting; "Sex was not one of my A-level subjects. It is only a mirage, floating in shimmering mockery before the bulging eyes of middle-aged men as they stumble with little whimpers towards the double bed, that somewhere there is a person or a position that will evoke from them sensations of which they dimly dream they are capable."[5]

After several attempts Pat found a convent which would take her, but before leaving she made a request of Quentin which he had been dreading for some time. She asked him to visit the Czech. Since his incarceration Pat had visited him every Sunday and on each occasion he would demand proof that she was who she claimed to be and not one of "them."[6] So now Quentin took on this arduous task, though only every month or two. At least the Czech accepted Quentin was who he claimed. "Who else could I be?"[7] But he found the journey arduous; two hours there; a two-hour chat with a man "I had never liked even when he was normal,"[8] and two hours back. Their time together was at least bearable as long as he didn't look out of the windows, where he would be likely see one of the other inmates exposing himself from the garden. They would chat over the three cups of tea that the Czech had laid out with the comment, "The place is an absolute madhouse."[9]

Despite the failure to get his book published, during the early 1950s Quentin seems to have been financially better off and was able to help his mother rent a room nearby, visiting her every evening to leave £5. On one occasion when talking about his father, she confessed that she had never loved him. Quentin retorted, "But, you hated him enough to marry him!" She replied, "Well, there was that."[10] Quentin continued to visit his mother regularly throughout the 1950s, often driven by his niece Frances. Baba Pratt died in 1960 at age 86, having happily outlived her husband by almost thirty years.

Quentin continued to live in his one room, and by now had long passed the four year barrier. He had to jump in the air to put his trousers on to avoid the dust getting on them. Quentin hated shopping; most of his clothes were given to him second-hand by friends. The only problem was shoes, these could not be altered. When he met someone new the first thing he did was to check their feet to see if they were as small as his. But food had to be purchased every day until he discovered Complan, a health drink designed for invalids which tasted like wallpaper paste, but was full of nutrients. This together with his pint of Guinness in the morning — "Because it makes the day seem shorter"[11] — would form a stable part of his diet for the next twenty-five years. There were often periods of several months when he would live on nothing else. I wonder what his doctor thought of this diet. Remember, he still had the same one who in the late 1920s had advised his parents that all he needed was a good lesson in life. If Quentin had been frail in his youth he was now exhibiting the constitution of an ox. How many people reading this could live on the diet he did even for a few weeks? As he got older his constitution seemed to get stronger still.

In 1952 Quentin encountered a man in a café whom he would christen Barndoor (real name George Taylor) because of his huge size. The man ordered food, but as soon as it was laid before him his head fell into it. He was exhausted. Quentin took him back to his tiny one-room flat where he slept until dawn. At the start they were not lovers; their relationship consisted of meeting a couple of times a week in a café. If George was tired he stayed the night in Quentin's room. After a while this progressed to him staying every weekend. "My life became a series of Saturdays for which I prepared and Sundays on which I recovered."[12] After a period of time George suggested sex "presumably to normalize our relationship,"[13] to which Quentin agreed. According to those who knew him then, these weekends were apparently pictures of domestic bliss with Quentin even cooking. However, in *The Naked Civil Servant*, Quentin describes at length how difficult he found living with someone again after so many years alone, even though it was only on the weekends. Finding the bed too cramped ("Never get into a narrow double bed with a wide single man."[14]) They took it in turns to sleep upon layers of accumulated dust on the floor.

Quentin, as I have already told you, hated shopping and cooking, but when George visited these activities were unavoidable. We can only imagine how much someone of his dimensions ate. "I found myself clawing away at the carcasses of dead animals until my nails were full of blood and I felt like a mangy old eagle,"[15] Quentin would lament. He had lived alone for so long that if he found his kettle facing the wrong way he became hysterical. He developed shingles, presumably due to stress.

It was on a summer day in 1955 during this period of domesticity that Harold Pinter dropped in from another room. He had been visiting a friend, an actress called Veronica Nugent who was then living in the same boarding house in Beaufort Street. She told Pinter, "Come upstairs, there's someone I want you to meet."[16] On entering Quentin's room he found him at the stove cooking bacon and eggs while a large man sat at a table reading a comic. They chatted away while Quentin attended to the man's dinner. On leaving Harold told his friend that he would never forget what he had just seen. Many years later Pinter told Quentin that it was at this moment that he was first inspired to write a play. Pinter's first play, *The Room*, was written two years later and is set in a snug, stuffy, rather down-at-heel bed-sit with gas fire and cooking facilities. In the opening scene a large man is sitting at a table being served bacon and eggs by a small, slightly built woman in a dirty dressing gown. (Quentin was famed for never washing his dressing gown).

Quentin's friends disliked and disapproved of Taylor. Hilda Lumley once said, "I've never understood your relationship with him."[17] It is true that George would not walk beside Quentin when they went out; he would keep a few paces behind and make fun of him to passersby; he would not even sit with him on a bus. Yet at other times in public George would engage in impromptu displays of emotion and would burst into operatic arias in cafés while holding his hand and telling anyone who would listen how long they had been together. Quentin's mother, however, does seem to have accepted George into her son's life and even sent him birthday cards. On Quentin's part this relationship seems to have been based on compassion or altruism. He describes George as "a poor wee thing"[18] who had been knocked about by everyone he ever knew. Quentin gave him a kingdom with himself as his slave.

Quentin said that in coming to know George he discovered a universal truth: "There is no great dark man."[19] Even under the skin of a man with the physique of an all-in-wrestler lie the same emotional insecurities that haunt us all. "Where we are led to think we will find strength, we shall discover force; where we hope for ruthlessness, we shall unearth spite; and when we think we are clinging desperately to a rock, it is falling upon us."[20] According to *The Naked Civil Servant*, George's departure from Quentin's life was instigated when he told George that the next weekend he would be staying with his mother. Apparently George took this badly and on leaving said, "I don't know what I've done wrong, even now."[21] Quentin tells us that he had done nothing wrong, he was "a man without guile. His only fault was that he existed."[22] Quentin does not go into further details of what must have happened, other than to remark that when you find that you have by accident bitten into a soft center it is impossible to put it back in the box. They had been together for four years, though by the end of their relationship they were no longer lovers; again this was George's idea.

Many years later he would say that the day George left was the saddest of his life. But he later married and had a family, so Quentin regarded him as one of his successes. In *The Naked Civil Servant* Quentin tells us that this liaison happened during the Second World War, and never gives his real name, always referring to him as Barndoor; presumably to guard his privacy. His real name would not be revealed for many years. Towards the end of his life Quentin would inform us that George was now dead, though he was twelve years younger than Quentin, so he must have maintained some form of contact with George or at least kept himself informed of his progress through some mutual acquaintance. The only piece of information about George that I have been able to find was supplied to me by Quentin's agent and manager, Richard Gollner, who shall appear later in this book. Quentin had told him that Barndoor had been a security guard at Heathrow Airport.

Quentin's funds were not unlimited so he took another job, this time in a display agency called Manhattan Displays, having been introduced to the firm's director by a woman who lived in the same boarding house as he. As I have said before, Beaufort Street seems to have attracted eccentric characters and Belinda Carlton certainly fits into that category. Although she worked as a secretary for Manhattan Displays, Quentin said she was rich, noisy and eccentric, so presumably her employment was merely a source of amusement for her, as was her choice of abode. She owned a small racing car and would drive at high speeds around London with Quentin as her passenger squealing with delight and edging her on to greater acts of daring. Once when two nuns were about to step onto the road he screamed, "Get them!"[23] In this job he seems to have done everything but mend clothes, though this could have been due to the fact that he was now the firm's sole employee. He thought up display gimmicks usually with moving parts which a sub-contractor would then try to make into reality. Unfortunately, he does not tell us anymore. Considering Quentin's intellect and imagination, what must these have been like?

One day during his employment there he was staring out of the upstairs window when he saw George Melly walking past with his wife. Quentin called down and they reacquainted themselves. The firm had just gotten in a batch of those pigs which stand on their hind legs holding a tray that you used to see outside butchers' shops and he was painting them. He told George that he was trying to give each one a slightly different expression. Quentin tells us that during his time there he painted the faces of four thousand dolls, made cocoa, washed dishes, typed letters and did filing as well as manning the phones, over which he was often mistaken for a woman. But his most important duty was trying to maintain peace between his employer and the outside world. Quentin tells us that she was rude to anyone who did not have more money than she, but countered this by being very good to Quentin. There was one exception to her behavior to those less financially endowed than her. A friend of Quentin's used to visit him while at work and moan about his problems finding a landlady to take him in. In what was evidently an uncharacteristic act she fed him and allowed him to sleep in her flat. Would she have been so generous if the man had not been a friend of Quentin's? However, this could not last, so Quentin contacted a couple he knew who ran a boarding house in the north of London. They were able to take him in, so now Quentin could visit three friends for the price of one bus ticket.

When work at Manhattan Displays was slack, which was often, Quentin and his employer would sit around drinking whiskey and playing Scrabble. Whatever the duties may have been and however he filled in his time was irrelevant to Quentin. He no longer expected anything from work or cared what he did and was just looking for something to relieve the monotony that posing had become. He stayed in this employment for four years from 1956 to 1960, but still continued to pose in the evenings. Yet again we must marvel at his stamina! It was during this time that the ban on him started to lift. Had the police gotten over their sulk? Things had changed so much that in one establishment a man was asked to leave for making fun of him. Six months after Quentin's departure the firm collapsed. Well how can a firm run without an employee? Why did Quentin leave? This was around the time that his mother died. The death of a parent is a significant event in anyone's life, and perhaps even more so in Quentin's; he had remained very close to his mother. Did it have any influence on his decision to leave, or had he simply decided that four years was long enough?

One day shortly after leaving the display firm Quentin was sitting in the garden of a friend's boarding house when she confided in him that she could not live like this anymore. Quentin, distressed at her emotional state — her oldest child was still only three — asked if she had any escape plans; she replied that there was an article in a paper about a contest to write a television play. Quentin declared that he would write for her a science fiction musical — *Take Me; Make Me Your Flying Sorceress* — with which she could win the prize. He also got a South American guitarist to write the music. When it transpired that three plays were needed he retrieved two from under his bed which had lain there for eighteen years. They did not win. Despite the failure, the guitarist was sufficiently impressed with Quentin's work to ask him to write the words for another musical he was composing. Initially the guitarist wanted to do a boy-meets-girl play, but this was something Quentin felt was beyond him; he did not know any boys who met girls, so they settled for a horror musical, *Evry Little Monster Wantster.* While Quentin enjoyed writing the words and enjoyed working with the guitarist he tells us it was doomed to failure, as the guitarist did not understand Quentin's jokes (was it a horror musical comedy?) and he did not understand the guitarist's music.

During these years Quentin maintained a busy social calendar among his many friends, one of whom was June Churchill. He still spent time with Mervyn Peake and his family; indeed, Quentin seems to have been able to extend his relationships with his friends to include their families. Quentin seems to have preferred to visit his friends instead of them visiting him. A single room which has not been cleaned for over a decade is probably not an ideal location for entertaining; when some friends did visit, Quentin would offer them a page from the day's newspaper to sit on to keep the dust off their clothes. There may have been other enticements to visiting his friends and he would often take a bath while visiting his writer friend Meadmore. For a while George Melly rented the room at the top of Meadmore's house and would find Quentin in the bath in all his naked glory.

Sometime during these years yet another portrait was done of Quentin, this time by the painter Theo de Rose. Once at an exhibition of the work of the painter Penelope Makyns, whom he had first met while posing at an art school, he was mistaken for the wife of the French ambassador. Penelope would be one of those who braved the dust to play chess with Quentin in his room, later sometimes even bringing her husband, Sir Peter Charles Oliver Harvey, who later became the second Baron Harvey of Tasburgh, an honor which had been awarded to his father for his services as British ambassador to France. Peter would also become the fourth baronet of Crown Point. What rarefied company Quentin sometimes kept.

It was towards the end of the 1950s that Paul Bailey first met Quentin. He had been invited there by Gordon Richardson. Quentin came into Gordon's room while Paul was there and was introduced. Bailey would maintain a friendship with Quentin for the rest of his life. He was then an actor and would become a writer and one of Britain's most distinguished novelists. In 2002 he would produce his own book as a tribute to Quentin. *The Stately Homo* is a collection of essays from Quentin's many friends.

After eight years of visiting the Czech, one day Quentin received a letter that the Czech was going to visit him. His initial relief at not having to make the journey soon turned to deepest despair. On entering Quentin's room the Czech kissed him and made it clear that he saw this as the culmination of their eight year relationship. "I found myself, at the age of fifty and more, fleeing like a crotchety nymph before a satyr of seventy."[24] After this the Czech made regular visits, usually bringing some present such as a suitcase full of maggot ridden apples. His visits dwindled in the following years presumably due to old age. He eventually hanged himself in his room.

Within a few months of leaving the display firm Quentin returned to full time posing for the first time in four years. He was shocked to find how much things had deteriorated. Students no longer went to college to work. "Now students enrolled for chaos. Work had almost ceased. The young people wandered through the corridors in droves, shouting, cursing, singing, necking."[25] Life drawing was now regarded by the students as too difficult and time consuming; by concentrating on simpler and easier tasks they could produce a greater volume of work with much less effort. For them, "no nudes were good news."[26] Moreover, his heroic poses were now ridiculed as outdated and as before they made the students work even harder. During a posing session in a school in Kent which Quentin felt was "a kind of cultural borstal,"[27] he noticed one student lying on top of another in a corner of the room. The teacher, on registering the shock in Quentin's eyes, made efforts to break up this passionate embrace. He had to resort to taking hold of the girl's hair and pulling her head off her lover's face. "There was a sound like tearing sticking plaster from a painful wound.... From eyes dull with debauchery, sunk in faces glistening with saliva, the two pupils gave their teacher a sullen stare.

Then, very slowly, they got up and returned to their easels."[28] The pupils now resented Quentin's presence to such an extent that he would regularly undergo a barrage of verbal abuse as he entered and left each establishment. Quentin found the whole scenario depressing.

In the following years he found himself being used more often for portrait classes; which, although considered a come-down, he accepted gratefully, as they were less physically demanding. His own explanation for this change was that although his face was aging as rapidly as his body, a good artist could still do something noble with "eyes that hang like an impending avalanche over the cheekbones. Nothing for which the life beautiful has a name can be read into a pot belly."[29]

13

Talking About Himself

"If only I could get some of the back pay?" — Quentin Crisp, *The Naked Civil Servant.*

On a day in August 1963 Quentin was sitting in his room in front of his gas fire in his filthy dressing gown breathing and blinking when the bell gave two rings. Quentin had now lived there so long that a note had been placed by the doorbell saying "Crisp, two rings."[1] It was his old acquaintance Philip O'Connor; they had not seen each other for fifteen years. Philip's autobiography, *Memoirs of a Public Baby*, had been published in 1958 and he was now working for BBC radio. He was putting together a series of programs about British eccentrics and wanted to do one on Quentin. Philip produced a tape recorder and asked him to say something about life and death. After being assured he would be paid, Quentin gave a long monologue on his life, starting with his early childhood and his rage at having to share his mother with his three other siblings. He discussed the genuineness of his outer appearance and how people often took it to be an affectation. Quentin talked and talked until the tape ran out. Commenting later to a friend on how he had been paid £40 to sit and talk about himself, he added, "If only I could get some of the back pay!"[2] A few days later Philip returned to Quentin's room with his boss. Quentin put some finishing touches to his interview and they left. O'Connor would later describe this it as being the best interview he ever did.

Months passed and Quentin heard nothing. He began to think that it was another failure, causing him to comment to a friend that it was "a wild idea in the head of Mr. O'Connor."[3] But eventually the program was broadcast, on 28 February 1964, entitled *A Male Artists' Model*, as the first in Philip's series on London characters. The broadcast was very well received. Critics called it the surprise of the week.

Some months after the broadcast a friend told Quentin that he had overheard a publisher who had been so impressed by Quentin's performance the publisher thought Quentin should write a book. After getting the publisher's name, William Kimber, Quentin, taking a rare step away from his philosophy of inactivity, phoned him and Kimber suggested Quentin write a two thousand word synopsis for a possible autobiography. When Kimber read this, he sent a courteous letter to Quentin saying that if his firm published the story it would be "bombarded from all directions with libel suits."[4] This came as a surprise to Quentin, as although he had always been totally open about himself, he was also always the soul of discretion when it came to other people.'

Quentin related this story to fellow passengers on a train while on his way to pose at Maidstone College. "Nothing shortens a journey so pleasantly as an account of misfortunes at which the hearer is permitted to laugh."[5] One of his fellow travelers was a teacher at Maidstone who suggested that he might be able to do something. A few days later Quentin was introduced to Donald Carroll. Carroll, a Texan living in Putney, had just set up business as a literary agent. Many years later in 1981 the two would write a book together, *Doing It with Style*. Quentin visited Carroll at his flat, where Donald asked Quentin to write a few chapters with which he could persuade the publishers. Quentin seems to have sealed himself in his room over the summer of 1965 working on these and did not even attend his niece's wedding on 12 June, when Frances Payne married Peter Ramsay. By Autumn Quentin had completed his work. With these chapters and some photos taken of Quentin by Angus McBean during the war, Carroll started a tour of the publishing houses.

In December 1965 Carroll's efforts paid off and Quentin signed a contract with the publisher Jonathan Cape to finish the book. He received a check for £100. "I nearly fainted."[6] Quentin spent the following six months writing the rest of the book, then handed the manuscript to Donald Carroll. Carroll handed it to the publishers, who handed it to a literary editor, Jane Miller. Over the following months she worked with Quentin at her home to get it ready for final publication. Tom Maschler, who was then managing director of Jonathan Cape, must have had aspirations for the new book, as he submitted the manuscript to two American publishing houses, however, both turned it down. Throughout this period Quentin not only worked on his book but also continued to model on an almost full time basis. By early 1967 the book was in its final editing stages and Quentin had received a total of £300 for his efforts.

In January 1967 Quentin first met Andrew Barrow, who would become a life-long friend. Andrew, whose name has already appeared in these pages and shall again, would later achieve his ambitions as a writer, perhaps his most famous work being *The Tap Dancer*. In 2002 Andrew would write *Quentin and Philip*, a joint biography of Quentin and Philip O'Connor, with whom he would also form a friendship. In this book Andrew describes his first impression of Quentin: "His face was both masculine and feminine, noble and ignoble, imperious and depraved. His hairstyle was like a charlady's or a duchess's. There was something utterly archaic about him yet he had the effect of a tonic."[7]

Shortly after this Quentin made his acting debut in a film based on Philip O'Connor's writing, called *Captain Busby*. This short film, about 15 minutes, based on Philip's surrealist poem of the same title, was shot in May 1967 at a railway station. Philip played the lead character and Quentin appears as an admiral. The film's premier was attended by both Philip and Quentin at the National Film Theatre on July 4, 1967. The film's director, Anne Wolff, was also in attendance. It seems to have been a mild success among the surrealist movement, but it did not cause a wider stir and indeed was quickly forgotten. To my knowledge Quentin never mentioned it.

Quentin wanted to call his book "My Reign in Hell." He felt that anyone, on reading it, would agree with him that he had followed Lucifer's path of reigning in hell (Soho) instead of serving in heaven (respectable society). However, after much debate, *The Naked Civil Servant* was finally published in January 1968. The first paragraph reads:

> From the dawn of my history I was so disfigured by the characteristics of a certain kind of homosexual person that, when I grew up, I realized that I could not ignore my predicament. The way in which I chose to deal with it would now be called existentialist. Perhaps Jean-Paul Sartre would be kind enough to say that I exercised the last vestiges of my free will by swimming with the tide — but faster. In the time of which I am writing I was merely thought of as brazening it out.[8]

The last sentence from *The Naked Civil Servant* is perhaps one of the most depressing and perhaps striking you may ever read in an autobiography: "I stumble towards my grave confused and hurt and hungry."[9]

Quentin would always say that he felt that the book's title was a mistake; everywhere he went he had to explain it, that it came from a conversation he had with a journalist who worked for *The Scotsman,* who while interviewing him asked if he was a famous model. Quentin replied that such a thing no longer existed, that models were now paid by the government and were just like civil servants except they did not wear clothes. In the following years Quentin would often repeat the story of how a friend of his was visiting her mother when she noticed a copy of *The Naked Civil Servant* on a table. On expressing her surprise at this, her mother replied that she didn't understand her daughter's reaction, as she knew she had always been interested in the civil service.

In his second autobiography, *How to Become a Virgin*, Quentin says that *The Naked Civil Servant* was not a "wild success,"[10] but this can be at best taken as a matter of opinion; it did reach a number of best seller lists and for a time people could be seen carrying it in the streets. Critical responses were certainly mixed; some found it to be full of self-pity while others found it totally lacking in self pity. *Gay News*, in its review, said that it would have been better for the gay cause if the book had been published posthumously, which as Quentin held was "a literary way of saying 'drop dead.'"[11] Throughout his life, Quentin seemed to be always at odds with the gay movement.

To celebrate his success, a friend whom he had known since the war years came up with the idea of having a dinner which people could be asked to pay ten shilling to attend. In *How to Become a Virgin*, Quentin makes it clear that he found this idea very embarrassing; "I could think of no-one that I would have the nerve to suggest should pay for the mere privilege of eating with me."[12] Despite Quentin's great misgivings, a room was rented in Schmidt's restaurant in Charlotte Street and people indeed attended.

One person was from the television world and on taking his leave promised Quentin he would try to do something for him. A month after this dinner the gentleman proved to be true to his word and invited Quentin to the Shepherd's Bush studios to take part in the BBC's *Late Night Line-up* program. One of the other guests was Fanny Craddock, whom he took to immediately. As he was preparing to go on someone asked him if he was nervous. He replied that he was not. "What have I got to lose?"[13] Indeed, he tells us he had only negative goals for the interview: "I wanted not to start every sentence with 'Well' or 'Er.' I wished to survive whatever was said to me without displaying embarrassment or shock."[14] As it transpired there was no need for him to have been concerned, as in other media he turned out to be a natural interviewee. It went smoothly; there were no difficult or uncomfortable questions. The interviewer only asked about his unusual appearance and his domestic habits.

He soon found himself being invited to do speaking engagements. Whatever the group he found himself talking to, he realized that his primary function was to entertain, but he also tried to guide and advise. If talking to aspiring authors he would repeat his advice — never read! When he found himself being invited to give talks in art colleges and universities, he would shock those present with his statement that all education was a mistake. "Cluttering one's skull with facts about any subject other than oneself I hold to be a waste of time. All general knowledge can be discovered in the nearest library."[15]

Most of his talks were, perhaps inevitably, delivered to homosexual and lesbian groups. To these he would try to deliver his warning against "forming an exile's view of reality."[16] Just because many homosexual men and lesbians thought of themselves as being outside of society looking in, they should not be fooled into thinking that everything in the real world was perfect; many of those inside were trying to get out. At these meetings he started to notice that while talking to male groups there would be some women present, at lesbian gatherings there would be no men. At one lesbian meeting a woman said to him "I suppose I shouldn't ask you this but why do the boys keep on at us to come to their meetings? I can't see any point."[17] Quentin's conclusions on this were as follows. The lesbian groups at that time were becoming more strident, more political, and felt that in order to be heard they had to present a masculine image. Homosexuals were then still regarded as feminine and therefore "politically ineffectual."[18] Of the gay world at that time, he says, "If I were asked to describe the differences between the sexes in the gay world, I would say that the men wanted to be amused; the girls sought vindication."[19] However, he still felt that such groups were a distinct improvement for gay people. "If there had been such an organization when I was young, I would have been a founder member. If there had been in existence any building in London where the very thing that made it impossible for me to feel at ease with other groups of men would have been taken for granted, I would have been on the doorstep before the place was opened."[20]

For these engagements he was usually paid the sum of £5, and, as he was always picked up at his front door by someone and left back there again and therefore had no expenses, this was an acceptable sum of money. He was also still posing, though now only part time.

After the publication of his autobiography he started to receive letters and phone calls on a weekly basis from total strangers. The letters were mostly from women and were usually a cry for help, while the phone calls were generally from men who were simply interested and wanted to know more. On one occasion Quentin was relating his amazement at these to a friend when she replied that she herself had written to strangers, because she was more likely to have something in common with a person whose work she admired than someone who just happened to be a relative.

With the publication of his book and his speaking engagements Quentin must have been at least to some degree better off financially. He was certainly busy. But despite this he continued posing. One might have expected him to embrace his new success and to apply all his time and energy to its pursuit. John W. Mills, who was still working with Quentin as a model, gave me the following insight. "His concern to continue working in this way was typical of his acceptance regarding fame and the lack of security it brought with it, security for him seemed to be the art school civil service, he trusted it and he was comfortable with those of us that reflected that secure appreciation of him."[21]

Although Quentin had now been posing for over twenty-five years, he still maintained his professional approach. He almost never broke his pose or even spoke to anyone during it. There were exceptions, and Mills related to me the following wonderful story which happened around this time and insight into Quentin's character, intellect and how his mind worked.

> I remember with pleasure an incident with a group of National Diploma students busy working in clay from Quentin standing in a classical pose. He suddenly said, "Sir, did you see the divine Sidney Poitier in *In the Heat of the Night?*" Silence followed; students were startled because Quentin usually did not speak when working. "What about that pig Rod Steiger?" he suddenly added. I replied that I had indeed seen the film and found it powerful, full of tense confrontational situations. "Steiger is the worst scene stealer on film of all time," stated Quentin vehemently. "There is only one other great scene stealer that one day someone will have the sense to team with him." A long silence followed whilst thinking caps were adjusted, then dramatically, "WHO do you mean?" cried the enthralled body of students no longer working but calling out the names of great film actors and actresses, only to be summarily rejected by Quentin. "Okay," I said, "Quentin, take a rest and let's see how we can resolve this." We rested and gathered around Quentin to work out this conundrum. Even more formidable actors' and actresses' names came up but none fitted, finally in exasperation Quentin said, "Someday someone will team Queen Elizabeth the Queen Mother with Rod Steiger. Just watch her at any public occasion, she always steals the camera attention by fiddling with her costume or by engaging a partner in discrete conversation, stealing the scene, just like Steiger but better." Alas, this was never to be, but what a typical Quentin observation.[22]

During the late 1960s age was starting to take its toll on Quentin's circle of acquaintances, partly because he was the youngest of his siblings, but also because while young, in order to appear more mature and sophisticated he had been drawn to those older than himself. He spent some time with Angus McBean in Suffolk to help him recuperate from a hip operation, Quentin once again showing the practical, domestic side of his character. In 1968 the youngest of his three siblings, brother Lewis, died in South America at the relatively young age of sixty-one. The following year his brother-in-law, John Payne, died, leaving Phyllis a widow.

One day Quentin was walking along Old Compton Street when a friend approached him and asked if he would like to appear in a program about Soho. By now there had been so many of these programs that his initial reaction was bemusement. However, he agreed on the basis that one of his philosophies was, "If we wish to be totally free from blame for our anonymity, we must never say no to anything."[23] By the time a man from the television world contacted him he had forgotten about this conversation. They met in a restaurant where Quentin was questioned about his experiences of Soho and how it had changed over the decades. Some weeks later the man phoned Quentin to ask him to go to a pub where he would also meet Denis Mitchell. Denis Mitchell's parting comment to Quentin was, "We must meet again some-time,"[24] which Quentin took to be the last time he would see him. He was wrong; over the following weeks he had many conversations with Mitchell, some in his room and some in Mitchell's home, until one day sitting in Quentin's room Mitchell said, "I think we'll make it all in this room."[25] It was at this point that Mitchell informed Quentin that the program would not be about Soho, but would be entirely about him.

In October 1968 Mitchell and a six-strong production team arrived at Quentin's room. The room was so small that the soundman had to stand in the hall maneuvering the microphone on a long boom through the doorway. For four days the normal routine of the house was interrupted, other residents moaning that they had to negotiate all the equipment and people to get to the bath room, as Quentin was filmed sitting around talking about himself and his life. The resulting documentary is truly fascinating, giving us a clear and unimpeded window into Quentin's life and thoughts, and is also proof to those who still do not believe that Quentin never cleaned his room. He tells Mitchell, "Unkind friends say that I have the dust brought in from Fortnam and Mason's. But it's not true, I simply don't clean the place."[26]

At the end as the crew is packing up to leave he gives us the following monologue delivered as a voice-over:

> If you're on a tightrope when you first set off you don't know how much play there is in the rope, but when you get into the middle between the ages of 20 and 40 the thing rocks like mad and it's too late to go back even to look back. But if you go on as carefully as you can, you see the other platform and then you just make a dash for it not bothering with what the audience thinks, or waving your arms or looking dangerous, and difficult and prodigious. What you grab hold of when you get to the other side [is] in fact the edge of your coffin. And you get into it and you lie down and you think, "my cuffs are frayed," "I haven't written to my mother." And then you think "It doesn't matter because I'm dead." And this is a message of hope. It will come to an end. It will come, we cannot be blamed for it and we shall be free.[27]

It is clear that Quentin then thought his life, if not already over, was at least rapidly approaching its end — he was now sixty. Fortunately, he could not have been more wrong.

This, like all the projects before, turned out to have a long fuse and the finished product was not shown until the end of 1969, when it was broadcast on Granada Television. It was extremely well received; the critic Maurice Wiggin called it "the moment one waits for."[28] Quentin was dismayed but not surprised that during the program no mention was made of his book. If it had been mentioned then the viewer would have assumed that the program was made to help sell his book. He was surprised, however, that no mention was made of his book in any of the reviews of the program published in the local papers. He was even more astonished when he discovered that the production company and his publisher were in agreement on this.

With the broadcasting of the documentary the letters continued to decline, but the phone calls became more frequent and now became unpleasant in nature. Many contained death threats while some were just a nuisance, often with more than one person on the other end. Once when he heard a distant voice ask if he was still on the line Quentin suggested that as neither of them had come up with anything witty to say, they might as well hang up. Some took the form of invitations to parties with "lots of lovely boys."[29]

The broadcasting of the documentary had another unexpected outcome: it sparked an idea in the mind of John Haggarty.

14

The Naked Civil Servant

"I have been trying to play the part of Quentin Crisp for over sixty years with total failure. An actor will do it much better than I have." — Quentin Crisp, *The Naked Civil Servant* (film) introduction.

In July 1970, Mitchell's documentary was given its second showing, this time as part of a series of Granada TV's *World in Action*. Around this time, based on an idea initiated by his agent, Donald Carroll, Quentin had started writing a book about style which would eventually be published under the title *How to Have a Lifestyle*.

In October 1970 John Haggarty started pitching his idea of making *The Naked Civil Servant* into a film. Quentin received a phone call from Jonathan Cape asking if the movie rights to *The Naked Civil Servant* were for sale. Quentin thought it was a joke until he was told that the enquiry had come from John Haggarty. Quentin phoned Haggarty, who assured him it was not a joke; he was completely serious. Haggarty introduced Quentin to Philip Mackie, whom he had persuaded to write the screenplay. After the appropriate legal contracts had been signed the three began regular meetings at Mackie's flat to work on the script. Several years later Quentin would design the cover for a play that John had written and which was performed in Leicester Square, though Quentin felt this was little repayment for someone who had changed his life so completely. Quentin spent that Christmas at Mackie's house to continue working on the script, and he would form a friendship with him which would last for many years.

By early 1972 the script was finished. Mackie's intention was that it should be made as a feature film, and initially things seemed to be going well. He found a director, Jack Gold, who thought it was "the best script I've ever read."[1] Shortly after this he also found his leading man. When Mackie first contacted Quentin to tell him about John Hurt, he said, "I've never seen anyone so willing to play a part."[2] This was quite true; John Hurt spoke of "the complete joy"[3] he felt on reading the script. But despite having a director and leading man on board, every studio Mackie presented it to turned it down. He even tried some of the American studios. Quentin was not surprised by this. He had suffered so many setbacks in his life that he took it philosophically, as always. He still found himself in demand for public speaking and he continued posing. He also had his book on style to finish. At one point apparently an unnamed millionaire said he would put up the full cash, estimated at three quarters of a million pounds, to have the movie made if Danny La Rue would star. Quentin was all for this idea and even suggested that it might be made into a musical. His idea was "laughed to scorn and the search for unconditional backing went blindly on."[4]

Quentin finished his book on style but had no better luck in getting it published than Philip Mackie was having with his film script; even Jonathan Cape turned Quentin's book down flat. Quentin shoved the manuscript under the bed and like so many other endeavors of the past forgot about it.

By now his Texan agent had returned home and he had acquired a new one. This gentleman, whom Quentin referred to as "The Hungarian," like so many others, came into Quentin's life by a rather chance set of circumstances. His real name was Richard Gollner. Richard told me, "He referred to me as the Hungarian because I am Hungarian, later he referred to me as Mr. Gollner. In thirty odd years we never got beyond that. His reason for not doing so, he told me, was that it was a habit of his, and that by not using anything more familiar he avoided generating hints of deep intimacy or indeed casual intimacy."[5] According to Quentin's account of their meeting, "The Hungarian" was living in the apartment above Donald Carroll's and Carroll had asked him to keep an eye on any mail delivered and forward anything worthwhile to him in America. Some of this mail was royalty checks for Quentin from *The Naked Civil Servant*. These he dutifully forwarded to Quentin and there followed an invitation to visit.

Richard gave his own version of how they met.

Donald Carroll edited *The Naked Civil Servant* and he lived above me in West Hampstead. After reading a proof copy of the *NCS* I identified Quentin's private school (public school) as the one I went to. Later, while having a drink with him at Donald Carroll's, he pointed out that he went to Denston, a horrible Alcatraz like school on the Derbyshire Staffordshire border, whilst I went to Abbottsholme, a very attractive, pretty red-brick school on the other side of the valley of the Dove river. I could see his school from my bedroom window. I became both Donald Carroll's and Quentin Crisp's literary agent when Donald Carroll moved to California. I became QC's manager much later, when I co-wrote, produced and directed *An Evening with Quentin Crisp, A Cure for Freedom*.[6]

Over the next few years Richard would be successful in finding work for Quentin writing articles in magazines and newspapers while his wife supplied

Quentin with regular dinners. Between these activities and posing he was able to make a living.

One day Quentin's friend Malya Woolf, was visiting and asked if he had anything her husband, Cecil, could publish. Quentin dived under the bed and brought out his manuscript on lifestyle. Handing this to her, he suggested that if Cecil was uninterested he should just throw it in the bin.

During the coming years Quentin maintained a close contact with Denis Mitchell, who in a way became Quentin's champion, conceiving of, and sometimes even paying Quentin for, various projects, none of which came off. Quentin for his part tried to come up with ideas Mitchell could use. Only one of these seems to have borne fruit. Quentin had brought his friend Joan Rhodes, the Mighty Mannequin, to Mitchell's attention, and in the resultant film which was shown at the end of 1974 Quentin appears briefly as her adversary in a game of Scrabble. Mitchell had now come up with the idea of doing another documentary about Quentin. While in the first one Quentin had talked about his life, in this Denis wanted to concentrate on Quentin's philosophy. Thinking that perhaps his writings on lifestyle could somehow be used to help with this new documentary, Quentin contacted Cecil Woolf and asked for his manuscript back. This request had an unexpected outcome; Woolf decided to publish the book. Quentin surmised that Cecil, thinking that Quentin wanted the manuscript back because a different publisher was interested, decided to publish it himself. Of this Quentin said he learned that "love does not cause jealousy; it is jealousy which engenders love."[7] So in March 1975 *How to Have a Life-Style* was published. In it Quentin states, "Style is not the man; it is something better. It is a dizzy, dazzling structure that he erects about himself using as building materials selected elements from his own character. Style is the way in which a man can, by taking thought, add to his stature. It is the only way."[8]

Although it would initially have a lukewarm reception, this book would become one of his most successful. It would be republished regularly for more than twenty years. Many people hold that if you want to know Quentin's philosophy of life, this is the book to read.

Alas, the second Mitchell documentary never materialized. What a great pity this was, it would have been a fascinating piece. Perhaps the events which immediately followed this overtook them both?

During the interim years Philip Mackie had twice renewed his option on the film rights for *The Naked Civil Servant* at £250 a time, which shows Mackie's belief in the project. But by now he had lowered his sights and was trying to sell his script as a TV movie. The BBC had turned it down three times and Mackie was becoming despondent, but his persistence finally paid off and he managed to make a deal with Thames Television in April 1975.

Things now moved with lightning speed. At the end of April, Quentin was taken to Teddington Studios to met Jack Gold and John Hurt. Quentin was delighted with Hurt; the two men got on very well from their first meeting. He was relieved when Hurt said; "I have no intention of merely giving a vaudeville imitation of Mr. Crisp."[9] John also twice invited Quentin to have lunch at his home. But apart from this he tried not to see too much of Quentin before the start of filming as "I didn't want it to be a mimic thing — an impersonation."[10] For the rest of his life Quentin would call John Hurt "my representative on earth."[11] The two men would remain friends until Quentin's death. Even when Quentin moved to America, John would visit him every time he went to New York.

Quentin was appointed technical advisor on the film, enabling him to make some more money, though he only gave advice on one scene. "I feared that Mr. Hurt might not know what an operatic business posing can become if you fling yourself into it."[12] John himself had been an art student in the past and had even once painted Quentin, though he was unaware of it at the time. Quentin also suggested the opening scene of the film where a young boy dressed in women's clothes — representing Quentin, dances in front of mirror. He felt this scene did not quite come off, as the boy looked at the camera instead of admiring himself in the mirror. He also shot an introduction to the film in which he states, "I have been trying to play the part of Quentin Crisp for over sixty years with total failure. An actor will do it much better than I have."[13]

Towards the end of the year while the film was in its editing stages, Quentin's new agent, Richard Gollner told Quentin that he had rented a theatre in which he intended to put on a play. This would fill the evenings, but he still needed something for the lunchtime crowd. He suggested that Quentin should fill this slot. So the King's Head Theatre's lunchtime slot was filled by Quentin Crisp, who presented his "straight talk from a bent speaker."[14] When he told friends that he had gone into the public speaking racket they replied, "When did you ever do anything else?"[15] His time there was not a great commercial success; sometimes his audience consisted of three people, but he did receive good critical reviews. In the *Observer*, B. A. Young called Quentin "not only a genuinely amusing man but a pretty wise one."[16] When after three weeks the evening play folded, Quentin asked to be released from his lunchtime slot as well. Though short, his three weeks had been a great learning experience for Quentin. He had always been a fast learner and he used his lunchtime performances to improve his technique. "I discovered that, while uttering one sentence, it was necessary to have a clear idea of what the next one would be so that I could concentrate not on what was to come but on the sounds already in my mouth. I found that I needed to pay great attention to their pitch, their volume and even the length of the silences between them."[17]

All of this activity had an invigorating impact on Quentin. In September he told Andrew Barrow, "I'm interested. I've perked up."[18] On 10 December there was a press showing of *The Naked Civil Servant* at Thames Television. The car which had been sent to pick up Quentin was late arriving and he missed the start. Afterwards when queried by the journalists for his thoughts on the film, he replied that it was "better than the real thing because it was so much shorter."[19]

Quentin was initially disappointed that *The Naked Civil Servant* had not become a film for theatrical release. He was mad about the movies. But in later years he came to realize that it had actually been a blessing in disguise. Had it been a film for theatrical release it would have been promoted as a gay interest story and very few people would have seen it, let alone been willing to pay the entrance fee to the cinema, and even many of those who might have been interested would not have wanted to be seen going in. As a television film it was automatically beamed into millions of houses and anyone who wished could watch it in privacy. Thus he and his story became much more widely known.

On 17 December *The Naked Civil Servant* was broadcast on Thames TV. Quentin watched it this time with some friends. In *How to Become a Virgin* he says, "It was the kind of programme that, had I been in no way personally involved, I would never have watched in a million years. I have long since ceased to be interested in homosexuality as a subject; there just doesn't seem to be anything left to say about it."[20] However, even Quentin had to acknowledge the excellence of the finished film. To say that on both the public and critical level it caused a sensation would be an understatement. Critic Nancy Banks Smith said that the film "justified the existence of television."[21] Clive James described Quentin as "some kind of hero."[22]

The next day he had his first high-profile television interview with Mavis Nicholson. He liked Nicholson from their first meeting and the interview went very well. By now he had realized that for an interview to be successful you had to find a way of talking intimately with your interviewer while also acknowledging the millions of people who were watching you. In later years he would say that it was one of the best interviews he ever did.

From here on he used TV interviews as a way of presenting his philosophy to the world. By 1981 in *How to Become a Virgin* he would tell us, "I no longer regard television interviews as ordeals that must be endured without flinching. They have become welcome opportunities for presenting myself and my ideas to the world—mini-parties which I enjoy and through which I try to offer entertainment to others. I could almost say they have become a way of life."[23] To get the best out of them he started to study how they worked. He came up with a number of guidelines on how to do them. Firstly, all that is required is that you look happy to be there. Secondly, if the interviewer asks what is the secret of the universe, you do not say "A good question. [You answer with a smile] I am happy to tell you there is no secret."[24] The answer is mundane but your lips are moving and you are smiling; you'll be asked back. Thirdly, suppose you have gone on a chat show with an interesting story about your mother and the interviewer asks, "How's your father? You have seconds in which to say. Thank you, my father is worn out dealing with my mother who!"[25] If you have something to say, you say it no matter what the question.

The film turned him overnight from an outcast to a figure of public affection. The tide he had been swimming against for sixty-seven years had finally turned in his favor. Whereas after the televising of the Mitchell documentary public reaction to him had been uneasy and cautious, after the film it was welcoming and accepting, even forgiving. He still continued to receive unpleasant phone calls and indeed the content of these became even viler, but the letters were now warm and friendly, even complimentary. It was the turning point. From this time on he would never look back. Photographers and journalists would give his bell two rings almost daily. He was a natural, posing for the camera and answering any questions with relish. To Quentin all secrecy was wrong; he wanted to tell everything, to reveal everything. He was an interviewer's dream. He once received a call from a friend who was indignant that a census taker had been asking him questions. Quentin replied that the census man had called him earlier and was sorry the moment he opened his mouth. Quentin's social life also quickly became jam-packed with invitations to parties, ballet, opera and theatre.

He was now recognized on the street; people would go out of their way to speak to him, a far cry from his face-to-face meetings of the past; a taxi driver refused to take his money, asking for his autograph in exchange. Quentin developed a great fondness for taxi drivers. He developed a theory about them. If you are someone who likes driving but hates people you get a job as a long distance lorry driver. You will never see anyone, except the occasional hitchhiker, whose ravaged body you fling into the ditch as you speed by. But if you like driving and you like people, you become a taxi driver and you will meet the entire spectrum of humanity. When a New York taxi driver once asked him what he did for a living, Quentin answered, "I'm in the profession of being." The driver replied, "Yes I do a bit of that in my spare time."[26]

A couple of days after the Nicholson interview he was at a party and was approached by the playwright John Osborne, who told him, "You've made sure that young man never gets a good part."[27] Osborne could not have been more wrong; the young man to whom he was referring — John Hurt — would never look back. He won an award for the film and it would launch him into a career which would see him lauded as one of Britain's greatest character actors. For some time afterwards John himself could not pay for a taxi.

The film, however, did not improve Quentin's relationship with the wider gay community. Quentin always seemed to be out of step with the majority of other homosexuals. When he was a young man other homosexuals tried to keep their true natures secret, and so to them Quentin with his manners and appearance was a threat. But we must remember that then homosexuality was a crime. Now forty years later things had changed dramatically. The law had changed and homosexuals were openly presenting themselves to the world. Homosexuality had become a "cause." People were now talking about the campaign for gay rights. In this new environment Quentin was seen as not being sufficiently militant. Also, his "struggle to ingratiate myself with the majorities grew to be horribly apparent."[28] While he was giving a talk to a gay group in Westminster, a member of the audience accosted him with the comment, "You used to be the Martin Luther King of the movement. What are these Uncle Tom sentiments you now express?"[29] But the truth was that Quentin had never been militant. What he had done was chosen not to live his life as a lie, but rather to live it being true to himself. Also by now as far as Quentin was concerned, "It is more than forty years now since I presumed to think that I represented homosexuality. Since then I have come to realize that I represent nothing grander than my puny self."[30] Quentin's message was that you cannot force the world to accept you if it is not ready, and if you do then all you will have achieved will be to become an object of resentment and even hatred to those very people from whom you seek acceptance. You can only wait until the time is right. It is not through constant force that acceptance is gained, but through boredom. This philosophy would bring Quentin into conflict with many members of the gay community for the rest of his life. But he would remain constant in his views. "I will not be nudged into a quarrel with the human race. Now that we've finally met, I love it."[31]

When Quentin returned to the King's Head Theatre in March 1976, his lunchtime performances were now so well attended that people had to stand.

In May, Quentin left England for the first time in his life. This trip was to St. Andrews University in Scotland to give a talk to the students. He found them more relaxed than those in England. He was picked up from the railway station and was very pleasantly treated throughout his brief stay. In *How to Become a Virgin* he observed, "The traditional English view of the Scots must have been based on the landscape. In fact the inhabitants not only of St. Andrews but of everywhere that I have been in Scotland are communicative, laughter-loving, and indulgent with foreigners to the verge of folly."[32] By the time he had returned to Beaufort Street he had traveled for eighteen hours in order to speak for only two, but he felt it had been worth the effort.

It was around this time that Quentin became engaged. He received a phone call from his long-time friend Anne Valery. One of her friends had become engaged and Anne was feeling left out.

> QUENTIN: So you wish for a fiancé of your very own?
> ANNE: Exactly. It'll be a secret and of very long duration. Possibly a liftime.
> QUENTIN: Indubitably.[33]

To repay his kindness she arranged for him to achieve one of his ambitions — to meet the *Carry On* actress Hattie Jacques, for whom it turned out Quentin was one of her heroes. He wrote about the event in the *Sunday Times* in May 1976. The two got on very well from their first meeting and became friends.

In August his show at the King's Head was upgraded to an evening performance at the New End Theatre. His previous one-hour show had been adequate for a lunchtime spot but would not be enough for a full theatrical evening's entertainment. Richard Gollner came up with the idea that at the end of his talk Quentin would tell the audience that there were cards placed in the foyer on which during the interval they could write any questions they would like to ask. When they returned he would endeavor to answer them. Thus the show was extended to two and a quarter hours in total and *An Evening with Quentin Crisp* was launched. This format would remain almost unchanged for the rest of his life. He performed at the New End for two weeks. Shortly after he left the theatre it was sold. When the owner was asked about this, she stated that Quentin's show had been the only one she had ever put on which made money. Quentin qualifies this by pointing out that his show required no expenditure in time, scenery or cash. All he needed was a chair and a table and he was "On."

In September Quentin took his show to the Edinburgh Festival, and during this run he made a quick trip back to London to be interviewed by the American Dick Cavett. Also on the show were John Hurt and Mary

Whitehouse. This program was to be shown in America to help prepare audiences for the first screening of *The Naked Civil Servant*. On his return from Scotland, Quentin received a visit from the former mayor of New York, John Lindsay, who arrived in his room with a film crew to do an interview with him. The two seemed to have gotten on well. Lindsay warned Quentin that if he came to America he must promise not to try to overthrow the government, and Quentin warned that he might just run for president. The subsequent interview was shown on a program called *Good Morning America* and was watched by eleven million people. In November 1976 *The Naked Civil Servant* hit American TV screens. It was very well received and won a number of awards.

At the end of November Quentin was invited to Belfast. He found the constant security procedures irksome, but this was offset by the organizers' efforts to ensure that he should be well treated. Every free minute was taken up with interviews and he found the questions asked here not as routine as those on the mainland. He was asked if it worried him that people might be coming to see him out of mere curiosity, to which he replied that the spirit in which they left was more important, though he surmised that the reason why most people came to see him anywhere was "to see how anyone so wicked can still move and speak."[34] In *How to Become a Virgin*, he makes an interesting observation about the "troubles." "At a posh party I attended, before I had uttered a word someone had protested, 'Things are not as bad as they are made out to be.' The terrible truth is that there is a sense in which the troubles are not bad enough. Life can go on indefinitely absorbing a few more pointless deaths every day. No major decision is forced on anyone."[35] He also summed up his trip to Belfast in typical humorous mode by stating that he had gone there in the hope of being shot at. "I jumped up and down in front of the soldiers but they ran away."[36]

Despite all of this new activity Quentin was still posing, showing once again his incredible stamina; he was now almost seventy. He was now also taking much higher paid appointments, posing for small groups and individual painters. Quentin had been posing almost continuously for thirty-four years. However, things had now changed somewhat, as John W. Mills related, "People were always anxious to interview Quentin after the book and the film, even turning up in the middle of a life drawing-modeling studio to get some kind of scoop. He always thwarted them, however, with much entertainment to 'the young things' who were keen observers and paramount in his concern and interest for their wellbeing."[37] Quentin makes no mention of this intrusion into his formerly secure and peaceful modeling world in any of his later books. Nor did he ever mention another change which had taken place in his modeling world during these later years. Quentin found himself being asked by teachers to sit in on classes with them. John recalls,

> My first invitation to Quentin to sit in on a tutorial happened during an episode of non concern, amongst students, for life study of any kind which was then considered "old hat" ... I had a tutorial later that day with a difficult student who was multitalented, good looking, but indecisive and a problem; it flashed through my mind that Quentin would provide the perfect foil to her indecision, etc. So I asked him if he would consider sitting in with me. "I would be delighted but only if the young thing doesn't object," he said. She had no objections and I hope enjoyed one of the most entertaining, revealing tutorials she would ever experience. It was so for me and Quentin in full flow is a formidable spectacle and in this case full of sageful care and sensibility. I was never in a position to ask what her response to the experience was, but I bet your bottom dollar she has dined out on it since then, as indeed I have. Subsequently Quentin sat in on many tutorials with me till we both left the teaching/art school model game.[38]

It was also around this time that John asked Quentin if he was writing another book. Quentin told him, "Yes, I am writing a children's book." However, for John, "Children and Quentin did not gel in my mind so I probed further." Quentin expanded on his plan thus, "You take a little from the Beatles lyrics and add a little Edward Lear or the Goon show and you have it made, children will understand, it's simple!"[39] Quentin's children's book never materialized. We must wonder if he actually did put pen to paper on this one and if so what it might have been like. However, as John told me, "Of course he could have been sending me up, but he was never malicious."[40]

During the summer of 1976 Quentin took time out of his now busy schedule to help nurse his sister Phyllis, who was then 76 and in very poor health. Phyllis had never really gotten over the shock of reading in *The Naked Civil Servant* that her youngest brother had worked as a male prostitute. She had been a vicar's wife for most of her life and perhaps we can assume that the discovery had been upsetting for her. She had also been very unhappy when Denis Pratt became Quentin Crisp. Despite all this, Quentin had maintained a close relationship with his sister throughout her life, and it was still sufficiently close for Quentin to have taken the time out and presumably lost quite a bit of money in doing so. Unfortunately, she did not recover and Quentin returned to Beaufort Street. Some friends noticed that the loss did affect him deeply. When one broached the subject with him he became completely silent for several minutes.

15

Traveling the World

"The moment I saw New York I wanted it." — Quentin Crisp, *An Evening with Quentin Crisp.*

The year 1977 would be his busiest yet. *The Naked Civil Servant* was now published in paperback and the publishing house, Duckworth, printed a new hardback version. This same publisher, evidently in a fit of overenthusiasm, even published his novel, *Love Made Easy*. This had been written some twenty-five years earlier but Quentin still had the manuscript under his bed. It received almost totally bad reviews and sank without trace. It survives today more as a curiosity piece. The novel does not seem to have been Quentin's forte. Despite this setback, he was now also working on a second novel, which would be called *Chog*.

During the summer he had started making the necessary arrangements to allow himself to travel abroad when the opportunity arose. He legally changed his name from Denis Pratt to Quentin Crisp. He acquired a bank account and a passport. His bank manager personally trimmed Quentin's passport photo on his desk with a penknife.

He played Lord Polonius in a film version of Shakespeare's *Hamlet* alongside Helen Mirren. In this highly unusual interpretation of the bard's work, Hamlet is played by identical twins David and Anthony Meyer; one plays the outwardly sane Hamlet, the other plays the tortured soul, and sometimes both appear on screen at the same time. Helen Mirren plays both Ophelia and Queen Gertrude. Although Quentin always insisted he was not an actor, his performance holds up well. It would become known as "The Naked Hamlet." For anyone interested, neither Dame Helen nor Quentin appear in the nude. It received some good reviews at the time. The back cover of the 1994 VHS tape release of the film gave some reviews, such as "Pure, unhampered vision ... a film not like any other." — *The Times*.[1] "A triumph ... extraordinary visceral appeal ... raw life, style and sense of imagination." — *The Guardian*.[2]

"An inspired interpretation of Hamlet's divided self." — *The Evening Standard*.[3] I have not been able to identify the authors of these reviews. The film did not become a wider success and survives today more as a curiosity. The VHS tape is still available online.

It was also this year that Quentin did his last session as a model for John W. Mills. John was about to leave teaching to work as a full time artist. It seems to be around this time that Quentin's famous felt fedora made its first appearance. Quentin had told John that the hat had been "given to him by a person who stopped him on the way to the art school at St. Albans, saying, "Here, you should have this, it will look better on you than me.'"[4] John also knew that Quentin was now seriously dreaming of living in America and so, as John told me, "I had never made a serious study of Quentin and the occasion plus the hat ... posed a special challenge, so we decided to make it a demonstration/master class for students still interested making such figurative/narrative work, 'How would you like Sir?' he said, 'Easy or difficult?' I chose difficult, much to his pleasure."[5]

The sculpture which John did that day of Quentin wearing his new fedora was later cast in bronze and sold at Sotheby's, which gave John life membership of the Chelsea Art Club. Indeed, the last time John would see Quentin would be a few years later at the same Chelsea Art Club, where they exchanged greetings briefly. John said, "I thought we might have occasion to talk, albeit briefly, so I didn't pursue things at that point, he was being guarded by minders at that stage too. As it turned out Quentin was on his way to Heathrow intending then not to return to the U.K. and we didn't meet again."[6]

In September *The Naked Civil Servant* was finally published in America. In the same month he had lunch with Arnold Schwarzenegger, who was in London to promote his film *Pumping Iron*. He told Arnold of his desire to live in America, because he had been "waiting to rule the world ever since I was born."[7]

But by far the most significant event of 1977 took place the following month when Quentin left Britain for the first time to travel to Toronto, Canada. The purpose of this trip was to be interviewed prior to the broadcast of *The Naked Civil Servant* on Canadian television. Of this event he writes in *How to Become a Virgin*, "If until that moment I had only suspected that the world had gone mad, the notion now became a certainty."[8] He arrived there on Columbus Day, which seemed fitting to Quentin, who by now felt very much like an adventurer discovering new lands. As soon he was in his suite at the Toronto Hotel the phone rang. The caller from the Canadian publisher's office set out the schedule for the next day, which consisted of

Quentin being rushed among four different radio stations. He was also interviewed by a newspaper called the *Body Politic*, which was the gay voice of Toronto.

From Canada he moved south to the USA. When he offered his passport to the American official, the man whispered in his ear, "Is it nice to be vindicated at last?"[9] Once past the border he headed to New York by invitation from the famous Broadway producer Michael Bennett, who wanted to buy the stage rights to *The Naked Civil Servant*. Bennett wanted to make it into a musical and David Bowie was said to be interested. Quentin was delighted and in full support. He got some idea of how luxuriously he was going to be treated when he was picked up at the airport in a Rolls-Royce. New York had always been the city of Quentin's dreams. "The moment I caught sight of it, I wanted it and stretched my arms through the car windows towards the skyscrapers like a child beholding a Christmas tree."[10] He spent two and a half days at the Drake Hotel in a suite which was "large enough to house a Catholic family."[11] He was wined and dined luxuriantly by Bennett, who took him to several theatres. The show which most impressed him was that of Victor Borge, who Quentin felt did even less on stage than he did but to greater effect. To try to raise further interest in Bennett's plans for *The Naked Civil Servant—The Musical*, he took Quentin to dine at Sardi's, where his presence did indeed raise a lot of interest. He was introduced to numerous celebrities, including the actor Max von Sydow.

On Quentin's last day in New York, Bennett visited him in his hotel room to present him with a large American flag. Quentin wore this as a scarf until he got back to England, where it would decorate his room until he eventually returned to America permanently. Richard Gollner had accompanied Quentin on this his first foreign excursion and found some unique hazards in sharing a room with him, as he related to me, "Quietly brushing my teeth one early morning, I discovered my teeth turn bright purple. I was using Quentin's henna [tooth]brush."[12] He also found that many Americans thought he was Barndoor from Quentin's autobiography. Richard said, "I'm extremely large; after *The Naked Civil Servant* was published when people first met me with Quentin they presumed I was Barndoor."[13]

This brief stay in New York greatly reinforced Quentin's love of America, its people and his desire to live there. He found the American people to be eager to speak, to listen and to endure whatever was needed to achieve happiness. They were interested in anyone who was different, and unlike the English, not only applauded anyone who was successful but actually wanted you to succeed because in your success they saw hope for themselves. If one man can do it, then so can they. In contrast to all this activity in America,

Quentin was very surprised that back in Britain, Jonathan Cape had no intention of republishing his autobiography. Looking back Cape's decision does seem bizarre. Others rushed in to fill this gap. Duckworth published another hardback version and Collins produced a paperback. He now found himself traveling around the country doing book signing sessions.

Quentin's star was now quickly rising and back in Britain his next step was to the West End and the Duke of York's Theatre. It was then managed by Brian (later Sir Brian) Rix. A play had just been cancelled and Brian was looking for something else to put on, initially as a stopgap. He asked Quentin what the first thing was that he said to the audience. Quentin replied that he had previously told the audience that he was going to deliver a straight talk from a bent speaker until someone objected to this on the grounds that it might give homosexuals a bad name. Rix then asked him what he now said, to which Quentin replied, "I say that I have been forbidden to say that this is a straight talk from a bent speaker."[14] He got the job.

The show opened on 30 January 1978. It was extremely well received by everyone. The *Evening News* called it "The most extraordinary entertainment in London!"[15] The only unhappy person was Cecil Woolf. Quentin was making use of a lot of the material from his book *How to Have a Life-Style* which Cecil had published and to which Quentin had given him the performing rights. However, the two remained on good terms with Quentin niggling Cecil, "Are you still in a huff?"[16] His new friend, millionaire Olga Deterding, held a party for him at her three-floor apartment, yet another example of how much his social life had changed in recent years. His run at the Duke of York's lasted for four weeks with Quentin earning £500 a week. During this time he also continued to pose during the day; how often have I felt compelled to point out his extraordinary stamina; and he would often arrive at the theatre by bus. Once during this period he was waiting for his bus to take him to the theatre when a group of youths accosted him and knocked his hat into the gutter. It must have been a very bitter reminder to him of his treatment in the past and that things had not changed that much, even though he now had his name in lights on a West End theatre.

It was while at the Duke of York's that Quentin got his Equity card. In his last, unpublished book, "The Dusty Answers," Quentin recalls this event. "When I was already on the stage, Equity came marching with its ragged banners down St. Martin's Lane with Miss Redgrave at the head! And they said, 'Why is Mr. Crisp working in a West End theatre without an Equity card?' And Mr. Rix, never at a loss, explained, 'Mr. Crisp is not acting. He's very sincere.' This was thought to be a specious argument and I was made to have an Equity card."[17]

During the run Quentin was starting to learn a lot about performing in front of large crowds, and when he was told that the actress Elaine Stritch, who was then in a London hospital, wanted to see him he took the opportunity of asking her advice about controlling the audience. Stritch's reply was, "Don't bother with any of that honey, just get them to like you."[18] One evening his old acquaintance Harold Pinter came to see his show and afterwards took him to dinner. When someone remarked that the world was finally accepting Quentin, Pinter replied, "And about time too!"[19] On 27 February his show transferred to The Ambassador's Theatre, where it ran until 17 March. After the Ambassador's he took his show on a tour of the provincial theaters.

In June he found himself on his way to Australia, "like other wrongdoers before me."[20] Quentin was highly dubious about this trip; he felt that Australians would have no interest in him. When his plane touched down in Sydney he was sure he would be able to slip off to his hotel without anyone noticing. How wrong he was. As soon as he stepped out of the airport he was bombarded by journalists and photographers. When he and his traveling companion reached their hotel they even discovered that a documentary was being made for local television about his arrival. Not only was he being blinded by the flash of photographers' cameras, there were more cameras behind that photographing the photographers. Although Quentin performed for ten weeks in Australia and visited almost every major city, he would later describe the tour as a "disaster."

In his second autobiography, *How to Become a Virgin*, he devotes an entire chapter to his experiences of Australia. But he says very little about his actual performances, instead talking about his experiences of the country and its people. He seems to have liked Australia. "They lack nothing. The streets beneath their feet are paved with opals. The air about them sparkles like diamonds. The atmosphere is so clear that the roofs of their houses are always as red as the day they were tiled; the walls as white as when they were first painted. Strangers kept saying that it was a pity that we had arrived in winter but, in fact, every day that we were there was warmer than an English May."[21] He was also dismayed that most Australians seemed unhappy with their country, often making disparaging remarks about it such as "We're so far from everywhere, aren't we?"[22] and "Australia is a cultural desert, don't you think?"[23] Quentin tells us, "I constantly tried to reassure my interviewers; I seldom succeeded."[24] During his ten weeks he gave numerous interviews and all bar one seems to have gone well. The one negative experience seems to have been caused by his interviewer's negative reaction to his appearance.

Although he does not mention it in his book, he also visited New Zealand. David Hartnell has had a highly successful career as a make-up artist living

David Hartnell with Quentin backstage before one of Quentin's performances in New Zealand (courtesy David Hartnell).

in various locations over the decades. He had spent most of the sixties and seventies in London but in 1978 he was back home in New Zealand. On 27 July, Quentin was appearing in a documentary about his life, which was being shot by New Zealand television, and David had been asked to do the make-up. Quentin was delighted with David's work and asked him to write down all that he had done. Quentin also asked David if he would continue doing his make-up while he was in New Zealand.

David was amazed at how youthful Quentin appeared, "I remember meeting him for the first time and thinking ohmigod I hope I look as good when I get to his age. His skin was like alabaster, as if it had never seen the sun, and he had very few lines on his face. He later told me that he never used creams on his face, simply tepid water and soap."[25]

David was equally impressed with Quentin's abilities with make-up and particularly his artistry when doing his hair. David said, "His hair was a work of art, to style; he insisted that he would do it himself. He simply lent forward and brushed his hair forward, then he magically — to this day I don't know how he did it — moved his fingers fluffing and ruching the front, tucking it back across his receding hair line and it was done. His hair was a masterpiece;

in fact, it was a complete work of art and nobody did his hair except the master himself."[26] Thus David got the opportunity to see Quentin both on and off stage. "He was a humble human being, nice to everyone he met, from the theatre cleaner to the celebrities that came back stage to meet him. He was also a very sharp businessman and knew exactly what was going on around him; he never let anyone pull the wool over his eyes. He knew he was one of a kind and he knew exactly how to hone his career."[27]

David also got the job of vetting the questions which the audience wrote down for the second half of the show. During the interval Quentin would come backstage and over a cup of tea, which David had made for him, would have a quick look at the questions. Quentin also had a number of stock questions which he carried with him just in case. David was curious that Quentin took his wardrobe back to his hotel after each show. "When I asked him why, he told me that he had very few clothes and they were all valuable to him."[28]

So why did Quentin view the tour as a failure? To Quentin it seemed that the ordinary Australian did not regard his homosexuality as anything significant. While waiting for a taxi in a Melbourne street he was approached by two pleasant and polite young men who had seen him on television. At the end of their chat one of them said in a matter of fact way, "So you're homosexual, big deal."[29] Had perhaps the tour been promoted too much merely on the fact of Quentin's homosexuality and relied on audiences to come because of that alone rather than on the exceptional and unique nature of the man himself? This argument is perhaps reinforced by Quentin's observations: "The sophistication of Australia was so complete that it did more than set the people free to come and see me; they felt sufficiently liberated to stay away."[30] So I think we can assume that Quentin was glad to return to England on 25 August.

It was sometime around then that he had perhaps the most unusual threat made against his life he had ever received. A woman expressed her intention to kill him as an act of mercy. This woman first sent him a very pleasant letter and then followed this up with a phone call to say that she was coming to London and would like to pay him a visit. To this he happily agreed. During the meeting which followed she appeared to be perfectly normal and they shared a pleasant time together. However, a few days later, Quentin came home to find a note from the police wedged in his door. This note advised him that the local inspector wished to talk to him urgently. Within half an hour this man and a fellow officer had arrived at his room to tell him they had received a letter from his visitor in which she stated that she was so overcome by Quentin's state of loneliness that she had resolved herself to kill him as an act of mercy and then kill herself. Quentin advised them to forget about the whole thing. He never heard from her again.

Quentin had now acquired an American agent. Connie Clausen was an interesting character in her own right, having started out in the 1940s riding elephants for Ringling Brothers and Barnum & Bailey Circus. Richard Gollner told me, "Quentin naturally warmed to [Connie], since apparently in her younger days she was a bareback rider in the circus. He said, 'That's probably the best qualification for being my New York agent.' I carried on being his agent outside the USA."[31] In 1960 Connie had written an autobiography, *I Love You Honey, But the Season's Over*, in which she talked about her experiences working in the circus. After the circus she had moved to Hollywood and from there to New York, where she worked as an actress on Broadway and television. She became a publicity agent for Macmillan publishing in the 1970s and quickly became assistant vice president. Sometime during the mid 1970s, I do not know the exact year, she fell down an open manhole cover in New York City, breaking, as Guy Kettelhack told me, "every bone in her body."[32] In typical Connie form, she turned this terrible episode into something positive and after receiving a substantial compensation for her injuries she opened her own publishing agency, Connie Clausen and Associates.

Connie had been in the audience for one of Quentin's shows during one of his trips to America and afterwards had introduced herself to him, expressing her emphatic wish to become his American agent. Connie would become much more than just his agent, and the two would share a close friendship over the next two decades, meeting once a week for dinner and a chat. Was she prepared for Quentin's next literary offering?

In November 1978 Quentin had finished his new novel, *Chog*, and handed the manuscript over to his publishers. I think it would be fair to say that they were shocked at its content. The story involves an affair between a prostitute and a dog, and tells the story of what befalls their progeny. Did his agents and publishers have no idea what he was presenting them with? Even Connie could find nothing good to say about it. Presumably his publishers felt in some way compelled to publish the book, but suggested that it might be somehow enlivened by the addition of some illustrations. Several people were approached but some were just not interested or were "too busy." Some who knew of Quentin's own abilities in this area suggested that the book would be of more interest if he illustrated it himself. In the end Jo Lynch was hired. Though the subsequent illustrations are certainly unusual, they do not serve to lighten the book and are in themselves disturbing, thought probably in keeping with the content of the book. Quentin was paid £2,000 for his efforts.

For reasons which he never uncovered, the American stage rights to *The Naked Civil Servant* were purchased by Hillard Elkins, not Michael Bennett, and so it was at Elkins' behest that Quentin returned to America on 7 October 1978. Initially Elkins had wanted to make the stage version as a straight play, but then, to Quentin's relief, reverted to a musical. David Bowie was still interested and Elkins was now engaged in discussions with him. On arriving in New York, Quentin stayed at the Chelsea Hotel and was there on the day that Sid Vicious allegedly murdered his girlfriend, Nancy Spungeon. Richard Gollner was still accompanying Quentin on his trips and related this incident to me: "We were staying at the Chelsea Hotel and saw Nancy Spungen's body being carried out after Sid Vicious stabbed her to death. [Vicious died before a trial could be held.] We in fact spent the evening before with Nancy and Sid in the Spanish restaurant next to the Chelsea Hotel for drinks."[33]

From here, in an effort to raise interest in Elkins' proposed musical and in his own one-man show which he would be touring with, he gave television and radio interviews beyond count in cities such as Boston, Chicago, San Francisco and Los Angeles. Andy Warhol's first law, that it is possible to be famous for being famous, was now given an adjunct by Quentin; it is possible to be interviewed simply because you are so often interviewed. Of the two media Quentin preferred television because he put so much of his physical being into what he was saying, and this was impossible to convey on the radio. He attended a party at the Waldorf Hotel given in honor of Bette Midler. When he was introduced to her they chatted briefly to allow the photographers to gather round, and then he turned to the largest one with a smile. Midler whispered in his ear, "That's right baby. Do the whole bit." Quentin would later say, "I have followed her instructions ever since."[34]

Quentin did his first American performance of *An Evening with Quentin Crisp* on 31 October at the smaller of the two Long Wharf theaters in New Haven, Connecticut. *Journey's End* was playing at the other. While not on stage he was lavishly treated, being wined and dined throughout New Haven. During the two-week run in New Haven he was twice invited to speak at Yale University, first by the staff and on the second occasion by the divinity students who had asked him to explain You-Know-Who. This second evening must have been particularly fascinating, and it is a great pity that no recording or transcript of it exists.

From New Haven he went next to Washington. Quentin was surprised at the effort the theatre's stage manager put into getting his stage set correct. When Quentin remarked that any old chair would do, the man replied that among other things, it must not have a fabric seat, as Quentin needed to be able to move around on it easily, and it must have arms on which Quentin could lean. He even brought in some real ferns to give the stage the appearance of a Dickensian lecture.

By now Quentin was beginning to settle into his newfound celebrity status. It was while in a restaurant in Washington, D.C., with his agent that he first commented, "Really I'm in the smiling and nodding racket."[35] In *How to Become a Virgin*, he writes, "Now, in public, like everyone who has been on the television, I wear perpetually an expression of fatuous affability."[36]

In his hotel room the phone buzzed off the hook with journalists wanting interviews or to know his opinion on something. One asked him, "What do you think will happen in 1979?" Quentin replied, "Everything will get worse." The journalist responded, "Marvellous. Thank you so much. Goodbye."[37]

From Washington he moved to New York, where he was given a room at the famous Algonquin Hotel. One morning while having breakfast in the hotel's restaurant a man came over to chat and introduced himself as the congressman from Minnesota. This was another example for Quentin of how different America was from Britain. "If you can try to imagine an English cabinet minister walking the entire length of a public place to speak to me, you will instantly see how far we have to go before we become a truly homogenised society."[38]

One evening a man arrived in his dressing room at the Players theatre and announced that he wished to make an audio recording of Quentin's show. After this man had sought and received approval from everyone needed, Quentin was taken, on 22 February, to Columbia Recording Studios where a live audience had been put in place. He went through his entire show while it was recorded on tape.

His run at the Players theatre was extended for a total of eleven weeks. One night while on stage the lights went out. It transpired that the theatre was on fire. The fire does not seem to have been severe, but the fire department arrived quickly. When all was again safe, Elkins, not wishing to miss any opportunity, asked some of the firemen if they would pose for a photo with Quentin. The resulting photo shows Quentin holding a glass as if about to give a toast, surrounded by the firemen. "By the knowing eye it can just be seen that they are sending me up but so gently that together we form one of the funniest tableaux in which I have ever been involved."[39] The photo could not be used for publicity for the show, as it would have looked like the fire had been staged as a stunt, but it did appear in a magazine called *Where It's At*.

He also got a job. *New York* magazine employed him as a book reviewer. This he enjoyed and did for the rest of his life. Publishers would later start sending him proofs of books yet to be published for a review that could be printed on the cover. For these he did not get paid, so he would reply, "Please feel free to quote me as saying anything which will advance the sales of this excellent work."[40] One publisher quoted him word for word on the cover, which Quentin thought was very brave. When someone once criticized his book reviews as saying as much about himself as about the book, he replied that the reader of the review not only wanted to know about the book in question but also about the reviewer. Why should anyone bother to read a review at all or give credence to what was said unless they knew something about the review's author?

During one performance he was asked if Jesus had style. Quentin replied that he had often been asked to express his view on God, but never before on his son. But he would not answer this question if it might offend anyone in the audience; to which a reply came, "Why stop now?"[41] During another show a woman came up on stage and, taking a gold chain from around her neck, placed it on his lap.

After his eleven weeks in New York, *An Evening with Quentin Crisp* moved to Los Angeles, California. Here he stayed at the Beverley Hills Hotel. One day while he was sitting by the pool of this lavish establishment a phone was brought to a man who was lying on a sun lounger nearby. It transpired that this gentleman was a doctor and the phone call was a cry for help from a patient. He told his patient that he would try to get to them later in the day, but couldn't promise, as they were terribly understaffed, before resuming his repose.

During his stay in Los Angeles Elkins and his wife invited Quentin to visit them at their home. Here a fellow guest advised him that he could make a lifelong career out of giving talks to universities. There were so many in America that by the time he had visited the last one he could go back to the first. By then the students there would have already been replaced by a new batch. Quentin took heart from this, as it opened up a possible new avenue for him. On taking his leave Mrs. Elkins told him, "I promised you America and you shall have it."[42] His run in Los Angeles was also extended. One of the Los Angeles shows was filmed, and is still one of the very few film recordings in existence of *An Evening with Quentin Crisp*. It would be released with an introduction by John Hurt.

While Quentin was doing one of his shows in America during 1979, David Leddick was in the audience. David was then worldwide creative director for Revlon and L'Oreal at Grey Advertising. He had read a review of Quentin's show in *The New York Times* and was so intrigued that he took his staff with him to see the show. Although David did not meet Quentin then, he did get his telephone number and called him. One of David's ways of encouraging and supporting artists was to pick an individual and give them $100 a month. David had decided to give this to Quentin. David says that

Quentin thought he was joking. But he was not and continued to give him the $100 from then on. This was the start of a friendship which would also last until Quentin's death. When David was in New York Quentin would have lunch at David's house.

I asked David about his donations to other artists and he replied, "I have great luck and I think it is due to my being generous. I have always been able to earn money fairly easily and I like to spread it around. I plan to die in a little white room with just a bed, a table and a chair. Like a Van Gogh painting. Without a cent left."[43]

Before he left America, *New York* magazine gave a party in Quentin's honor.

From America he moved north to Canada and back to Toronto. He found that he was still as in demand in Canada as he had been the previous year and in fourteen days was interviewed twenty-one times. He stayed at the Waldorf Astoria and performed *An Evening with Quentin Crisp* at the Workshop Theatre. During his stay in Toronto he was able to reacquaint himself with a former boss — the lady who had run the display firm where he had painted the faces of thousands of dolls. She was now running a shop which specialized in cats, not the real thing but calendars, cards, and the like. He also found another old friend in Canada: the landlady who had run the boarding house to whom, while he was working in the display firm, he had sent his destitute friend, and whom he had tried to help by submitting plays in her name to a television competition. Evidently she had found a way out of her predicament.

Quentin did not return to Britain until early April 1979; he had now been away for six months. He found that the papers were declaring his American tour a triumph and discussing the upcoming musical of his life with David Bowie starring. EMI also decided to produce a British version of the audio recording of his show which had been made in New York, and he was taken on a whirlwind tour of Britain to promote it.

In September 1979 *Chog: A Gothic Fable* was finally published, though with almost no publicity. This received even worse reviews than *Love Made Easy* had. In *Punch* Jeffrey Bernard, who had known Quentin in Soho, wrote, "I tried to work out what disgusts Quentin Crisp so much but gave up after a few seconds."[44] Perhaps one of the kindest reviews appeared in the *Observer*: "Quentin Crisp's new mock-gothic novel sports the familiar sour malice."[45] But perhaps one of the most bizarre things about this episode was that the novel was published in Japan as a children's book and sold eighteen thousand copies. It was, fortunately, his last novel.

After this Quentin seems to have taken up Elkins' guests' advice and rounded off 1979 with a return to Canada to spend three days lecturing at the University of Alberta.

Back in Britain in 1980, an era had come to an end. Vi Vereker sold her boarding house to a man who increased everyone's rent. Vi had been finding the house a burden for some time and Quentin had even once tried to persuade the other occupants to club together to buy the house. This was not successful. By now all the old Beaufort Street stalwarts had left, even Gordon Richardson.

In February 1980 he was interviewed on the popular British chat show *Friday Night, Saturday Morning*. This show was innovative for its time in that it changed interviewers every few weeks, and those who accepted the challenge were allowed to pick their own guests. Thus Quentin was interviewed by Ned Sherrin on 22 February 1980.

Of the many interviews Quentin did throughout his life, one especially worth mentioning occurred on 6 June 1980. English composer and keyboard player Morgan Fisher had started his career in 1968 with the pop group The Love Affair, which had several hits, including the number one *Everlasting Love*. Throughout the seventies he had been composing music for various projects including London's Institute of Contemporary Art. From 1973 to 1977 he played with the British rock band Mott the Hoople. Morgan was putting together an album called *Miniatures* which consisted of fifty-one one minute pieces and wanted to do one with Quentin Crisp. He visited Quentin in his room at 129 Beaufort Street where Quentin laid out a shawl on a chair so Morgan could sit down before getting some orange juice and digestive biscuits for them to eat while they talked. "We had agreed (with not a little glee) that it would be ideal for him to read a piece in which he described his loathing of all music, 'Stop the Music for a Minute.'"[46] After he had the recording done Morgan asked Quentin if he could ask him some questions, and the resultant thirty-five minute interview is one of the best Quentin ever did. Perhaps it is because it is in his own domain that Quentin is unusually relaxed and open, or perhaps because Morgan has a very relaxed style of interviewing. It is more like hearing two old friends (although they had only met for the first time that day) having a casual chat with no agenda, and neither party is worrying about what people might hear them saying. Morgan told me, "Perhaps he was relaxed and off guard because it was recorded after the business of the day was done — the recording of his track for my *Miniatures* album. I simply said, 'May I ask you some questions?' (for no special purpose) and he generously agreed. The tape recorder happened to be still running."[47]

How often have you heard Quentin openly laugh and chuckle? He talks about his experiences on aging (he was then seventy-one) in a down-to-earth and practical way that I have never heard him do anywhere else. During the

Quentin outside 129 Beaufort Street, 1980 (photograph by Morgan Fisher).

interview a lady phones him and after hanging up Quentin gives us a fascinating insight into the type of, often bizarre, communications his new found
fame brings him; how he had become a kind of on-call agony aunt whom
people felt they could disturb any time of the night or day. The interview
finishes with Quentin talking at length of his love of America and his wish
to live there permanently. "In New York you can hear the heart of the world
beating. Wonderful!"[48] Morgan's album *Miniatures: A Sequence of 51 Tiny
Masterpieces* was released in 1980.

Quentin's plans to live in America were now progressing, and he told a
friend, "I long for New York like a bridegroom longs for his bride."[49] That
summer he returned to California again and from there went back to New
York. In the autumn he returned to Los Angeles. Quentin was now spending
more time in the U.S. than in Britain.

Quentin had now become reacquainted with his former literary agent
Donald Carroll and the two collaborated on a book, *Doing It with Style*, which
was published in 1981. The introduction states, "Ever since the day our distant
ancestor looked up and noticed for the first time that some people were blessed
with a certain indefinable quality that set them apart from others, that

Quentin in his room at 129 Beaufort Street. His famous gas fire is to the right, 1980 (photograph by Morgan Fisher).

endowed their every act and utterance with a special fascination, we have referred to these people as 'having style.' Whatever they do, they do it 'with style.'"[50]

The publisher sent the two men on a three-week authors' tour of the United States, attending book signings and doing over sixty radio and television interviews. As in the past, the two men got on very well together despite the rigors of the trip. Carroll would later tell how he was given a "master class in courtesy and good manners"[51] by Quentin one evening in Los Angeles when Quentin answered the phone in their suite. The caller was someone whom Carroll did not wish to speak to and he told Quentin, "Say I'm not here, say I'm dead, say anything."[52] Quentin returned the phone to his mouth and said, "I'm afraid Mr. Carroll can't come to the phone at the moment, but if you are willing to talk to me I will say exactly what he would have said." Carroll tells us, "The caller was instantly charmed; I was suitably chastened."[53]

Quentin had also now finished his second autobiography, *How to Become a Virgin*, which I have already quoted from many times. This would be published the following year—1981. In this he advises that television is the only means by which one can become a virgin. If you have done something which society frowns upon, do not hide it away, do it on television and the next day people will not shun you, they will cross the road at the risk of their own lives to say, "I saw you on the telly."[54] At the end of the book he states his intention to move permanently to America, and in the last says, "Perhaps the wisest course of action for me to adopt will be to lie down on the White House steps and, when the occupant opens the door, to start whimpering those lines engraved round the plinth of the Statue of Liberty: 'Bring me your huddled masses yearning to breathe free.' If ever there was a huddled mass."[55]

On a February afternoon in 1981 Quentin was on the corner of Second Avenue and Seventh Street in New York when he bumped into a young lady called Penny Arcade. Penny would become one of the most significant figures in his life. How often such chance encounters had a major impact on Quentin's life.

As a teenager Penny had her theatrical debut in Kenneth Bernard's play *The Moke Eater* before becoming a superstar for Andy Warhol's Factory featuring in the Morrissey-Warhol film *Women in Revolt*. Penny had recently returned to New York after many years globetrotting.

In the spring of 1981 the "patron saints of hooligans,"[56] Vi Vereker, died aged eighty-five, and in April, Quentin returned to Britain to make his final arrangements to live permanently in the United States. Quentin knew that to live in New York was very much more expensive than London. In England his £16 state pension was adequate, but in New York it wouldn't last a day. So if he was to achieve this brave new life for himself, he had to be able to work, and to do this he needed a green card. His lawyer had been working on this for some time, but it would be the actor Derek Jacobi, who was a friend of one of Quentin's American "spies," who would physically bring his card back from New York. Nothing now stood in his way.

I asked Richard Gollner why he thought Quentin moved to the U.S. His answer is interesting and thought-provoking:

> It was certainly true that one of the reasons he went to New York was because a great many people in the U.K. started to envy him. He often drew interesting parallels between England, where success is envied, and New York, where success is celebrated. His accommodation in New York was as grungy and in terms of square footage, the same as the one in London. What London and New York shared is that way before he was famous, not to say notorious, people really enjoyed spending time with him. I for instance spent a lot of time playing chess with him. But it was very difficult for people to spend time with him without coming up with some idea or scheme to be able to stay around him. That in the end became very restricting for him. In New York he could of course start anew.[57]

16

America, Here I Come!

"I shall leave the room as if I had never been there. I shall wipe the slate clean. And that will be very nice."— Quentin Crisp, in *Quentin and Philip: A Double Portrait.*

Since he had returned from America in April, Quentin had continued doing his one-man show until finally, on 13 September 1981, he was able to leave his room in Beaufort Street for his beloved America. In an interview shortly before leaving, he said, "I shall leave the room as if I had never been there. I shall wipe the slate clean. And that will be very nice."[1] He would be seventy-three years in three months. We must not underestimate the courage required to make such a move, though it came as no surprise to his friends, who had always known him to be a man of immense courage.

When he had visited the U.S. the previous year he had made arrangements with a man who had told Quentin that he could stay with him indefinitely when he moved permanently. Quentin had written from England to this man advising him of the date of his arrival. The man had not replied, leaving Quentin to assume that everything was fine. However, when he arrived in New York and rapped on this man's door, he would not open it. Perhaps he had not known Quentin well enough to believe he would actually do it. Quentin contacted the man, who had acted as his manager when he had last been in America. This man proved to be a true friend and allowed Quentin to sleep on his sofa for the next six weeks until he found a permanent place of his own.

One of Quentin's spies in New York, John Ransley, who, many years previously had lived for a period in the room above him in Beaufort Street, found Quentin a room on the second floor of a lodging house called The Eastwick, on 46 East Third Street in the Lower East Side of Manhattan. This room was even smaller than his one on Beaufort Street and had a telephone but no door bell. Callers had to ring from the phone box on the corner, then Quentin would go downstairs and let them in. In his introduction to *Resident*

Alien, Quentin's third autobiography, Donald Carroll would describe this location as "one of Manhattan's most insalubrious neighborhoods ... alongside drug dealers, pimps, derelicts, Hell's Angels and all manner of low life."[2] Yet Quentin would live here for the rest of his life without once being accosted. Of his Hell's Angels neighbors, Quentin wrote, "They have a bad reputation, but they've never murdered me. When I take my washing to the Chinese laundry on First Avenue, I pass between their house and the row of Harleys marshalled out side. I walk with bowed head to show that I respect their supremacy and they leave me alone."[3]

The room looked out into the center well of the building, which meant that no natural sunlight could enter. There was a small hotplate and a small sink, but he did not have enough space for a table and would use his bed as his desk. He shared a toilet and shower with the occupants of the other five rooms on his floor. Here Quentin would also follow his philosophy of never cleaning, and as the years passed the dirt slowly built up to its four year peak as it had on Beaufort Street.

The only thing he confessed to missing about his room in London was his asthmatic gas fire, and he found his room cold during the harsh New York winter months. Initially he also missed Bovril and Germolene, two products he had difficulty getting his hands on in New York. But soon friends back in England were stepping in to fill the breach by sending him parcels of the stuff, and they would continue to do so for the rest of his life.

Many friends were worried when he agreed to have his name and number in the telephone directory. But Quentin replied, "What, I ask the world, is the use of a telephone if my number is unlisted? It means that no one will ever be able to call me; I will have to call him. Think of the expense."[4] The talk show host David Lettermen asked Quentin if he did not receive a lot of calls from weirdoes, to which he replied that he could hardly object: "I am the weirdest of them all."[5] After this interview he did receive a number of teasing calls for the next six months, and even a few death threats. These he took calmly, as in England he had received such calls almost daily.

Many of the calls he received were merely amusing. One night he was awoken by a lady calling from Australia who, after a trip to the hairdresser, had realized that her hair was now shorter than she had originally wished and asked Quentin's advice on what could be done about this. Another night he was disturbed by a man who asked Quentin if he had ever suffered from a sexually transmitted disease and if he knew that Greta Garbo had died. Quentin replied that, no, he had never suffered from a venereal disease and yes he was aware that Miss Garbo had died. The caller replied, "I suppose that means we shall all die."[6]

Friends who met him now in New York all described him as "very happy" despite having to wear galoshes to cover the holes in his shoes. America took him in and the American people took him to their hearts. I asked David Leddick why he thought that was the case. He replied, "He was a very dear person. You couldn't help liking him because of his basically sweet nature and he did need looking after. There was something of the precocious child about him. And he was also outspoken, stood up for his and other's rights and was brave. These are all qualities that Americans like to think are theirs."[7]

His first winter in Manhattan he came down with a bad attack of rheumatism which became so severe he needed hospital treatment. He also developed bronchitis. He would suffer from both ailments for the rest of his life. Were these conditions brought on by the coldness of the New York winters and apparently inadequate heating in his new room? In typical form, he did not allow this to interfere with his new busy American life. His fame grew so quickly that one day he received a letter addressed "Quentin Crisp. New York. America." There would be few days when he was not attending some function or other. He commented to a friend that if he could live on peanuts and champagne he need never buy food again.

Later that year, 1981, he gave his stage acting debut as Lady Bracknell in the Soho Repertory Theatre's production of *The Importance of Being Ernest*. This would be the first time he had appeared in drag for fifty years. In autumn the same year he took his one-man show to Sweden. Unfortunately I have been unable to find out any details of this trip, other than from Quentin himself, who wrote that this was a mistake.

In December 1981 he was back on stage playing the older Lord Alfred Douglas in Professor Eric Bentley's play *Lord Alfred's Lover*. This part must have brought Quentin a certain sense of satisfaction. It was Lord Alfred (the Marquess of Queensbury) who brought about the downfall of Oscar Wilde in the now infamous court case. Eric Bentley has extremely fond memories of working with Quentin. Quentin had been unable to learn all the lines of what was a very long play and so Eric changed the format to pretend that Lord Alfred (Quentin) was reading from his memoirs (actually the play's script) which he held in his hands. Eric remembers:

> The show had to stop rather frequently while Quentin adjusted his large magnifying glass; he could only read the script when this glass was at the right distance both from the page and from his eyes....
> Which perhaps suggests that he ruined the show. But he didn't. To the contrary. For the whole two hours of its duration, the eyes of the audience were glued to the action on stage, largely because Quentin sat enthroned there the whole time. (It is a play that probably should have been called *Lord Alfred Douglas Comes Clean*.) If Quentin wasn't an actor, he was something that had great value to the performance of this play. I called him my Rock of Gibraltar."[8]

Eric remembers an incident which happened during the play when a young actor started using obscenities, which included calling the stage manager a faggot.

> I got really flustered and angry and fired him, raising my voice as I had never done in my life. Why am I bringing up such sordid details? Because, when I turned to Quentin hoping maybe that he would do some shouting too, he looked me candidly in the eye and said, very quietly, "I shall remain perfectly calm." That was Quentin. Physically rather slight, mentally he was tough as nails. I think all gay people who knew him sensed this. The straights didn't. They took his queenly, "effeminate" style to intimate, if not actual weakness, then at best delicacy. The joke was on them."[9]

Quentin's one-man show was now in almost constant demand and he toured throughout America. The only place he was not appreciated was in San Francisco. "the critics could see how overcome I was and made fun of me.... When I explained that ... in my opinion, every theatre-goer throughout the world was a middle-class middle-aged woman with a broken heart, the people of San Francisco's love for me died in an instant."[10] During the interval of a show in Los Angeles he was handed a book to sign and when he asked what name he was told Roddy McDowall. "You're Roddy McDowall!" he cried, and McDowall asked, "You remember me?" Quentin replied, "You divorced Lassie!"[11]

In the Spring of 1982 he met Guy Kettelhack, who was then employed as an assistant to Quentin's agent Connie Clausen. Thus started a friendship which would last for the rest of Quentin's life. Connie appointed Guy to produce a book about Quentin and the two spent much time together while Guy collected material for this. Guy was an influential figure during Quentin's years in America both professionally and as a friend. During his six years working for the agency Guy booked Quentin into a wide range of theatres and managed to get him more money for his appearances, "fed by my conviction that he was worth ten times what anyone was offering."[12]

Richard Gollner, who remained Quentin's British agent after his move to America, told me, "The most difficult thing about representing Quentin over the years was that he said 'Yes' to any work offers he was given, without discriminating in any way. His motto was 'to be invited is to be loved.' Unfortunately that left me to be the baddie, who on many occasions had to inject a degree of reality, not to mention lack of availability into his mix."[13]

The Wit and Wisdom of Quentin Crisp, compiled and edited by Guy Kettelhack appeared in print in 1984. He states in the introduction:

> The joy of compiling *The Wit and Wisdom of Quentin Crisp* came not only because of the wealth of material at my disposal but because Mr. Crisp is one of those rare people who speak as they write ... the words fell onto the page as gracefully as they had been spoken.... Mr. Crisp's style and personality are the results of a life-time

of conscious choice and meticulous honing.... But there is far more to Mr. Crisp than carefully constructed artifice. Style and sincerity are the same thing in him (as he says they must be in any true stylist), and his incisive opinions and observations are completely served by the wit and grace with which they are expressed. You may find yourself falling off a chair laughing at a "Crispism" but you'll haul yourself back up astonished at what you've learned.[14]

Guy would become known as a "Crisp expert." He would occasionally be called upon to try to smooth feathers ruffled when Quentin would express one of his strong opinions on some subject or other. Guy would also become the executor of Quentin's estate.

It was Guy who introduced Quentin to Tom Steele, which led to Quentin getting a job as a film reviewer for the magazine *Christopher Street*. To someone as in love with the movies as Quentin, being paid to watch them must have been like letting a kid loose in a candy shop. He developed a friendship with Tom, who was the magazine's editor. The two would become regular cinema companions. Tom once described going to the movies with Quentin as being "almost a holy ritual."[15] Sometimes if the film was just too bad Quentin would actually fall asleep. On one such occasion a woman tapped Tom on the shoulder and said, "Your father has fallen asleep." To which Tom replied, "He's not my father he's my lover."[16]

Another of the most influential of his new friendships he made in America was with the British singer and actor Sting. Sting would immortalize him in his song *An Englishman in New York*, and Quentin also starred in the video Sting did for the song. He can be seen walking through New York streets and at the end talks about his desire to meet everyone in the world before he dies. Sting would describe Quentin as one of his heroes. A couple of years later Quentin would appear in Sting's film version of the Frankenstein story titled *The Bride*, where he played Frankenstein's (portrayed by Sting) assistant.

Now that he had fully settled in the U.S. he would often talk about his desire never to return to England. As more time passed he would start to talk openly about how he hated England, about how badly he had been treated there. Perhaps the contrast of how well he was now treated and respected in the United States brought the abuse he had experienced for most of his adult life in England into sharper relief.

Throughout his eighteen years in the U.S. he would never miss an opportunity to make pronouncements on its wonders, especially those of New York. He continued to state that he was in "the smiling and nodding racket,"[17] and would repeatedly declare, "I was a loser. I still am but now it's become a profession."[18] He now was happy. When anyone would challenge him that he could not always be happy he would reply, "There are times when I'm neutral."[19]

Quentin and Tom Steele doing their rat-face (photograph by Raymond Luczak, courtesy Tom Steele).

To show the difference between English and American attitudes, he would tell the story of how one day he was stopped while walking along Third Avenue by a large black man, who, looking him up and down exclaimed "Well, my, you've got it all on today!" before walking off laughing. Quentin remarked, "And it was true I did have it all on, and yes I did look ridiculous, but what the heck."[20] As Quentin would often point out, no one in England would have said that. In England they would stand in front of him, their faces inches from his, saying, "Who do you think you are?"[21] He felt this was a rather stupid question. "It must have been obvious that I didn't think I was anybody else!"[22]

Perhaps his most repeated observation was, "In America everyone is your friend."[23] Once when he made this statement in an interview with Terry Wogan during a return trip to England, Terry retorted, "Yes for twenty minutes." To which Quentin replied, "What else do you need! In England you have to make friends, it's very tiring. And once you've made them you get stuck with them, which is even more tiring. In America you never get stuck with anyone. Three weeks is a meaningful relationship."[24] That was all he needed.

Connie Clausen and Quentin at his seventy-fifth birthday party (courtesy Michael Andersen-Andrade).

His one-man show was becoming increasingly popular, and in the summer of 1983 he performed for six weeks at the Actors Playhouse in New York, where his show was re-titled *How to Make It in the Big Time*. Later the same year he did a four-week run at the Ivanhoe Theatre in Chicago. Financially he was now making enough money that he had acquired a Wall Street financier to look after his investments. He had also stopped lifting his British pension, which was now left to accumulate in an English bank.

Paradoxically in the years after Quentin moved to the U.S., he started developing a closer relationship with his family. Within his first year there he was contacted by his great-niece, Michelle Goycoolea, his late brother Lewis's granddaughter. She visited him in New York and they would form a close relationship; over the years he was a regular visitor at family events at her home in New Jersey. He attended her wedding in July 1986 and would be there for the christening of her children. In March 1998 he attended the christening of Michelle's third child, who would be called Ian Quentin Crawford. In the photo showing Quentin holding his new great-great-nephew, though he has his eyes closed, he seems perfectly happy and relaxed. He only had one piece of advice for the newborn, "Don't let the name give you any ideas."[25] In 1983 his sole surviving sibling, Gerald, had died at the age of eighty. Thus Quentin became the eldest member of his extended family. In a strange way, he became the patriarch. Over the coming years he would develop closer relationships with his nieces: Frances Ramsay in England and his brother Lewis's two girls, Denise (named after Quentin christened Denis) and Elaine (Michelle's mother) who lived in South America. In his will he would leave whatever money he had to his three nieces, though he would often joke that he had to die soon in order to leave them anything at all.

He spent Christmas of 1983 at his friend Donald Carroll's home with Carroll's wife and family and showed a softer side to himself when he purchased a Christmas present for Carroll's son, but at the same time showed his lack of experience in these family situations by asking Donald's advice on how to present the gift. Years later Donald would write of this time Quentin spent with him: "One couldn't avoid the suspicion that he was having fun of a type that he had thought closed to him."[26]

In America as he had throughout his life in Britain, Quentin still found himself at odds with many in the gay community. He still expressed his dismay at the level of militancy which was now inherent in the gay movement, and still insisted that he no longer had any interest in homosexual issues. Quentin often repeated his statement that he represented no one but his own puny self. He caused perhaps the biggest rift in the early eighties at the height of the AIDs epidemic. Quentin believed that the gay community, by talking so much about AIDS, was contributing to the already existing hysteria associated with the disease, reinforcing the belief that it was a "gay-plague." They were providing fuel for the "anti-gay" brigade. Quentin felt that the gay community should try to play down AIDS; that it would pass. Unfortunately the only headlines anyone saw were that Quentin Crisp believes AIDS is a fad.

Quentin was now working on his latest book, *Manners from Heaven*. In researching this he read every book on etiquette he could find and made the interesting discovery that prior to the Second World War half of every such book consisted of instructions on how to behave in the presence of ladies. However, there now were no ladies, in his view. This he commented on while being interviewed by a female televisionary (perhaps not the wisest thing to do), who, taking great exception to his comment, turned to her audience with the question, "I don't think we're putting up with that are we girls?" The audiences replied "No!"[27] Quentin reminded them that it was they who had decided to become people. "Courtship happened because women were more precious as well as more frail than mere men. If the world is going to contain no women — only people — it will rapidly become faster, harsher, louder and the only subjects ever discussed will be sport, sex and money."[28] By his way of thinking, "To say what we think to our superiors would be inexpedient; to say what we think to our equals would be ill-mannered; and to say what we think to our inferiors is unkind. Good manners occupy the terrain between fear and pity."[29]

For Quentin money was sacred and therefore it followed that employers were to be treated with respect and not questioned. This was probably a legacy of his middle class upbringing. If told to go somewhere and work he went unquestioningly. So in May 1984 he returned to England for the first time in two and a half years to appear on a television program with Molly Parkin. He seems to have been very unhappy with this program stating that it was "one of the most ill-conceived and under rehearsed items ever."[30] An unusually harsh comment from Quentin. But it did not deter him from returning to Britain just a few weeks later, this time on a tour to promote *Manners from Heaven*. He does not seem to have blamed Molly Parkin for what he perceived as the failings of the previous program as he attended a dinner she organized for him to help promote his new book. During the following days he traveled to several English cities where he did book signings, theatre appearances and gave interviews. The busy schedule seems to have taken a toll on him and he declared that he was tired and was glad when it was all over and he could return "home."

He was busier than ever in 1985 and now more in demand in films. As I have already mentioned he played Dr. Frankenstein's (portrayed by Sting) laboratory assistant in *The Bride*. He also guest starred in an episode of *The Equalizer* titled "Early Light" with Edward Woodward, in which he played a small-time crook called Ernie Frick.

In March 1985 he learned of the death of his old friend "Miss Lumley who can do no wrong,"[31] though in later years their relationship seems to have become strained and he had now re-christened her "Miss Lumley who can do no wrong — in her eyes."[32] What had caused this deterioration in once a remarkably strong and loving relationship, probably only she and Quentin really knew. In later years she apparently had often commented on the furniture she had provided Quentin when he had to vacate his room above her ballet studio, implying that Quentin had given her an inadequate sum for it.

In April 1985 Quentin made another transatlantic trip to perform his one-man show in Dublin at the Gate Theatre. To publicize this he was interviewed by Gay Byrne on Ireland's top television program, *The Late Late Show*. He explained to Gay that the purpose of his performance was to try to show the people of Ireland how to be happy, to which Gay replied that if Quentin had any tips on this, he was sure the people of Ireland would be eager to listen. It seems that they indeed were eager to listen, as he was very well received in Ireland and his show was a great success, so much so that he was offered further dates in other Irish cities but was unable to take them up.

Later that year he received correspondence from the National Portrait Gallery in London to say that they now had a collection of portraits of him. He wrote to Marguerite Evans, whose 1943 portrait was included, "The whole idea of me becoming a fragment of English history after the way I was treated there is a source of amazement to me, but I cannot say it lessens my hatred for England."[33] This collection also included one of the photos taken of him by Angus McBean during the Second World War.

In 1986 Phillip Ward was living and working in Manhattan. One February day his secretary, Kathy Hurt, told Phillip of a conversation with Quentin when she met him while standing in the queue at the East Village post office. Phillip had known about Quentin ever since he first watched *The Naked Civil Servant* in 1975, a seminal moment in his life. Phillip relates this incident:

> My mother and a few siblings were gathered about the living room watching television. Bored with game shows, Mother stood up and moved toward the television set to turn the dial. She stopped at the local public television station where a movie had just begun. It was *The Naked Civil Servant*, and "the" Quentin Crisp was introducing the movie with teacup in hand addressing the viewers. Mother left the dial on that station and returned to the sofa to watch the movie. My stomach wrenched in fear that others in the room would see the delight in my eyes while watching this man's life unfold on the screen. It was as though he was addressing me directly. It was a directive to be one's self at all cost without apology. "Be" was the answer to life's adventure.[34]

Phillip asked Kathy to arrange a dinner date, and thus started a friendship which would become very close as the years passed. Phillip tells us, "I was overwhelmed by his generosity of spirit and kindness — and his honesty of heart. And despite his spoken adversity toward love and being loved, Quentin exuded unconditional love to those he trusted and believed in. Because of this and over the years that followed, I enjoyed an intimate and close friendship with Quentin Crisp, and one which I cherish daily."[35] Particularly during the last years of Quentin's life Phillip would be a steady support, allowing Quentin

Phillip Ward with Quentin Crisp (courtesy Phillip Ward).

to continue his literary contributions after he lost the use of his left hand to carpel tunnel syndrome. Quentin would dictate his work into a tape recorder, then Phillip would see that the words were typed up. At the end of his life Quentin would make Phillip his executor.

In 1987 he had a small cameo in the film *Fatal Attraction*, where he met the stars Michael Douglas and Glenn Close. He played a guest at a literary party during which the two star characters first meet. Unfortunately, this scene was cut from the released film, but as Quentin said, "I lived a little while."[36] Working on the movie brought him to the attention of the film's assistant director, Jonathan Nossiter. Jonathan became determined to make a movie about Quentin and his efforts would pay off a couple of years later. This movie will be discussed later. In the same year he narrated a short feature, *The Ballad of Reading Gaol*, which was based on the famous poem by Oscar Wilde. Considering how much Quentin disliked Oscar Wilde, it seems strange that he took part in such a venture. Quentin would probably have simply said he did it for the money.

Wilde stated that in all things it was style which mattered, not sincerity, while for Quentin sincerity was at the very core of true style. It seems that it was from this differing opinion which Quentin developed his dislike for Wilde, though perhaps it also came from the fact that people often compared Quentin with Wilde, something which, considering their diametrically opposite viewpoints on style, must have rankled Quentin greatly. He definitely did not see himself as a twentieth century Oscar Wilde, and as the years passed he would often go to greater and greater lengths to explain why. In his last autobiography, *Resident Alien*, he gives perhaps his most fervent denunciation of Wilde, stating, "The thing that I deplore about Mr. Wilde was that he never came to grips with how sordid his life had become. When the names of five or six boys whom Mr. Wilde knew only in Braille (they were procured by Lord Alfred Douglas and met Mr. Wilde in darkened rooms in Oxford) were read out at his trial, he was still bleating about love and invoking the fair name of Mr. Plato, who died a Greek philosopher and came back as a spinster's alibi."[37] It was this, together with the falseness of Wilde's style, which in Quentin's view led to his inability to cope with a relatively short prison sentence, after which he fell apart completely, dying at only forty-two in exile in Paris.

In May he was back in England being interviewed by Terry Wogan to generate some advance publicity for an extensive tour of his one-man show starting in Covent Garden. However, his feeling for England had not changed, and when back in his beloved America he wrote in a letter to Margaret Evans, "Of all the places on the face of the earth, England is the one that I wish to visit least."[38]

The good ship Quentin hit some rocky ground in the winter of 1987 when he lost some of his investments in the Wall Street crash. How much damage this did to his overall finances is not known. Quentin never discussed his financial situation with anyone (except presumably his accountant); remember his mother telling him that money was never to be spoken of. But considering Quentin's attitude — "Money is for saving not for spending"[39] — it must have been an upsetting blow. The fact that throughout his time in America he continued to live the life of a pauper in his single room in the cheapest area of Manhattan probably served to soften the loss. His day-to-day lifestyle could not really suffer. However, he was still in great demand and no doubt was soon refilling his coffers.

Towards the end of 1988 he was back for another tour of England. This one was being billed as a "Final Visit." He would be eighty on Christmas Day. He did a number of interviews, including a return chat with Terry Wogan, and played to packed houses at every performance. He also attended a number of farewell dinners, the last of which was held at the Chelsea Arts Club on 28 September.

Nineteen eighty-eight also saw the publication of his next book, *How to Go to the Movies*. The bulk of this book consists of a reprint of his film reviews for the magazine *Christopher Street*. In the first few s Quentin lays forth his opinions and observations on the nature of stardom, the stars of the golden age of Hollywood compared to those of the day, and on the nature of the new Hollywood. These are fascinating essays and show Quentin's deep and profound understanding of the film industry and the nature of stardom.

> I seldom remember my dreams, but I recall every frame of every movie I see and my fantasy life used to be lived chiefly in the cinema. However, a regular diet of celluloid is fast becoming difficult to obtain. In the 1950s it was prophesied that television would kill the movies. It didn't, but it helped to drive the industry mad.... The trend has been away from a steady flow of seldom first rate but very acceptable pictures to a few productions upon which so much money has been squandered and on which so many expectations ride that a kind of financial hysteria has set in. The producer, the actors, and the audience have all been led to believe that each new release will be the greatest ever. It is as though every sexual union between a husband and wife must be the most shattering experience or the marriage will fail.... It is the continuous appreciation of a director's work or an actress's performances that are the deepest joy of moviegoing."[40]

The following year, 1989, he produced another book, *Quentin Crisp's Book of Quotations*. Here he gathered together one thousand quotes and observations made over the centuries about homosexuality, from both homosexuals and heterosexuals, which chart the changing attitudes through time towards homosexuality. "The fact of homosexuality never changes; but as homosexuals change what they think they deserve, heterosexuals spend their lives adjusting to it. It therefore seems infinitely worthwhile and even urgent to record all these fascinating vicissitudes of relationships, these shifts of moral emphasis that disturb our lives ... expressed in the words of people who throughout the ages stood on both sides of the barbed-wire fence."[41]

Also in 1989, Mavis Nicholson made her way to New York to do a "sequel" interview with Quentin, fourteen years after her original groundbreaking one the day after the televising of *The Naked Civil Servant* in England in 1975. Although fourteen years had passed, the two are very relaxed in each other's company, and you can tell there is a level of affection between them. In almost all interviews Quentin simply did his routine, but with Mavis he is more open and interactive. This makes for a very relaxed and genuine interview with Mavis showing great respect for her subject. It was filmed in Quentin's favorite diner, which had opened just for the occasion. In this interview Mavis asks the question she had dodged fourteen years earlier — "Why do you think you are a homosexual?"[42] To my knowledge this is the only time he was asked this question in an interview. He answered,

> Well the true answer is I have no idea. But you can say certain things which may help. I am a textbook case, for those who read textbooks. Within minutes of being

254-0508

QUENTIN CRISP
Waif. Ret.

46 East 3ʳᵈ Street   New York City, NY 10003

The business card which Phillip Ward presented to Quentin on his eightieth birthday (courtesy Phillip Ward).

born I had pneumonia so I was an object of special concern to my mother. My father, perhaps for that reason and also because I was the youngest and therefore an added expense, disliked me and this meant that I was not provided with a masculine pattern for facing the world. I lived in a woman's world, in my mother's world among my mother's friends. And my mother introduced me to a very romantic life. I can remember that she read to me from the works of Tennyson. So I lived in a world of beautiful ladies and brave knights and chivalry and all that rubbish. So that I never learnt how to live in the real world. And I think that meant that I made the most of my weakness, my femininity. At a time when my brothers wanted to be wonderful things like engine drivers and the captains of iron ships I only wanted to be a chronic invalid."[43]

During the interview Quentin makes the following telling observation about the difference between his life as it was in England and how it was now in the U.S. In England he never spoke to anyone unless he already knew them, for fear of the reaction he might meet, and he would never go into a restaurant without first knowing what it was like — he might have been thrown out. In America within minutes of leaving his room he would have found someone speaking to him and he would, without thinking, go into any restaurant expecting that he would be welcomed. He told Mavis, "I'm done with England."[44] The interview was released under the title, "Mavis Catches up with Quentin Crisp."

By the end of the 1980s Quentin was becoming increasingly aware of his age. "As time goes by we begin to look like airline food, a good imitation of what we used to be, but dehydrated."[45] He regularly spoke to friends of how tired he felt. Considering the schedule he maintained, this is not surprising. For many years Quentin had been telling everyone how he welcomed death, but now in his ninth decade his words had extra weight. He wanted a significant death and often said how it would be great to be murdered. "After all as a test of how important you are to someone being loved isn't a patch on being murdered. That's when someone really has risked all for you."[46] The advancing years and fatigue did not slow him down, however, he knew how fortunate he was to have finally achieved his dream and was going to make the most of it. He regularly spoke of the joy he now felt with his life in America and the kindnesses he received. The only way he had to repay all of this, to show his gratitude, was by making himself infinitely available. So he rarely turned down any invitation unless it clashed with another one or was simply impossible to get to. Many friends expressed their concern that by saying yes to everything he was leaving himself open to be exploited. Quentin himself said that he expected to be exploited. Perhaps to Quentin, this was just another way of showing his gratitude to America?

17

Becoming a Film Star

"Being in a film is like giving birth. For a few hours ... you swear you will never go through such an ordeal again, but when sufficient time has elapsed ... you have another baby or make another film." — Quentin Crisp, *Resident Alien.*

Although by the start of the 1990s Quentin was already in his eighties, this did not slow him down one little bit. The nineties would prove to be his busiest decade ever. He maintained a schedule which would have had most men half his age on their knees with exhaustion. In one month alone during the summer of 1990, he visited eight U.S. cities.

His one-man show was in more demand than ever. He continued his prodigious literary output; he had started a diary in the *New York Native* magazine; he started contributing film reviews for *The Guardian* newspaper as well as *Christopher Street;* he was constantly being asked to produce articles for all manner of magazines and newspapers.

But perhaps most surprisingly the next few years would see him establishing himself not just as a film star, appearing in over a dozen movies, but also as an acclaimed actor. Considering how much Quentin loved films we can only surmise how great a pleasure and sense of satisfaction this must have brought him. The little boy who had sat in the cinema theatre with his mother, mesmerized by what he saw on the silver screen; the young man who had regularly been beaten up in the street by thugs and oft hospitalized; the middle aged man who had taken to "the forgetting chamber"[1] to escape his life; this man was now rubbing shoulders with Hollywood stars like Glenn Close, Max von Sydow, Michael Douglas, Tony Curtis, Wesley Snipes, Patrick Swayze, Denzel Washington and Tom Hanks; this man now had his name flashing on that silver screen!

He also became in demand for television advertisements. Over the next 10 years would appear in commercials for a diverse range of products including deodorant, jeans, spectacles, perfume and even cigarettes — though his advertisement for cigarettes may be the only one ever made for that product in which the "star" refuses the offer of a cigarette. And of course he continued his great love — the television talk shows, which he would appear on as often as he could. Quentin often expressed the view that eventually everyone in America would either be interviewed or be interviewing someone else. "There is just so much television time in America and you will never switch on your TV set to hear a voice saying, 'as we have nothing worth watching' ... And the chat show is the cheapest way to fill it."[2]

He continued to be at odds with many in the gay community and was openly opposed to the idea of gay marriage. "Wild, pink horses would not make me turn the adjective 'gay' into a noun."[3] As the decade progressed this relationship deteriorated further. Quentin was not opposed to the gay movement as such, but his objection was the same as before. It was the movement's continued and increasing militancy, the "marching, protesting and grumbling,"[4] which dismayed him. He would continue to repeat his warning against forcing the world to accept you against its wishes. Indeed, Quentin was opposed to all forms of militancy. When someone once said to him, "What is worth having is worth fighting for," Quentin replied, "That which we can only maintain by force, we should try to do without."[5] Somewhat less explicably, he also found that some homosexuals were unhappy with him because he regularly stated that he had not had a sex life for many years and was very pleased about it. Quentin was greatly dismayed once when on a talk show with an elderly lesbian, even older than he, proudly stated that she still had a sex life. He once said that if he had still been sexually active he would not have come to America. Quentin believed that had he still been a practicing homosexual he would not have been granted entry into America or given resident alien status.

He was constantly being invited to attend events — movie premiers, parties for various people or projects, gatherings of various gay organizations. For most of these, all that was required of him was to be seen to be there and enjoying himself.

In the early 1990s a new avenue opened up for Quentin in the shape of cruise liners. He would perform on a number of these, though they must have been taxing, as he was confined to a ship and could not get away from his audience for several days at a time.

At the opposite end of this scale in terms of both numbers and physical space he performed in front of four thousand people in New York's Central Park. One member of the audience in Central Park was Bette Bourne, who took him to a party afterwards, and who would play him to such acclaim in the stage play *Resident Alien* in 1999 and onwards.

In the summer of 1990 he was asked by the Ronald Firbank Society in England to produce an article explaining what had gone wrong with sex. "The answer is that sex suffers from the same malaise as television: there is too much of it, with the result that it repeats itself. Halfway through what you assumed was going to be a new episode, you realize that it's a rerun: you know how it will end. After that, it's difficult to remain interested."[6]

The same year Quentin asked Penny Arcade's permission to name her as his "anima figure" for an article in the *London Sunday Telegraph*. The *Oxford English Dictionary's* definition of anima is "Jung's term for the feminine aspect of a man's personality." For Quentin, Penny was the woman he most identified with, his soul mate. In typical tongue-in-cheek form, Quentin commented in the article, "Most people would be horrified to be publicly identified as my soul mate, but Miss Arcade is impervious to embarrassment."[7] It was very rare for Quentin to make a statement like this about someone and shows how significant Penny had become to him. The only other comparable instance I can think of was his statement about John Hurt being his representative on earth. By now Penny had become one of his closest friends and his regular public escort. Quentin often said, "I make it a point to attend all of Ms. Arcade's shows."[8]

He guest-starred in a made-for-television movie called *Flowers for Matty* based on the long-running television show *Kojak*. Telly Savalas reprised his role as the lead character and Quentin played a character called Mr. Isabella.

Since getting to know Quentin while working as assistant director to Adrian Lyne on *Fatal Attraction*, Jonathan Nossiter had been determined to make a film about him. By 1990 his efforts had borne fruit. Quentin was initially uncertain and asked his friend Tom Steele to meet Jonathan. After being reassured, for Quentin much of 1990 was taken up with the production of *Resident Alien*, which was to follow his life in America. The film features many of his friends, including John Hurt, Sting, Guy Kettelhack, Penny Arcade, Tom Steele and more.

Most of the film involves Quentin sitting by himself or with a group of friends discussing the nature of fame and what fame means in America. There are scenes of Quentin speaking to various groups; sometimes the audiences are from the gay community; sometimes members of the audience are openly hostile. The film also shows various people, some friends, some not, discussing their views on Quentin. In the scenes between Quentin and John Hurt they are shown walking along New York streets and sitting chatting in Quentin's room. At one point the two are watching clips from *The Naked Civil Servant*, which is playing on Quentin's tiny television set which is sitting rather precariously on Quentin's bed. They watch the scene where Quentin (played by

John) is badly beaten up by a gang of queer bashers. Both men are emotionally moved by the scene. The two men are so relaxed and easy in each other's company and the affection (dare I use the word love?) between them is palpable and deeply touching.

For Quentin, 1990 ended on a high note when one of his friends, the Countess Erme Klent-de-Boen, organized a party for his eighty-second birthday in the prestigious El Morocco Theatre–Night Club in New York. It was billed as his eighty-first birthday party — to make him feel better.

Quentin would travel to many U.S. cities throughout 1991 to help with preliminary showing of *Resident Alien*. He made the first such journey to Seattle, where it seems to have been well received. His next journey was to Boston, where it was shown to a full house, after which Quentin was quizzed by the audience and the following day interviewed by the *Boston Globe*. In New Jersey it was not well received. One woman commented "Did you see him? He hasn't changed his clothes since the film was made!"[9] After the film when Quentin faced the audience, one woman began her critique with, "I thought the least boring bit was...."[10] The next showing at New York University went better. The university did a course on filmmaking, as most of the questions asked were technical ones, can we assume most of the audience were film students. His last sojourns were to the Archives cinema and the Angelika (where it was shown twice), both of which are in New York. "The film is now on its own: no more publicity can alter its fate. For the director's sake, I wish this venture well, but for myself, I am inevitably somewhat blasé about its chances of making money or bringing anybody fame. Because of my great age, my future is now (if it hasn't already passed)."[11]

Resident Alien was finally released for general viewing in October 1991. It had mixed reviews, some critics comparing it unfavorably (and perhaps unfairly) to *The Naked Civil Servant*. It is a very different film, made from a different perspective and a different viewpoint. As Quentin commented, "I merely presumed it was an attempt to depict my life in America, to show how it had fulfilled my dreams of it."[12] The other criticism was that it failed to show or reveal anything new about Quentin. But as Quentin again commented, comparing *The Naked Civil Servant* with *Resident Alien*, "That earlier television play was completed when I was already sixty-six — long past the age when I could be overtaken by any major change other than decay."[13] Quentin had been an open book for years — there was nothing new to reveal. It does, however, give a very interesting and enlightening view of his life in America and has some poignant moments.

Although Quentin had thought he had finished his tour of duty with *Resident Alien*, he was wrong. It was extended for many months. He made a trip to Boston again at the end of December 1991, to the Coolidge cinema, where it was shown twice. The showings went well and the trip was a pleasant one. "I never had an unoccupied moment and never walked anywhere. The questions asked of me were all friendly, but more or less a matter of routine, except that one young man wanted to know what I would have done with my life if I had been under no obligation to earn money. I replied that I would never have gotten out of bed."[14] In June 1992 he went to Rhode Island to lend his presence to a screening at the Avon Cinema and then to Baltimore. Both excursions seem to have gone well. "The audience was extremely friendly and only asked benign questions."[15] Even in the summer of 1993 he was off to Toronto where the film was being shown as part of that city's festival and where he was "interviewed from ten in the morning until five in the afternoon."[16] His final journeys were to Austin and Tampa, where *Resident Alien* was being shown as part of the city's gay and lesbian film festival.

Early 1991 he voiced the character of Balthazar in a version of Shakespeare's *Romeo and Juliet* in which the entire cast is made up of cats with only one human character, a bag lady played by John Hurt. The director was Armando Acosta, whom Quentin described as "looking like Mr. Michelangelo's idea of God but not so worried."[17] After his customary lunch Acosta took Quentin to a recording studio where over the next two and a half hours he "tried to coax from my flaccid vocal cords some hint of music, some breath of magic."[18] Quentin's reaction to the whole experience was "one of complete bewilderment.... Why ever was I being asked to recite poetry which had tasked the skills of great actors?"[19] On learning that his voice was to be heard beside those of such exalted actors as Sir Ben Kingsley (Father Capulet), Dame Maggie Smith (Rozaline), Robert Powell (Romeo), Francesca Annis (Juliet) and Vanessa Redgrave (Mother Capulet), his thoughts were, "How angry they will be."[20] At the end of the recording session a publicity photo was taken with Quentin holding a large white cat: "Presumably this creature was the juvenile lead?"[21]

Quentin was totally opposed to the commonly held view among homosexuals which had become known as the "separate but equal" concept. In this many homosexuals feel that the only way they can or should live is in self-contained gay communities. Quentin felt that pursuing this idea was taking homosexuals in the wrong direction. "If Mr. Bush announced that he was converting Indiana into a reservation for homosexual people and that we must all go and live there: I would burst into tears.... If I think about my life, I see it as a slow journey from the outer suburbs of ostracism almost to the heart of the world — assuming it has a heart. I would not wish to be shunted into a siding."[22] In his view the only thing which homosexuals did differently from other people was in the way they spent their evenings. "If all anyone ever talks about is their sex life no-one will have anything in common with anyone."[23]

Perhaps one of the most unusual examples of this idea occurred in 1991 when he was invited to attend an exhibition being held at Yale University, the content of which were designs, by the students, for a school for gay teenagers. "My father never took the slightest interest in me or my education, but if he ever had moved his thin lips to ask me of what my studies consisted and I had replied that I was building a school for a bunch of homosexual children, he would at once have demanded the return of my school fees."[24] It also saddened Quentin that the students' attempts to explain their work were unintelligible. "I had not hoped for deathless oratory, but I had also not expected a flow of 'ums,' and 'ers,' and false starts from the lips of the most privileged young men in the world."[25]

Quentin's most auspicious acting role was undoubtedly when, in 1992, he portrayed Queen Elizabeth I in the film *Orlando*. This inspired piece of casting is now regarded as his greatest acting role and the one for which he is remembered. Quentin was by then eighty-three, but the director, Sally Potter, was impressed by his stamina and professionalism. In an interview for Paul Bailey's book *The Stately Homo*, when asked why she chose Quentin Crisp for the role, Potter replied, "Because he is the true Queen of England."[26] Indeed, he was her only choice for the role. "Nobody else was even considered."[27]

When she first approached Quentin to play the part she visited him in New York. "I remember the first time I met him to talk about whether he might do it or not, we read through the scene once, and I asked him if everything was clear, and he said, 'I understand it completely.' That was the end of the discussion, and nothing more needed to be said."[28] Working with him, she said, was "sort of idyllic. He was patient, professional, punctual.... I'm not sure I gave him in-depth direction at all times because it wasn't necessary. There was this feeling, with Quentin, that one looked him in the eye and sensed complicity. His beady eye indicated suffering and incredible intelligence behind the role-playing."[29]

His scenes for *Orlando* were shot in England during March 1992. On 9 March he took off "timorously,"[30] he says, for England. It would be the first time he had been back in Britain for two and a half years. On his arrival in London he was put up at the Chelsea Arts Club, the very same place where a farewell party had been given for him two and a half years earlier. At breakfast the next morning someone commented, "Thought you were never coming back,"[31] to which he replied that he was doing it for the money. On a pleasanter note, Tilda Swindon, the film's star, welcomed him with a bouquet of flowers and a gift.

Quentin found the work physically exhausting. "On my first day of work I realized instantly that I was doomed to a life of agony."[32] It required him to wear heavy Elizabethan costumes which trailed the ground behind him and were so tight they raised a blister on his stomach. "Never in the history of dress design has so much glass been affixed to so many yards of tat."[33] The costumes were so cumbersome that he had to be helped to get out of his trailer, as he couldn't see where he was placing his feet. His back ached and on one occasion he fell backwards in a chair, banging his head off a wall and stretching his back muscles even further. Although everyone involved could not have been nicer to him, he was glad when the ordeal was over. "I returned home in a state of total nervous and physical collapse on the 24th."[34]

Quentin had by now developed a refreshing approach to cinema acting. "I try not to memorize lines because it's so very difficult, and when you memorize them you have to say them and it all gets rather dead if you're saying lines you think are in the back of your head."[35] But I think we need to take this with a slight pinch of salt.

In 1992 Quentin appeared in the last performance of Penny Arcade's anti-censorship show *Bitch! Dyke! Faghag! Whore!* together with singer-songwriter-actress Marianne Faithful. This event was also notable because it was during this show Penny asked Quentin to promise to live to be one hundred, to which he acquiesced.

In the summer of 1992 he received a phone call from a gentleman who turned out to be the grandson of Quentin's only cousin, Morris Washbourne. Morris had gotten married and had four daughters. One of these had married an American artist and settled in Baltimore. It was one of her three children who had made contact with Quentin. He and his girlfriend were in town and wished to meet him. When Quentin met them at his local diner he expressed his bemusement that they not only knew of his existence, but despite having changed his name and moved to another country, that they were able to find him. His first cousin twice removed replied, "We've all known about you for years. You were the homosexual in the family."[36] This announcement shocked Quentin. "On hearing these words I had one of those rare glimpses of myself as others see me. I had never before thought of myself as the family's dark secret, the black sheep, the skeleton in the cupboard."[37]

For some time Penny Arcade had been trying to persuade Quentin to return to the stage. He had declined on the grounds that he had said it all before. Finally in the autumn of 1992 she persuaded him to try out a new format stage show. The two sat on comfortable chairs on a stage set up to approximate a living room, with fireplace, table and tea trolley. The show consisted of Penny interviewing Quentin. Although initially set for a series of five Sunday performances, it became such a success that it would be rerun for years under the title *The Last Will and Testament of Quentin Crisp*.

Over two cold weeks in the winter of 1992 he attended a number of preliminary screenings and did a television interview, in an attempt to generate advance publicity for the film *Romeo and Juliet* to which he lent his voice, along with various luminaries of the film world. The film features a cast of cats with John Hurt as the only human actor. These screenings seem to have gone well. Quentin relates, "I am happy to report that the interest of the audience was aroused. A moment comes in the film when a cat, which has forced its way into a cage and snatched up a bird in its mouth, is compelled to release its victim on being hit by a car. On seeing the bird fly away, everyone cheered. On realizing the cat was dead, everyone groaned."[38]

Towards the end of 1992 and for much of 1993 Quentin made several trips to U.S. cities to attend previews of *Orlando* to help promote the film and be interviewed. These started when he attended the first screening at the end of 1992 through to the summer of 1993 when he went to Cleveland where, after the showing, he spoke to the audience and answered questions about the film and his part in it, and the following day gave a television interview. From there he went to Miami, where he was interviewed by local journalists and then to Dayton, Ohio, where he again faced the audience.

For several months after its general release he had to endure people walking backwards in front of him on Manhattan streets while genuflecting and kissing his hand. And for the first time his performance won him critical acclaim. People started to realize that Quentin Crisp could act. Quentin was typically dismissive of it all. The film was "unashamed festival material [which I] wouldn't have went to see in a thousand years had I not been in it."[39]

If you are thinking what a hectic life Quentin was now leading, it is perhaps timely to remind you again that he also had a listed telephone number so anyone anywhere in the world could phone him. Quentin always answered his phone no matter what time of day or night it might ring. When he first got a telephone in England he said he felt he had to answer it in case it might be a message from "you-know-who" and when he picked up the receiver would say, "Yes Lord."[40] On one cold winter's morning in 1992 he was first awakened at half past six by a stranger who then went on to apologize for not realizing that it was still early morning. "I would have thought that the fact that the world was still in utter darkness might have warned him."[41] At half seven he received a call from another stranger who asked him what was the difference between right and wrong. "I quoted the hero of one of Mr. Munro's stories who admits that he has forgotten the difference between good and evil but excuses this lapse by admitting that his mother also taught him three ways of cooking lobster and that 'you can't remember everything.'"[42] The stranger seemed to be content with Quentin's response and rang off. At half past eight he received a call from Australia, by which time he knew he was not going to get any further sleep and got out of bed.

Though 1992 was a highly significant year for Quentin, it also had an unfortunate outcome. He began to realize that he was losing his hearing. "I stood for a moment at the open window of my room and, except for the very faint wail of a distant police car siren, there was no sound to be heard.... Then I sat down and began to turn the pages of a newspaper in search of its cross-word puzzle and it was as though I was handling some kind of flannelette. At last it dawned on me that I had become almost totally deaf." He was much dismayed at this discovery. "I liked the sounds of Manhattan."[43] He was also unhappy because this now "deprives me of the pleasure of long telephone conversations — especially with strangers."[44]

In January 1993 Quentin made two trips to Philadelphia, where for a larger than normal fee, he made a cameo appearance in the film of the same name which would win Tom Hanks his second consecutive Oscar. The director, Jonathan Demme, thanked him personally for agreeing to appear in the movie, in which he did two scenes as a guest at Tom Hanks' parties. In the first he was required to try to do the Madison. In the second he was thankfully allowed to remain seated throughout. Considering how mad Quentin was about the movies, it is safe to assume he loved being in them. However, the process of achieving this, he did not find easy. "Being in a film is like giving birth. For a few hours after, while the memory of the suffering is clear in your mind, you swear you will never go through such an ordeal again, but when sufficient time has elapsed and the memory has faded, you have another baby or make another film. In the case of filming, it is the money that is the lure. For two weeks of suffering you are paid sufficient wages to live without doing anything in Manhattan for six months. What the lure of childbirth is I cannot imagine."[45]

David-Elijah Nahmod and Neil Ira Needleman were high school friends who had ambitions to be film makers. But they had no money. They did have a short story written by David called "Aunt Fannie." David was then living in New York's East Village and he often saw Quentin out walking. Of course he knew who he was — he had seen *The Naked Civil Servant* and *Orlando*. Neil adapted David's story into a screenplay and they decided on the bold move of shooting the story using video equipment but still needed a 'name' to help generate interest. David then took the next bold step and called Quentin. When David put the proposition to Quentin, that he play the title character, he was stunned by his reply: "I say yes to everything, as long as you're buying lunch."[46]

Connie Clausen's seventieth birthday party in 1993. In front at left is Connie's best friend Norma Lee Clark (Woody Allen's personal assistant) and at right is Connie. In back left to right are Michael Andersen-Andrade (Connie's son) and Quentin (courtesy Michael Andersen-Andrade).

So Quentin played Aunt Fannie for the lunches. David remembers how he took Quentin to various East Village shops to buy his wardrobe for the part of Aunt Fannie. The shops' keepers, who all knew him of course, were not in the least perturbed watching Quentin trying on old ladies' clothes. David also remembers how, as they walked along the street, people would regularly stop to express their admiration for him, shake his hand, ask for autographs and take photos. "It was amazing, I felt like I was with true royalty."[47]

The film was shot in an old farmhouse owned by Neil which was situated in Westchester County, New York. In the film Aunt Fannie is a deceased elderly lesbian who hauntingly advises her young gay nephew, played by

David-Elijah Nahmod, to accept his true nature and find love. During the actual filming David was impressed by Quentin's professionalism and the way he approached the task. David told me, "He just showed up fully prepared and played his role."[48] Neil remembers how his family fell in love with Quentin. Neil's late wife was then selling cosmetics and gave Quentin some samples.

Quentin was invited to attend a preliminary screening for cast and crew of the film *Philadelphia* and was surprised by what he saw. "I thought I was in a jolly film. I was wrong. *Philadelphia* is one of the most tragic films I have seen."[49] Although Tom Hanks would win his second Oscar for his performance, it is Denzel Washington whom Quentin praises. Washington, he says, "to the naked eyes seems slight but, to the camera, is monumental. He is a truly great actor. As with Miss Garbo, filming him is like photographing thought. With the use of a few words we see him starting out hating homosexuality and ending up at least feeling sorry for Mr. Hanks."[50]

On Christmas Day 1993, his eighty-fifth birthday, Quentin delivered his controversial *Alternative Queen's Speech*. This was shown on Channel 4 in Britain at the same time as the Queen's Speech and caused quite a stir, though as Quentin later said, if anyone was upset by it, they did not have to watch. Quentin had only agreed to do this if he was allowed to say whatever he wished. The speech was delivered from a suite in the Plaza Hotel in New York. Throughout the speech he promoted America: "I do this because America is the land where I think, despite its faults, is where the best of you should be."[51] And he went on to say, "I left England's lonely streets over ten years ago. Here there are no nice people from Tonbridge Wells eager to chill what is left of my marrow with iceberg stares."[52] But he did not shrug from discussing the country's defects.

> The American youth are violent because they have no inner life, they have no inner life because they have no thoughts, they have no thoughts because they know no words and they know no words because they never converse. They would not be heard above the din that rocks the dim cellars where they gibber and twitch. They have one word a year which means I don't like this and another which says I do like this. If you ask the young in what sense their little friends are cool, they say nothing. They cannot embellish their thoughts."[53]

He continued, "Though I regret this it does not in any way reduce my love for America."[54] Of Americans in general, he said, "They are a truly open handed people, free with their time, their money and their availability."[55] He ended his speech with, "My advice to the British is to pack tonight, set out tomorrow like the Portuguese explorers of old for the land of the blessed. We are waiting for you."[56]

For a short time afterwards he received a number of phone calls from journalists of various English newspapers expressing their disapproval that his *Alternative Queen's Speech* had been broadcast at the same time as the real *Queen's Speech.* "I have refrained from quoting Miss West, who, when told her radio program was obscene, replied 'They could've turned it off.'"[57]

One winter's day Quentin was sitting in his room breathing and blinking when his phone rang. The voice on the other end, that of a policeman, said, "We can't get in. There are no front doorbells." Thus began, as Quentin said, "One of the strangest episodes of my life...."[58]

Quentin went downstairs and was met at the front door by not one but three New York officers, whom he escorted up to his room. For some reason they proceeded to search his room and while doing so the phone rang again. This time the voice stated, "The ambulance is here."[59] Despite stating that he had not ordered such a vehicle, the police escorted him back downstairs and out the front door, where he found a large number of the local residents, his landlord and Stephen Sorrentino (with whom he had an appointment and with whom he would later star in the movie *Homo Heights*). Now in the street one of the policemen stated that as it was snowing, they should get into the ambulance.

On arrival at the hospital he does not seem to have been treated with much consideration or respect, according to Quentin. "My body was handled as though I were already dead, flung unceremoniously on to a wheeled stretcher, raced into an elevator where the other passengers stared at me coldly."[60] When he arrived at his bed things did not get any better. There he was stripped of all clothing including the bandages he had to use for his eczema. According to Quentin's account, at one point during all this, one of the doctors told him, "You sure go with the flow."[61] After having been given some injections and other treatments, he was eventually allowed home.

Of the whole experience Quentin summarized, "All I know is that when there is anything wrong with you, go to a faith healer, go to a witch doctor, go to a herbalist, go to a chiropractor, go to an analyst; but don't go to hospital."[62]

Why did he allow himself to be treated in this way? Certainly as the doctor commented to him, he always went with the flow. In his younger days in England to have protested his treatment in any way could have resulted in him ending up in a hospital. But this was decades later, a different country, and he was now a worldwide celebrity. He would tell this story often, always stating that he had no idea why the incident occurred. But someone must have called the police and presumably they called the ambulance.

However, I have been able to find out more about this incident. Penny Arcade has been able to fill me in on some of the background and expand on the story.

Penny told me that during the winter of 1992 Quentin had been very ill, suffering from repeated bouts of influenza. Some of his friends were becoming very concerned. Some were trying to persuade him to go to the hospital and were on the brink of calling an ambulance. Quentin hated hospitals and doctors. He contacted Penny for help. Penny told me, "I understood QC's aversion to hospital and promised that under no circumstances would an ambulance be sent for."[63] Penny's boyfriend, Dr. Robert Reder, was a doctor. "QC liked him and above all did not believe that he was a real doctor because of his good looks, long white hair and sartorial splendor. Dr. Reder was a cardiologist, and had a charming way about him that QC responded to, so QC, protesting that Dr. Reder could not possibly be a detested doctor because he did not wear a white coat, allowed Dr. Reder to examine him, and he prescribed some medications for the flu."[64] So Penny was able to say that Quentin was now under doctor's care, which eased others' concerns and took the tension out of the situation.

The following year Quentin had become friendly with a woman who had become a kind of assistant to him. According to Penny this lady had become somewhat proprietorial about Quentin and so when he again fell ill with influenza that winter of 1993 she, against his wishes, called an ambulance. He called Penny for help, but by the time she arrived Quentin was already on his way to the hospital, so she followed the ambulance. When Quentin got out of the hospital she took him to his local diner, where over dinner Quentin swore to Penny that he would never again allow anyone to get into that position of power over him. "He and I already had a track record of my respecting his wishes regarding his health as far as hospitals were concerned."[65]

Apart from the bronchitis and asthma, now Quentin was also having increasing problems with the use of his left hand due to carpel tunnel syndrome. By the early 1990s his left hand was almost useless. His doctors had suggested an operation but he replied, "When I cut my wrists I will do it myself and it would be forever."[66] Phillip Ward related how Quentin, with Phillip's help, dealt with this new problem:

> This prevented him from using his trusty companion: the typewriter. Luckily "My useless hand!" was not his dominant right hand and he was able to continue to scratch out his compositions. Mr. Crisp received many offers for articles and reviews, but he needed assistance in providing them hard copy. Along with the Demon Machine and Mr. Crisp's clear dictation, I was able to transcribe his voice as quickly as he spoke the words. Thus, I became his "Left-Hand Man" and typed and readied his manuscripts for publication over a number of years.[67]

By 1994 David-Elijah Nahmod and Neil Needleman were ready for their next film project. This would be a feature length movie called *Red Ribbons*.

This story concerns a group of friends who gather at a memorial service for a friend who has died of AIDS. Of course they approached Quentin again. This time he played the character of Horace Nightingale III not just for the lunches, but also for a 5 percent share in the profits. Georgina Spelvin played the deceased's mother and has very fond memories of her time working with Quentin. She arrived on set with her copy of *The Naked Civil Servant* clutched in her hand. "Would you please, please, please sign this for me Mr. Crisp?" Quentin replied, "Why I'd be delighted to, my dear, if you will kindly give me YOUR autograph. I've never met a porn star before. You know, you don't

Quentin and Georgina Spelvin on the set of *Red Ribbons*, 1994 (photograph by David-Elijah Nahmod).

look like a porn star. You look more like one of those ladies who lunch."[68] This film was shot over several hot summer weekends in a Brooklyn apartment crammed with actors and equipment. Though it was very hot Neil remembers that Quentin never complained about the heat, never perspired and always looked dapper. "He remained calm and dignified throughout. What an amazing professional!"[69] In one scene Quentin is sitting with his partner apparently drinking tea. Neil told me that Quentin's cup was actually filled with Guinness.

After the day's shoot Neil would drive Quentin back to his Lower East Side room. One day they were stuck in heavy traffic so to try to alleviate the boredom Neil, who was born in Brooklyn, decided to tell Quentin some of the history of the area, of "the Dutch influence in the architecture and the Parisian influence in the street design." Quentin replied, "Oh, there's nothing worse than Brooklyn."[70]

Around this time Quentin was giving a number of public speaking engagements at New York's Downtown Gay and Lesbian Center and Neil decided to tape them. He discovered how brave and blunt about his opinions Quentin was. On one occasion he berated the gay community for making martyrs out of those who had died of AIDS, pointing out that society does not do this with people who have died of other diseases such as cancer. He also made his oft repeated comment on how gays are always moaning about how they are treated. He pointed out that they had a center where they were not just free to congregate but where they were also free to be themselves. When he was a young man in England the gay community had no such luxuries. The audience were clearly unhappy with what they were hearing. David-Elijah Nahmod had to try to soothe their ruffled feathers by pointing out that Quentin was not just entitled to his own opinions but had earned the right to voice them if he wished.

Before one such engagement Neil asked Quentin what would happen if he introduced him as his son, to which Quentin replied, "Oh, I don't believe they'd believe that for a minute."[71]

Red Ribbons has now been released on DVD and includes the short story, "Aunt Fannie." It also contains Neil's videotape of one of Quentin's Gay and Lesbian Center talks.

David maintained a contact with Quentin after the film, going to see *An Evening with Quentin Crisp* and occasionally phoning him to see how he was.

Quentin had now lived in America for thirteen years and was such a familiar sight in Manhattan that he was recognized everywhere he went. He had been interviewed by *Hello* magazine and for the photo was dressed in a spotless white suit. *Hello* gave him the suit as a memento of the great occasion. One day during the hot summer in 1994 he decided to wear it. He was sitting in a restaurant when a woman came up to him and said, "You remind me of Quentin Crisp." To which he lowered his eyes and replied, "We all try to dress like him. He was such a wonderful role model."[72]

That same summer he received a letter, written on pink paper "Never open a letter written on pink paper!"[73] from a woman calling herself Francesca, who claimed to have painted a portrait of him some fifty years ago when he was a model. In her effort to jog his memory she related how she had brought him coffee during breaks. She evidently wished to renew their acquaintance and asked him to meet her at LaGuardia Airport. They went to her hotel room, where she immediately grasped hold of him and demanded that he kiss her. She was around seventy while Quentin was then eighty-five. She next demanded that he hug her. Quentin admonished her with the words, "Don't press your luck."[74] Quentin tells us no more about this woman, other than her liking of animals, "which is always a fatuous claim, as some animals are lovable and others are downright fiendish."[75] I cannot help but wonder if she was the same one who all those years earlier, during the Second World War, had professed her love for him and even threatened suicide if he did not reciprocate.

Though Quentin professed to having difficulty telling one perfume from another—"I would claim they all smell alike"[76]—in the summer of 1994 Calvin Klein used him to spearhead the advertising campaign for his new unisex perfume, CK1. When Quentin arrived at the studio to shoot the commercial it involved a number of people, including Quentin, standing together while an almost-naked young man crawled around among their feet. Quentin, on observing this scene, casually asked, "What does it all mean?"[77] Mr. Klein wisely had Quentin repeat this as the line in the advertisement.

For Quentin 1994 would be another busy year in front of the camera. He had a brief appearance this time as himself in the film *Naked in New York*. The film follows the lives of a college couple, played by Eric Stoltz and Mary-Louise Parker, as they try to create a career for themselves in the world of art and how their struggles impact their relationship. Other star turns included Jill Clayburgh, Tony Curtis, Timothy Dalton, Kathleen Turner and Whoopi Goldberg. Despite the star studded cast, the film was mauled by the critics and can even be found on some "worst movie of the year" lists.

He appeared in *Stonewall 25 — Global Voices of Pride and Protest*, a documentary film made for the 25th anniversary of the Stonewall Riots which occurred in Greenwich Village in New York in 1969. These are frequently viewed as the first instance where members of the gay community fought back against the persecution of sexual minorities and marked the beginning of the gay rights movement in the United States. Others who appeared in the film included Sir Ian McKellan, Joan Rivers and Lee Grant.

He also appeared in *The 28th Instance of June 1914, 10:50 A.M.*, a documentary profiling the lives of the eccentric gay artists David McDermott and Peter McGough, who lived without modern amenities as part of their striving to create their art.

18

Going Out with a Bang

"My life in New York has been infinitely wonderful. I am very happy living my winter years here.... At least for right now I am too busy to die." — Quentin Crisp, afterword to omnibus edition of his autobiographies.

Quentin was now in his late eighties and his age together with an increasing severity and number of ailments started to reduce the pace of his life. He would often comment on how he was now perpetually tired. During these final years his eyesight also started to fail him. He started to develop cataracts. Phillip Ward recalls, "This hindered his ability to easily scribble a letter or compose an article without discomfort, or even read without the assistance of a magnifying glass. Mr. Crisp was too vain to wear his eyeglasses. And he had eyeglasses! Yet, he'd never dare be caught in public with them resting on his undeniably English nose. It was not his style, and we all know he had style!"[1] Despite all this he continued to lead what by anyone's standards would be called a very full life.

Quentin had now also started to embrace the information technology age. Ward continued, "Mr. Crisp was totally fascinated with the computer, yet he was genuinely frightened by it and its potential. But then, he celebrated in the machine's ability to enhance the size of font so that he could read the words more clearly and comfortably. He definitely felt that the computer screen was much better than the typing paper rolled into his trusty typewriter! Plus, he was able to see the letters without use of his handy lorgnette, which was often dangling from his neck and about his chest. It was a marvel for him to watch the words appear across the wide computer screen. His face lit up with childish electricity; a total excitement of wonder! Work on the Demon Machine was the Grand Cookie Jar for writing for Quentin Crisp. Bad vision and old age certainly was not kind to Quentin Crisp's penmanship, but neither could stop him from writing! He even answered e-mail. I maintained his e-mail address on AOL, which was HRH QCrisp, and he answered postings regularly."[2]

During these last years he still found himself in demand in films. From 1995 to his death he appeared in over a dozen movies. In 1995 he made a brief appearance as a New York pageant judge in the film *To Wong Foo, Thanks for Everything, Julie Newmar*. This film follows the adventures of three drag queens (played by Wesley Snipes, Patrick Swayze and John Leguizamo) as they travel to New York for a beauty pageant. The same year he had a cameo as a tramp in the film *Desolation Angels*, which follows the downward spiral resulting from a feud between two best friends, one of whom blames the other for raping his girlfriend.

He would give his last feature-length acting performance in Sara Moore's *Homo Heights*. Sara told me she had originally intended this to be a TV series, but then decided to turn the script into a feature length movie. The central character in the movie is called Malcolm, an aged cabaret entertainer, who in an altered reality is being held captive by the head of the gay Mafia, The Donna, Maria Callous. His friends set about concocting a plan to give Malcolm what he wants most in the world, his freedom.

Sara, who is friends with Stephen Sorrentino, wanted to cast Stephen as The Donna "knowing somehow that this very handsome, macho guy from Long Island would make a terrific battle cruiser sized drag queen." When Stephen read the script he told Sara, "This is Quentin!" She acquiesced, "And indeed it seemed I had written a character that was very much like Quentin yet in another dimension, almost a cartoon version of him."[3] She didn't know that Stephen and Quentin were in fact friends. Stephen passed the script to Quentin. "The next thing I know my phone rang and a voice said: 'Miss Moore, this is Mr. Crisp. I'd love to do your movie.' My response: 'Stop it, Stephen! This isn't funny.' Being a master of many voices, I truly believed it was Stephen taking the mickey and impersonating Quentin, which he can do flawlessly. But the ensuing silence and then a repeat of those very lines made me aware I was indeed speaking to the living legend himself. From that moment on, I knew the film would be made."[4]

Even with Quentin on board Sara was having problems getting the finances to start her movie. As time passed she became concerned that Quentin might be losing interest, so she decided to visit him in New York.

> It was taking some time to get all the finances together and I feared that his interest would lag. So after sending him the latest draft, I flew home to New York and we agreed to meet at his café. It was a snowy January day and usually I would arrive at the diner well before Quentin (or "Mr. Crisp" as I initially called him until we got closer) and get us a good table in his favorite

spot, the Plexiglas-enclosed area near the sidewalk. But this time, as I came toward the diner, I saw that Quentin was already there, seated alone. He had his monocle up, the one he always wore around his neck, and he was reading my script. I stopped there in the falling snow and just watched him for a few moments as he looked up every now and again to look for me. I knew right then that I just wanted to savor this moment — me there in the falling snow, a young writer with a dream, watching this truly great man reading my words. I let it sink in. A snapshot for the soul. Then I went in and all the fantastic stories began.... I am forever grateful.[5]

Quentin had faith in Sara's project and did his own part to help raise funds for the movie by making several trips as the film's spokesman.

When funds were finally available and during working on the film, which was shot in Minneapolis, Sara, like those who had worked with Quentin before, found him a professional and a delight to work with. "He was magnificent all during the *Homo Heights* adventure. He was our darling and there wasn't one person on that set who wasn't utterly amused and in awe of him. His genius shone through all that he said and did and he was a complete riot with the telling of stories. I think we all fought over who'd get to sit with him at dinner or spend time with him after the day's shooting, too."[6] Quentin was now well in his eighties and not in good health, but this was not evident during filming, as Sara related, "He was the perfect professional and you'd never have known if he wasn't feeling well. We were all very, very aware of his age and limitations, yet none of that ever emerged on or off the screen."[7]

Sara also found Quentin a great personal help during filming. "I was going through some personal crises during the filming and though I tried very hard to mask this, it was Quentin who actually reached out and said exactly the thing I needed to hear: 'Sometimes you must put your heart aside. Just remember where it is and go get it later.' That sticks with me through any and all heartaches to this day — very empathetic, practical and British. Keep calm and carry on, as the old saying goes."[8]

Quentin attended the film's premieres in Minneapolis and in New York. Sara maintained contact with Quentin after the film with regular phone calls and lunches together in his favorite diner in New York. Sara had hopes of *Homo Heights* becoming a series of films with Quentin continuing to play Malcolm, but it was not to be.

Meanwhile he modeled jeans for Levi Strauss and trainers for Nike. His advertisement for Impulse body spray would appear in a list of the top one hundred television commercials. But he rarely left the U.S., declaring himself to be too old for world travel. There were exceptions.

In May 1995 Quentin made a trip to Austria with Penny Arcade. This was to put on their show, *An Evening with Quentin Crisp and Penny Arcade*, at the Vienna Festival. The show was a triumph, performed at the Mozart's Theatre to a sold-out house of 1,700. A review of the show described it as "Dry, wise, eloquent: This is the kind of humor one likes to listen to, but much too seldom hears live. The questions were asked by the American performance artist Penny Arcade. She provoked lots of originality from Mr. Crisp regarding trans-Atlantic differences, the role of sex, and the never-ending theme of AIDS and activism. All who were able to attend this experience listened with animated looks. And they knew that they were witnesses of a rare happening at the festival."[9]

He returned to Britain in 1996, first to Scotland to help promote the launch of a whiskey which had been named after him. Since moving to America he had become particularly fond of whiskey and visitors to his room would often comment on the generous portions he poured himself and them.

Later that year he returned again on a book promotion tour for *Resident Alien*. Billed as his third autobiography, *Resident Alien: The New York Diaries* would be his last book, with "The Dusty Answers" to be his final installment. Published in 1996, *Resident Alien* consists of entries from his diaries from the *New York Native* and covers the five years of his life from 1990 to 1994. It has an introduction by Donald Carroll, in which he states, "It is no exaggeration to say that Quentin Crisp could well be the wittiest man alive,"[10] and ends with "Quentin at the age of eighty-six is still cheerfully holding the door open for latecomers to his party. Do come in. I promise you a good time."[11] In his foreword, Quentin says that if he had gotten his way and called his first autobiography "I Reign in Hell,"[12] then this one would have been called "I Serve in Heaven," "for Manhattan has far exceeded my expectations of happiness."[13] The book hit the best seller lists in the U.S. and Britain. Although Quentin states, "I, who have not worked in many a long year,"[14] as you read the pages you will be amazed at the pace of his life in America.

With his appearance in three movie releases, 1996 would also be one of his busiest film years.

The Celluloid Closet is a fascinating and intelligent film documentary which charts the changing attitudes and portrayal of homosexuality down through the history of American cinema. Narrated by Lily Tomlin, the cast included Quentin, Tony Curtis, Whoopi Goldberg, Shirley MacLaine, Tom Hanks, Susan Sarandon, Gore Vidal and many others. He again achieved star billing in the film *Homo Heights*, aka *Happy Heights*. His second star billing of that year came in the film *Men Under Water*, a buddy movie which follows the friendship of two men, one a slum landlord who wishes to make movies and a plumber who works for him.

Quentin was now eighty-eight, but his pace had not slackened and he continued his policy of never saying "no" to anything if possible. As an example of his policy of infinite availability, on the last day of 1996 he received a phone call from photographer David Whitworth who was in New York and who had long been an admirer. They arranged to meet the next day, New Year's Day 1997, at his favorite restaurant, where they ate and chatted for three hours. David gave this account:

> He made me laugh when he said that he had recently been to see *Sunset Boulevard* and as he was leaving, one of Ms. Paige's entourage asked him if he would like to come backstage because Elaine would like to meet him. "Oh," he said, "Oh but I am not worthy," and left without meeting her. We chatted about current music; he said he loved Madonna, he still receives a bottle of champagne each year on his birthday from Sting. I asked him if he would mind writing a little quote for me on the back of the restaurant bill. He thought first, then wrote, "You don't have to win," and signed it Quentin Crisp. Time flew by and he said he would have to be getting back, I offered to walk him home and asked if he would mind me taking a few photographs of him walking home; he said he didn't mind at all.[15]

In 1997 he played the character of Simon in the film *The Electric Urn*, which is set at the end of the millennium when New York is controlled by fascists. The resulting backlash against all things cultural has driven members of the New York nightlife (including Simon) underground. The same year his voice was heard as the narrator of the short film *Little Red Riding Hood* directed by David Kaplan and starring Christina Ricci as the title character. This eighteen minute black and white film presents an unusual adult version of the famous fairy tale using humor, startling imagery and dance. The film would go on to win a number of awards, including one for David Kaplan at the Avignon Film Festival, where he was awarded the Prox Panavision, the festival's grand prize for short films. The film's photographer, Scott Ramsay, also received the festival's Eastman Kodak Vision Award for best cinematography.

The death of Quentin's long time agent Connie Clausen in September 1997 at the age of seventy-four was another blow, an especially bitter one. Connie had been at home by herself when she suffered a stroke. She was in a coma when she was found three days later. She did not regain consciousness and died soon after. Guy Kettelhack and Quentin both gave eulogies. Quentin expressed his gratitude that someone as vital and full of life as Connie had not lingered on an invalid. Not only had she been his agent for twenty years, but they had formed a very close friendship. Connie's son Michael told me that his mother "considered Quentin a dear friend and her most special client."[16] She left a gulf in his life which could not be filled. Her agency, now called the Clausen, Mays and Tahan Literary Agency, continued to represent Quentin. At this point Charles Lago entered Quentin's life. Lago, who was a

Quentin outside his apartment house in Manhattan, New Year's Day 1997
(photograph by David Whitworth).

A shop near where Quentin lived sells movie memorabilia, New Year's Day 1997. The picture second from the right in the window is of Quentin taken some twenty years earlier (photograph by David Whitworth).

former English policeman, along with Chip Snell, ran a tour management agency called Authors On Tour. With the agreement of Quentin and the Clausen Agency, Lago saw to it that during the last two years of his life Quentin was kept busy. He re-instigated Quentin's one-man show after an absence of some years and found that it was still in demand, with Quentin now flying all around the United States performing it. Some of Quentin's relatives were roped into typing out the transcript of the show from old recordings so Quentin could re-learn it.

Quentin was by now undisputedly a very old man; he was approaching ninety. He would discuss his advanced years often. When asked to what he attributed his longevity, he replied, "Bad luck!"[17] "When I got to America I hoped I would die before my shoes wore out, but now my clothes are threadbare and I am threadbare too."[18] It seems by then Quentin knew he was not going to be around for many more years; indeed, he phoned Penny Arcade and asked her, "Miss Arcade, I know I've always promised you to live to be one hundred years old but I was wondering if you would give me a dispensation so that I only have to live to be ninety."[19]

But his mind was still as sharp as ever and so were his views, which would sometimes shock and offend. In 1997 when he was asked by a journalist from a London paper that if a test could be done on a baby in the womb and it was shown to be gay, should the baby be aborted? Quentin replied without hesitation, "Of course!"[20] This comment caused such a furore that his publishers were considering canceling his contract. Guy Kettelhack was, as before, called in to try to soothe the situation by trying to get Quentin to issue a counter statement of some kind. However, Quentin's only reply would be, "What did they expect me to say?"[21] As for Guy himself, "I never thought Mr. Crisp needed an apologist. He said what he believed perfectly clearly. The adamantine truth at the center of every observation I heard him make, his unerring insight into human motive, have always, to my mind, been perfectly expressed."[22]

Quentin was surprised that his comment had caused such a fuss. He had often said that he wished he had never been born and repeatedly spoke of himself in the most derogatory ways. He repeatedly described himself as "a sad person's idea of a gay person."[23] He often expressed puzzlement as to why anyone would wish to live the life of a homosexual if given the choice. But we must try to put some of these statements into perspective. Quentin was born at the beginning of the twentieth century and faced the world as a young homosexual in the late 1920s and 1930s, when attitudes and treatment of homosexuals were dramatically different. He was regularly beaten up in the streets and left unconscious in the gutter while those passing by looked the other way. He was refused entry to cinemas, restaurants, pubs and clubs. His home was anywhere that would be prepared to take him in or that was so bad that it could not be offered to a "real" person. His friends were anyone who would put up with the disgrace of being seem with him. He had to endure on a daily basis a barrage of hateful looks, insults and missiles thrown by those he was merely walking past. His choice of occupation was severely limited and he went for regular periods without employment or money, sometimes fainting in the street from hunger. He found homosexual sex disgusting and repellent. He said that had he known what he would be expected to do he would have immediately taken the veil. Of his first experience of sodomy, he said it "was like having a colostomy operation without an anaesthetic."[24] In later life he would describe homosexual intercourse as uncomfortable, often painful and messy. Perhaps then we can understand why he answered the question as he did.

But perhaps the comment which caused the most anger and righteous indignation was when, after the premature and tragic death of Lady Diana in a car crash in France, he said that she was trash and got what she deserved. Some people felt that Quentin sometimes said things in order to start an argument. If this is so, then he certainly succeeded in that instance. He himself said that it lost him the love of all the homosexuals in America, though for years it had seemed that many homosexuals had no love to lose for him. When asked later why he had made a statement which had made him so unpopular, he only replied that he did not say anything to be popular, he said things because he meant them. Most of Quentin's statements were double-bluffs, even triple-bluffs designed to make people think, to try to point out some aspect of the world that he felt needed greater examination and possibly through this to change for the better how people lived and behaved. As he is now himself deceased we cannot ask him further, and so it will probably remain an enigma.

In the last years of his life he often talked about how someone had explained to him that he was not a homosexual but a transsexual. He did not tell us who had made this diagnosis. He said that if he had known this when he was young, he would have had the operation and lived his life running a flower shop. "And no-one would have known my guilty secret."[25] As with everything he said, we must not take this statement at face value. Whatever Quentin might have done with his life, whatever sex he might have been, he would have had an impact on all those who met him. He would have left his mark on the world.

If Quentin had one regret at the end of his life it was that he had not become an American citizen. He wished to die an American in America. He would often express this regret but explain that because of his great age, he could no longer learn all that was necessary to pass the citizenship exam. If he was to learn it all, by the time he would sit for the exam it would all be forgotten.

Despite his now great age and increasing physical frailty, during these last couple of years he was still in demand for film cameos, many of which would not be released until after his death. He continued to be as professional as ever, somehow overcoming everything to deliver a performance. In the short film *American Mod*, which follows three Mods as they spend an evening in New York, he once again wears women's clothes for the part of an elderly grandmother. In *Barriers*, a film about a young boy's struggle to survive as he grows up in the sometimes harsh environment of Manhattan, he plays the part of Nathan, an ancient store clerk. This film would win the Artistic Achievement Award at the Huntington International Film Festival for its director Alan Baxter and writer Charles Ricciardi. In *Love in Tow*, he has a brief cameo in which he delivers a line which was written specifically for him: "I don't think Mr. Klien ever quite had the knack for women's panty hose."[26] This film would win the Best Comedy award at the U.K. Filmstock festival in 2000.

He had a nice cameo in *Famous Again*, written and directed by Neil Ira Needleman of *Aunt Fannie* and *Red Ribbons*. It is a story about an old man who used to be a famous film star but who is now forgotten. Until, that is, he writes a book in which he falsely admits to having abused his son. The book becomes a best seller and he ends up being interviewed on national television. Quentin plays a prison inmate who has murdered his younger gigolo lover. Neil had written the part specifically for Quentin. "It was really a non sequitur scene that I included for one reason only: I wanted to work with Mr. Crisp again. And he was fabulous in the scene, as usual."[27] The film also features David-Elijah Nahmod and Georgina Spelvin.

During the making of *Famous Again*, Quentin as always kept everyone amused with his stories, anecdotes and observations on life. For Neil, his favorites were those in which Quentin compares America with England: "In America, if you tell your friends you're getting up a cabaret act, they'll say, 'What are you going to wear?' 'What songs will you sing?' 'Do you need me to play piano for you?' 'Where will this take place so I can tell my friends?' In England, your friends would say, 'For God's sake, don't make a fool out of yourself!'"[28]

Another of Quentin's English-American social comparison stories which he told Neil and which he told often is worth repeating here.

A woman, intending to make a long journey by rail, went to a main-line terminus in London and, as she was early, entered the station canteen. There she brought a cup of coffee and a Kit Kat. Then she had to negotiate the change, the Kit Kat, the coffee, her shoulder bag, and her suitcase while she looked for somewhere to sit. The only vacant seat that she could see was at a table where someone was already seated, so reluctantly she sat there. After putting down her case and sliding her bag from her shoulder, she put some free sugar and milk into her cup. The Kit Kat was lying in the middle of the table. The moment she unwrapped it and laid it out on its sheet of silver foil, the man opposite her leaned forward, broke off a piece, and ate it. Deeply affronted, she also broke off a piece. Then, while she was taking a few sips from her cup, he took another piece, leaving her only one last bit. This she quickly devoured. Then the stranger went to the counter and brought himself a cream bun which was a spiral confection with a little disc of cream on the top. At that moment the woman's train arrived, so she hastily reversed the original ritual, hitched her bag on her shoulder, took her suitcase, and as she passed her enemy, she snatched the lid from his bun and ate it defiantly. Then she boarded the train and, as it moved off, she put her case in the luggage rack, sat down, took her bag on to her lap, opened it, and there was the Kit Kat. The one on the table had, of course, been his, but because he and she were both English and had never been introduced to one another, neither could say "What the hell are you doing with my chocolate biscuit?"[29]

Over a dinner with Guy Kettelhack in London in November 2009, I also asked him if all the stories about the dirt of Quentin's room were true. Guy assured me that it was all true, but also emphasized that actually Quentin kept his room perfectly orderly and organized; everything in neat piles or rows, and that Quentin always knew exactly where everything was.

Quentin had now been living in his one room in Manhattan for seventeen years and, as in England, still refused to clean it. Many people simply cannot believe that this was true, but it was. Andrew Barrow, in his book *Quentin and Philip: A Double Portrait*, gives an excellent and somewhat disturbing description of just how grim Quentin's room was when he visited him in October 1998.

> It is extremely small, as small as a prison cell or hospital cubicle, and so crowded with boxes and packing cases that there is scarcely space for the bed and armchair.... Everything seems to be caked in an oily black debris worse than dust. On the left side a filthy old-fashioned sink with a dirty mirror above it. In the middle of the room there is a small fridge and a TV. On the floor beside the bed is a telephone. On various shelves and surfaces there are discarded kitchen utensils and even a sort of frying pan on a hob. On the windowsills there are cups and other drinking vessels.... A bookcase beside the sink is stuffed with useless books which he is too polite or lazy to throw away, and on the floor are dozens of bottles of make-up, fixative and medicine.... Only the presence of a bottle of champagne and an unopened bag of luxury groceries give a clue that somebody far from run of the mill lives here."[30]

Some of his friends were starting to become concerned for him due to his advanced age and increasing frailty and tried to persuade him to move to somewhere more comfortable. But Quentin simply stated that he was too set-tled where he was and any move would be too great a hassle. He would also argue that there was the financial element of moving to be considered. Quentin never seemed to acknowledge that he was by now, by most standards, at least a moderately wealthy man. In *Resident Alien* he says, "If I knew that I would die sometime during the next two years, I could live in a palace riddled with standard of living, but unfortunately I don't."[31] Quentin, even towards the end of his life, simply would not spend money unless he had to. Despite the squalor of his living environment, he was still invincibly middle class in many of his attitudes. Or was it just that Quentin, like many people who have once known extreme poverty and now have money, will not spend it for fear of ending up poor again? It would not be until his death and the reading of his will that many people, even close friends, would find out how much money he had accumulated by living on peanuts and champagne.

In December 1998, his ninetieth birthday, he started a six week run at the Intar Theatre. During the run he became very ill and would later say that he thought he might die. Phillip Ward remembers how "he struggled getting to the theater on time by taking a bus up Third Avenue and then across 42nd Street to the theatre, despite a taxi allowance given him by the producer. 'Money is for saving, not for spending.' He was determined not to fail or to disappoint Mr. Glines and the theatregoers who paid money to come see him. Quentin never missed a performance, despite his ill health."[32] Was this the start of his final declining health? His question and answer sessions which formed the second half of each performance were recorded by Phillip Ward and will form part of his final book, The Dusty Answers, which is to be published by his last editor, Phillip Ward, of *Crisperanto: The Quentin Crisp Archives*.

However, his health was now deteriorating rapidly. Although he had suffered from a number of ailments for many years now — eczema, bronchitis, rheumatism, and an almost useless left hand — he had somehow soldiered on, he had always been a man of incredible willpower. Despite all of this he was still very mobile, his incredible stamina still in evidence; visitors to his room on the second floor often commented on the speed with which he would sprint up the stairs, leaving much younger men to catch their breath.

19

The Death of the Significant Quentin Crisp

"I look forward to being extinct. I've outlived my wardrobe." — Quentin Crisp, in *Quentin and Philip: A Double Portrait.*

One of Quentin's performances at the Intar Theatre on January 24, 1999, was filmed by documentary filmmaker L. Brandon Krall and eventually would be released on DVD in 2009. Brandon told me how she found that Quentin resembled her grandmother in many ways, "although they were very different in significant ways as well. It was their generation, they were raconteurs and had a certain restrained elegance and humor that I greatly admire."[1] Watching this DVD it is self-evident that Quentin is now very old and very frail; however, his mind is still as sharp as a steel trap and his rapport with the audience is undiminished, perhaps ever greater. Brandon said of the film, "Mr. Crisp's audience identifies with him easily at the age of 90 like a grandparent who just wants us all to be happy. Having lived through the better part of the 20th century, his *messages of hope* are full of human tenderness and irony; there is a reparative wisdom and forgiveness in his prescriptions for each of us to progress through stages of 'making,' to 'doing,' finally to arrive at the 'profession of being.'"[2] Brandon also told me, "I think we love him in part for his insistent originality, his soloist's flight taking us out of our accustomed atmosphere to see with existential clarity the Zen-camp reality of the human condition."[3]

The six-week run of *An Evening with Quentin Crisp* ended in the first week of February 1999 and had been such a success that it attracted the attention of two English promoters who flew to New York to try to persuade him to bring his show back to the land of his birth. But Quentin could not be persuaded. Months later he would tell Tim Fountain that he simply could not face returning to England and that his health was now so precarious that he doubted that he could physically cope with such a journey.

In February 1999 he told *The Guardian*, "My body is dying on me. I wear it like an old overcoat. It's horrible. You start to smell. The smell of death."[4] In his foreword to the omnibus edition of his autobiographies, published to celebrate his 90th birthday, he wrote: "My body is falling apart as I write this missive to you.... I am very ill with prostate cancer, an enlarged heart and eczema (to mention just a few of my afflictions). So I don't expect to live much longer."[5] He now also had a hernia which caused him great pain and discomfort and which he boasted as being as big as an orange.

He still talked about having a significant death. He did not want the response at the news of his death to be "Isn't he dead? I thought he was dead."[6] His oft talk of suicide seemed now to be an option he no longer proposed, excusing his lack of trying with the words, "I can't throw myself under a car or leap from a skyscraper. It's very difficult — you see, I'm a nancy."[7] However, he did continue to express his delight at the prospect of being murdered. The more grotesque and sensational the nature of his murder the better. "In America the truly great are always murdered."[8]

During his last year he had started to clean out his room, as he did not want his relatives having to work through all the rubbish. Throughout 1999 when friends called him they would often find him in extreme discomfort and sometimes in such pain that he had to hang up the phone. During one interview he leaned back and folded his arms across his chest and said, "I shall soon be in my coffin, in eternal sleep. Won't that be wonderful?"[9] Although he had for years been telling everyone that he was looking forward to death, it is clear that he knew he was now dying and genuinely longed for it. Despite this, he continued to tour with his show throughout 1999, and even as late as October did a week in Cleveland, Ohio, and then Chicago, Illinois, which ran into November at the Leather Archives and Museum, though these would prove to be his last ever performances.

During the last two years of his life Quentin had been working with Phillip Ward on his last book, to be titled "The Dusty Answers," which I have already mentioned. The book was recorded on tape either in Quentin's room or in Phillip's apartment on Christopher Street. As Phillip has commented, "Quentin was bringing closure to his life and wanted to have the last word on it."[10]

The prospect of impending death seems to have galvanized his dream of dying an American in America. He was evidently now prepared to put his failing memory to the ultimate test and had started the process of becoming an American citizen. We can only assume that he now felt he had nothing to lose and if he did manage to pass the exam he would have achieved his final dream. During this year Phillip Ward was helping him to study the required booklet to prepare him for the citizenship test. Regrettably, he did not get the chance to sit for it.

He was also now becoming concerned with making changes to his will. Many of the will's beneficiaries were dead. Phillip Ward told me, "He wanted to make sure that all his life savings were secured for his family and that his copyrights were in proper hands. Recent demands had been made on him to alter and make changes to his will, requests which he didn't want to do, and this frightened Quentin very much. Also, he wanted to reward those who had been kind and helpful to him over the years by awarding them $5,000 each."[11] During the summer and autumn of 1999 Quentin had made the changes he wished with Phillip working as liaison with his lawyer, Mr. Roth. The final will would be ready just shortly before his death.

In March, Tim Fountain and Bette Bourne traveled to New York to visit Quentin, to discuss the play they were creating about him and ask his permission to put it on. They spent two hours in his room and found him in good form, delivering a performance which Tim found "a breathtaking and fantastically contradictory display, delivered with huge generosity and charm, never once seeming belligerent or hectoring despite the strength of many of the opinions."[12] Quentin gave them his full blessing.

Mid–1999 he posed for his waxwork model for Madame Tussauds. He wondered to friends if his model was to be placed in the house of horrors. Although the plaque for his waxwork image reads "Am I now immortal?," he stated clearly that he would not be around when it was finally unveiled to the public.

When his friend film producer June Lang had lunch with him around the same time, she found him in a contemplative mood. She knew he was not well. He expressed his wish not to be forgotten. "I assured him there would be no chance of that: that he had indeed left his mark on the world."[13] He talked about his thoughts on death. "I tried to laugh and joke and smile but my heart was not in it. I knew he would not live much longer but I also knew he was ready to go."[14] It was the last time she would see him.

Early in 1999 Charles Lago had booked Quentin on an extensive British tour which was to include Manchester, Liverpool, Brighton, Leeds, Birmingham and London's West End, but by late 1999 he was by anyone's standards not just a very old but now also a very, very sick man. There has been much debate about this tour and why he embarked on it. Tim Fountain's play *Resident Alien*, in which Bette Bourne plays Quentin, was opening just a few days before Quentin's first performance was scheduled, and it has been proposed that, although he had originally been in favor of the play and given Tim his full permission, he had now changed his mind and was concerned that the play was going to mock him. It has been further proposed that

Quentin's model at Madame Tussauds wax museum. The accompanying plaque reads, "Am I now immortal?" (photograph by David-Elijah Nahmod).

Quentin wanted to come back to England to present the "real" thing as a counter to this play.

A number of people have said that he expressed concerns about this play to them. Penny Arcade told me he was upset. He told her, "I don't want it, and I'm not having it! They are going to portray me as a drag queen like Bette Bourne. I only was in drag once for a birthday party. It is absurd." Penny tried to calm him. "I then explained to Quentin that Bette was an actor long before he did Bloolips (Bloolips was QC's only experience of Bette). I also told QC that Bette had seen a video of our performance together in Vienna thru his friend Sheyla Baykal and I explained that Bette was an excellent director and one of the only people I had ever trusted to direct me and my writing, which Bette did in 1988 for my long run in Bid for the Big Time at the Ballroom in NY. Quentin was impressed by that."[15] By 5 November he seems to have calmed down enough to tell *The Evening Standard*, "Of course I don't mind at all that they're doing this play."[16]

Far from mocking him, this play is a lovingly written and superbly acted tribute to Quentin which has won many awards and has played all over the world to the present writing.

Quentin did not initiate this British tour, it was set up by his agent. Quentin never picked his own itinerary; he went where he was invited or told to go. That his first date on this tour was in the same city and just days after *Resident Alien* opened can only be pure coincidence, or if indeed this was deliberate, then it was not Quentin's doing. He had not been back to Britain for years and had said repeatedly that he was finished with England. June Lang told me, "Quentin told me many times how much he hated England ... he swore he would never go back."[17]

Tom Steele told me that during a conversation Quentin told him, "This will kill me."[18]

Penny Arcade recalls how he burst into tears while talking to her about it, he was so upset at the prospect. Penny was so dismayed at this situation that she tried to intervene with his agent. She contacted the agent making her view plain that if Quentin made this trip it would kill him. The agent seemed sympathetic and agreed to cancel the trip. Penny emphasized that if this was to work he must tell Quentin that the trip had been cancelled due to some organizational problem. However, shortly afterward she received a phone call from an angry Quentin who admonished her for interfering. According to Penny, Quentin told her that his agent had not only said he was going to cancel the trip but would never employ him again.

Phillip Ward also remembers the day Quentin lost his temper — not something he did often if at all. Phillip recalls,

I arrived one day to work on "The Dusty Answers," Quentin greeted me with fury in his tear-filled eyes and anger in his voice asking why I had joined Miss Arcade in canceling his tour of England. I was surprised and befuddled. I had had no communication with Miss Arcade or anyone, other than my partner Charles, in discussing anything about Quentin, his health, or his upcoming tour. But, apparently, my name had been invoked during cancellation discussions with Mr. Lago, which he then relayed to Quentin, who then released his fury in my direction.... I had nothing to do with it and had to quickly convince Quentin that that was the case, of which it certainly was. To throw back to Quentin his own philosophy, "I want what you want" was exactly what I wanted. If he desired to go to England, knowing quite well the dangers the two flights would give his ill heart, he should definitely go. He had lived his life as a singular being and done it by and for himself for nearly ninety-one years, so why begin now allowing others to dictate what his life should be. Quentin would not have any of that and immediately called Mr. Lago to set the English tour back in motion. It was an action he wanted to do.[19]

When another friend, Simon Hattenstone, then a staff writer with the *Guardian*, tried to make him feel better by saying that at least the audience would be adoring, Quentin replied, "No, no, no! They hate me in England, hate me!"[20] He told his niece, "I have begged, pleaded and wept in an all out effort not to be sent to England."[21] In a phone conversation with Andrew Barrow he said how he was being forced to return to England. But, "I must do what the policeman says."[22] (The policeman was Quentin's nickname for Mr. Lago.) Andrew replied, "Weren't you meant to murder a policeman?"[23] This was a reference to the ending of *The Naked Civil Servant*, where Quentin discusses various means of ending his life. He says, "Wishing to go out in a blaze of ignominy, I shall limit my activities to killing a policeman."[24]

However, Phillip Ward told me,

> Quentin wanted to go to England, despite all the wails he may have given to most everyone who spoke with him during this time. This includes close friends and relatives, collaborators and editors, agents and managers. Quentin told us what we wanted to hear, and that was always the case, that he did not want to go to England. But, I do know that he wanted to go and he had my blessing, which he wanted to hear, despite my concern and fear that he would die during the adventure. He could die anywhere, it didn't matter to him as long as his body withered and fainted toward extinction soon and quickly.[25]

It seems that even at this late stage it was not absolutely certain Quentin would make the trip. In *Quentin and Philip*, his friend Andrew Barrow said, "During October there was a great deal of worry and confusion about the trip, which naturally increased when Quentin spent a few days in hospital and then announced, 'Not only are they sending me to England, I am being sent to dreadful places like Leeds and Manchester.' The trip was cancelled and then reinstated."[26] Was this the incident when Penny Arcade tried to intercede with Quentin's agent? However, Phillip Ward told me that Quentin was not in a hospital at any time during 1999.

Resident Alien debuted on 10 November to great critical acclaim. Andrew Barrow saw it three days later and telephoned Quentin to assure him that it was "wholly respectful."[27]

Six days before his departure for England he signed the executorship of his estate over to Phillip Ward, it had for many previous years been the responsibility of Guy Kettelhack. Phillip Ward related to me how Quentin had worried about this change. "Guy Kettelhack had been a dear friend to Quentin Crisp and business associate while working at Clausen Literary Agency. In the later years, however, especially after Guy left the agency, his regular communication and interaction with Quentin was not as frequent as times before.... He fretted much about it and did not want to offend Guy as he had been a wonderful friend over the years. I offered to be his executor, only if that would make Quentin's decision easier and concern less stressful."[28] Quentin also signed his new will, which apart from the various $5,000 donations, left the bulk of his estate to be divided evenly between his three nieces. On signing this he said, "Now I can die."[29]

Days before his departure he told Penny Arcade that if he died in America he would only make page ten. So was he aiming to achieve two things, embracing his own demise and a significant death?

In the last days before he left for Britain he gave several interviews to English newspapers in which he repeated that he considered his death to now be very close and also emphasized his desire to die in New York. However, the prospect of impending death had thankfully not dulled his mind or his views, which were as sharp and frank as ever. In an interview done for *The Independent* on 18 November, he could not help but have one last swipe at the gay community. He told his interviewer, David Usborne,

> I think that gay people have really gone too far. When I was young, you never mentioned it. Now you never talk about anything else. If I was to say that I came here and had a meal and was photographed and was interviewed, a real person would say, "Were they nice, did they pay for your meal, what did they ask you?" But a gay person would say "Were they gay?" And if I say I don't know, I didn't ask them then the whole thing would have been a waste of time as far as they were concerned. Quite extraordinary. I don't think gay people want to be integrated. Because you're integrated if you say "I'm gay" and people say "And then?" That's not what gay people want. They want to say "I'm gay" and have the whole room say, "Oh, do tell us about it. It sounds so interesting."[30]

He spoke to Richard Gollner. "He called me three days before he died. I urged him not to do this [the England trip], but he said rather weakly that he'd already agreed."[31]

David-Elijah Nahmod phoned Quentin two days before he left for England and found him in apparently good form. When David asked if he needed anything Quentin replied, "You're very kind. But some lesbians brought me some chocolate, so all is right with the world!"[32]

The Thursday night before Quentin's departure Phillip Ward was still helping Quentin with the citizenship booklet and told me how he decided to give Quentin a short test. "Teasingly that evening, I tested him on some of the questions and he did very well with not missing one answer. If only he had taken the test, he would have been one-half the way toward full happiness. The other half would have been fulfilling his desire to meet Elizabeth Taylor. His contributions to AmFAR (the Foundation for AIDS Research), were partly due to this wish of his, with hopes of one day a close encounter with his favorite movie star."[33] Phillip also thought Quentin was agitated that evening. "I suspected Quentin was not taking the heart medicine I had delivered to him a couple days earlier. He felt why take them, especially if they were to prolong his life when he only wanted to die."[34] Quentin then had dinner with Phillip and his partner Charles Barron and ate a hearty meal washed down with Scotch and water. They talked about his life and its impending end. After dinner they walked Quentin back to his room. Phillip recalls, "I kissed Quentin on his cheek and said, 'Have a safe trip, sweetheart. Hurry back home! I love you, Quentin.' And he said, 'Thank you. You are very kind. And I love you too. Goodbye.' I stood at the bottom of the stairs and watched him climb the first flight, huffing and puffing, with his right hand grasping the railing to help pull himself up the stairs. I remained in the lobby listening to him continue to his floor. His grunts and sighs still sing inside my head remembering him that night. Intuitively, I felt this was the last time I would see Quentin. He was not coming back alive."[35]

The next morning Phillip phoned him to wish him well and success with the tour. Penny Arcade also phoned him for the last time. "I want to say goodbye to you forever now in case you die in Manchester. I have been very fond of you over these many years."[36] Later that day Quentin left his beloved New York for the last time.

Quentin was now so frail that when his plane landed at Manchester Airport he had to be taken off in a wheelchair, pushed by his companion Chip Snell, who had been accompanying him on his tours throughout 1999. They were met by the tour's English promoter, Mark Ball, who had arranged to drive them to the house where they would be staying. Quentin preferred to stay in private houses rather than hotels and this had been arranged. They were to stay in a house in south Manchester owned by Emma Ferguson. Unfortunately, Mark lost his way and after some time had to phone the house for directions. Emma met them in the center of town and Mark followed her to her house, arriving around eleven A.M.

In his documentary *The Significant Death of Quentin Crisp*, Tim Fountain talked to Emma Ferguson about that day. Tim asked her what she thought on seeing Quentin. Emma replied, "Not well, I mean not well! I was shocked when I saw him. I expected him to be old, to look old, but he looked ill."[37] She related how only herself, her son Keir, and Chip, whom he was traveling with, were there that day. "I asked him if he wanted any food, any cooking, but he said no, he didn't feel well, he felt sick. So he just wanted to go to bed. That was about half past six, seven."[38] Tim asked her what happened the next morning.

> We woke early, I listened to see if there was any noise, if he was awake, to see if he wanted the bathroom or tea or breakfast. When Chip got up at about half eight I said I want you to go to see if he wants breakfast but Chip said, "Oh no he likes a lie in." At nine or half nine I said I really want you to go and see if everything's ok or if there's anything I can get for him. So Chip went up to wake him then and then shouted down, "Emma I need you to come upstairs." I just walked into the room and just by looking at Quentin I knew that he was dead."[39]

In his later biography of Quentin, Tim expands on this. Emma had lit a real fire in her lounge which Quentin seems to have been cheered by. She prepared tea and crumpets for him. Quentin seems to have had a pleasant conversation with Emma's son Keir in which they discussed spiders and scorpions. Mark Ball was in the house at that point. Quentin then said he wished to sleep but did not want to try to climb the steep stairs and so went to sleep on the lounge sofa under one of Emma's quilts. At approximately one P.M. Emma had to go out of the house and on returning two hours later found Quentin distressed. Alone in the house, he had been unable to get upstairs to the bathroom and had had an accident. Emma cleaned up and sometime after this Chip also returned. She gave them both tea and brandy. By seven P.M. Quentin was again feeling sleepy. He declined Emma's offer of food and said he wanted to go to bed. With considerable difficulty Emma and Chip managed to help Quentin to get up the stairs "on his bottom, one step at a time."[40] At around three A.M. she thought she heard Quentin go to the bathroom. In the book Tim relates how Quentin was found dead with a bottle of his angina pills in his hand and several pills scattered over the bed. He also relates how the brandy bottle from which Quentin and Chip had drunk the previous night was discovered beside the bed three days later. It had apparently been half full after their drinks that evening but was then empty. Emma didn't know how it had got into to Quentin's bedroom. On the bedside table was a glass and two nickels.

Quentin would have been ninety-one on Christmas Day.

With regards to the two coins, Phillip Ward filled me in on these. "It was two U.S. quarters, not nickels, that Quentin had left on the bedside table. It is an Old World tradition to place quarters on the eyes of the dead, and was something which Quentin practiced nightly by placing two quarters on his bedside table. He even did this ritual at home and on our travels together."[41] Also, with regards to the empty brandy bottle found beside Quentin's bed three days later, he told me, "There is no way Quentin could have carted the liquor bottle up the stairs by himself. He needed his right hand to pull himself up and forward, while holding the left hand crooked and close to his person, thus being unable to grip any sort of bottle either in the hand's clutch or the crook of the elbow. Impossible."[42] He also told me, "I was informed by Chip upon his return with Quentin's ashes that several individuals surrounding Mr. Crisp's tour had gathered in the dying room the night following Quentin's death and had a celebration in which they finished off the bottle of brandy that had been shared with Quentin upon his arrival in Manchester the night before."[43]

The post-mortem report recorded his death as due to a massive heart attack. Despite the amount of alcohol he had apparently consumed during the last twenty-four hours of his life, no mention was made of any alcohol in his bloodstream.

Quentin knew how ill he was and that he did not have much time left. It is hard to believe that his agent was not also fully aware of his state of health, and he bore much criticism for sending so sick a man on such an arduous trip. He had not been booked on a direct flight and had to change at London for a flight to Manchester, making the journey even longer and more exhausting. His former agent and friend Patrick Newley, speaking after the death, said, "When I spoke to him two or three weeks ago in New York he was clearly not happy about coming over here for the tour. At his age it was too much. I rather think he might still be alive if he had not come across here."[44]

Indeed, while his agent has been much criticized we must concede that he would not have sent Quentin to England if he had believed it would kill him. Why kill off a lucrative asset? Ryan Levitt, the tour's publicist, was adamant the final decision to go to England was Quentin's. "We gave him the opportunity to cancel four weeks ago and we felt strongly that he would, but he said he wanted to tour England one last time."[45]

There is another possibility. Did Quentin finally accept his journey to Britain because he knew he had very little time left, and that the trip would probably kill him? June Lang told me, "In my opinion, this was Quentin's way of planning his death."[46]

Someone was critical because Joan Crawford, whom he much admired, died drunk and alone. Quentin replied that seemed to him like an ideal way to go. "If you cannot arrange to die in private you may have to die and be polite at the same time. It may not be easy."[47] Had he indirectly managed to do just that? Quentin had also often commented that if you could afford to buy enough alcohol to ease the unpleasantness of the dying process then why not do so? However we must be careful here; he had made arrangements to have dinner on 29 November with his old friend Elizabeth Wyndham, whom he had first met at St. Martin's school in 1956; he had also made a hospital appointment to have surgery for his hernia when he returned to America (though how likely was he to survive such a procedure?). So he was not absolutely certain that death awaited him in England. Also, when his body was found his pills were scattered over the bed, so we must assume that when he had his heart attack sometime during the night he had tried to take his medication. Some ten years earlier he had, even then, told Mavis Nicholson, "In theory I long for death, but as I say this if I looked up and there was a great crack in the ceiling I would move, because your body wants to live in spite of everything."[48]

On Monday, 22 November, his death was front page news both in Britain and America (not page ten as he predicted). There were few newspapers in Britain which did not carry the story and many of the broadsheets such as *The Guardian* and *The Times* had the news on their front pages. *The Independent* printed his interview done with David Usborne back in New York before he had left for England. Even Buckingham Palace issued a statement expressing sadness at his parting. In America his death was the second item on the CNN news network. In Manhattan's Lower East side many restaurants and shops displayed a photo of Quentin in their windows and some even lit candles for him. Soon people also started leaving flowers outside the house at East Third Street where he had lived. The next day John Hurt was presenting an Evening Standard award and broke from his role for a few minutes to pay his tribute to Quentin, ending with "Bless you, Quentin. You're one of the greatest philosophers who ever lived."[49]

Quentin's body was cremated in a secret ceremony which was listed under a false name. His ashes were flown back to America where they were scattered around the streets of Manhattan where he lived.

Phillip Ward and his partner Charles now started the task of clearing out Quentin's room. Phillip told me,

It took two months to deconstruct Quentin's apartment, as the dust was uncomfortably thick. Shifting things about created a fine cloud of dust that prevented any prolonged amount of time in the room. The building's super, Hapi Phace, was eager and ready to move in immediately the day of Quentin's death, but he had to wait until Charles and I cleared out the space, which took us until the end of February 2000, whereupon Hapi immediately claimed stake. After all, Quentin's room was the largest in the building, and Hapi could now leave his tiny closet-of-a-room and move into larger quarters. Also, Quentin's telephone number was directed to our apartment, initially to collect calls from various people expressing their condolences to Quentin's family. Then it was used to allow people to respond to the planned memorial invitations sent out by the family and the estate, which we planned for March 3, 2000, at Cooper Union's Great Hall. After the memorial, Quentin's number was then switched over to be used as the phone number for *The Quentin Crisp Archives*, where it continues to be used today for both the archives and issues related to his estate."[50]

In a rather bizarre turn of events, which is perhaps fitting, and which Quentin would have probably laughed at, the mattress which had borne Quentin's body in sleep for the previous eighteen years was retrieved by the designer Miguel Adrover. From the cloth covering he created an overcoat to be displayed with great success on the New York catwalk during Fashion Week in February 2000. Miguel is an unorthodox designer. When, in November 2009, I interviewed him about his creation, he told me he had actually always wanted to live in a tropical jungle. His inspiration as a designer came from BodyMap, Ralph Lauren, Vivian Westwood and HessNatur and his drive as a designer was to create clothes that anyone could wear. Miguel told me that when he had lived in Manhattan he and Quentin had virtually been next door neighbors. They frequented the same diner where they often chatted over a cup of tea. "He was a really polite and funny person, and extremely sophisticated."[51] Miguel had found the mattress lying in the street and immediately knew he must do something with it. He told me how he and his assistant had to wear face masks and rubber gloves when cleaning the mattress cover, but they still got rashes. Miguel actually made an overcoat and a skirt from the cover which caused a stir on the catwalk, but that was not the end of the story. The New York Metropolitan Museum contacted Miguel. They were of the view that the Quentin garments were in fact part of New York's history and asked Miguel if he would donate them to the museum, and so they became a permanent exhibit.

While sorting out Quentin's estate, Phillip discovered that he had for some time been writing checks for a number of AIDS charities. This was something which he seems to have kept secret from even his closest friends. Even with this generosity when Quentin's new last will and testament was finally processed it was revealed that he had left his three nieces $650,000 dollars and another $600,000 from investments and savings.

In Britain, on 9 January 2000, the BBC broadcast a live recording of Tim Fountain's play *Resident Alien* on Radio 3 as a tribute to him.

In March 3, 2000, over seven hundred people packed the Cooper Union's Great Hall in New York for *An Evening for Quentin Crisp*, which was organized by Phillip Ward. Phillip's choice of venue was highly significant. "Quentin would have marvelled and grinned with knowing that all of us who participated in the memorial spoke from the same lectern as Abraham Lincoln when he addressed the New York City public in a speech that garnered him the nomination to become candidate for president of the United States. The stage is often used as a platform 'of the people, by the people, for the people' and significantly so Quentin Crisp!"[52]

For over two hours they listened while over twenty of his friends and colleges spoke from that lectern. Among those present were his three nieces, Frances Ramsay, Elaine Goycoolea and Denise Pratt-Reiner; his friends Penny Arcade, Guy Kettelhack, Phillip Ward, Louis Colaianni, Eric Bentley, Tom Steele, and many more.

Frances said of her uncle, "I did not meet him until my first visit to London when I was 15. I had been told he was eccentric, but this did not really prepare me for his outrageous appearance. However, I quickly realized that he was someone really special.... He was always generous and genuinely interested in all the family. I shall always lovingly remember him as my Uncle Denis."[53] Academic and writer Professor Eric Bentley described him as "one of the toughest, strongest men I have ever known."[54] Penny Arcade told the gathered crowd, "He grew up to be himself and that is the greatest thing that anyone can achieve."[55] John Hurt spoke via video link, saying, "He was a philosopher and he is the only philosopher to my knowledge that actually lived his philosophy. He was a major, major figure of the twentieth century and he wasn't like anyone, he was literally unique."[56]

In April 2000 the National Film Theatre put on a season of his films as their tribute to him, which included such rarities as *Hamlet* and *Captain Busby*.

I can think of no better way of ending the story of his life than with this extract from his foreword to the omnibus edition of his autobiographies: "I would hate to leave this world without saying that I have had a good ride of it all.... I have made it to the Big Time with an abundance of smiles."[57] Comparing this sentence with the last one from *The Naked Civil Servant*—"I stumble towards my grave confused, hurt and hungry"[58]—will show just how much his life had changed in the interim thirty years.

While we should of course mourn his loss to the world we must remember that he had lived a very long and exceptional life and that he truly welcomed and indeed wished for death. In his last work, "The Dusty Answers," he tells us,

> I'm tired of it already, and I hope that death is just nothing. And as death approaches, I welcome it. I open my arms to it because my life has become wearisome, physically wearisome. I am covered with sores from my eczema. I creak all over my joints from rheumatism. I have cancer of the prostate gland. I have a bad heart. What more could go wrong! Lose all my hair? I visualize death as coming more or less as spontaneously, but I shan't do anything, that the world will go dark, that I shall feel cold, that I shan't be able to hear anything, that it will go silent and dark. And that I shall float away and not yell when people say, "Quentin! Quentin! Are you there? Are you alive?" I shan't answer. It'll be wonderful![59]

There can be no doubt that Quentin Crisp was the most famous homosexual of the twentieth century, perhaps of all time. It could also be argued that he did more to enlighten the world about homosexuality than anyone else. Yet especially in the last decades of his life he found himself often in open opposition with many in the gay rights movement. But to leave his epitaph at that would be to do him the gravest injustice. He was a totally unique human being. I doubt that I would be challenged when I say that it is unlikely there has ever been or ever will be anyone quite like him again. He overcame a lifetime of verbal, emotional and physical abuse, degradation and subhuman treatment to become a worldwide celebrity. Loved, respected and admired by millions for his intellect, humor, humanity and courage. But above all he was a profound and unique philosopher. His impact on the world cannot be underestimated and will continue to be felt for many decades and beyond.

His impact on those he met was profound, as Sara Moore told me, "Knowing Quentin changed my life entirely. Working with him will always be an extreme high point in my own very eccentric career and life. He made me, as he did so many others, feel not so alone in the world. He was an extraordinary person and those of us lucky and blessed enough to spend real time with him know we were in the company of a bona fide genius. And that genius was housed in a human soul so good and vulnerable and genuine."[60]

Perhaps I should leave the last word on Quentin Crisp to the writer Ronald Harwood, author of the play *The Dresser*, who first met Quentin in 1954 at one of Gordon Richardson's parties on Beaufort Street. "If I were asked to write his epitaph, I would suggest, simply, 'Quentin Crisp was in every way astonishingly beautiful.'"[61]

Afterword

When I first launched my Web-site in early 2000 there were three other sites about Quentin; however, two of these subsequently folded. It seemed that the world could so easily forget Quentin and what a loss that would be. I must admit that I did not feel particularly hopeful.

I am sure Quentin would have just told me not to bother. Throughout his long life he always insisted that death was the end. There was nothing after. When Mavis Nicholson asked him if he ever thought about an epitaph, he replied, "Well, everyone says that but I don't think about it because I will be dead. And what does it matter. You see people who say, 'What do you want to have written on your tombstone?' They think that they will look down from a cloud and count the people at their funeral. They won't, I've got news for them, they'll be dead!"[1] However, in the last years of his life he did seem to give it some thought. When asked by his friend Louis Colaianni how he would like to be memorialized if his image were produced in stained glass, he replied, "I should like to be seen with a pen in one hand and a book in the other, winking."[2] Although he had once said, "The absolute nothingness of death is a blessing. Something to look forward to,"[3] towards the end he also seemed to acknowledge the possibility of an afterlife to the extent that when, shortly before his death, he was asked by an interviewer who he would like to meet in the afterlife, and he shocked the man by replying, "I want to meet Pol Pot and sit down with him quietly and ask him what he thought he was doing."[4]

I could not forget. Maybe the truth was that it meant too much to me personally. I could only do what I could. Now here we are ten years later celebrating his centenary and I could not have been more wrong.

Resident Alien, which was broadcast on Radio 3 on 9 January 2000 as a tribute to Quentin, has continued to be performed around the world. In 2008 it was put on in New Zealand as part of their Heroes Festival with actor John Watson playing Quentin. John has plans to tour with the show. In February to April 2009 it had a ten-week run at the New End Theatre in London, the same theatre where Quentin first performed *An Evening with Quentin Crisp* in August 1976, as a centenary tribute to Quentin, with Bette Bourne reprising his role.

We have also had three more plays about Quentin.

Carved in Stone, written by the late Jeffrey Hartgraves, features some of the most famous gay literary figures of recent history, including Oscar Wilde, Truman Capote, Tennessee Williams and Quentin Crisp. It debuted to great success and critical acclaim in San Francisco in 2002. Although, sadly, Jeffrey passed away prematurely in 2008 from cancer, the play has already had a second run. It was on again at the Asylum Theatre in Los Angeles for eight weeks starting in June 2009 with Leon Acord reprising his role as Quentin Crisp. I think it is safe to say it will be delighting audiences again. When I interviewed Leon in 2007 he told me that he would like to return to the role on a regular basis. "The great thing is, I can't grow too old for the part!"[5]

Quentin and I: The New Mini Musical is a one-man show performed by David Leddick with music by Andrew Sargent and lyrics by David. It debuted in April 2005 in Miami Beach and had a second run in New York in March 2006. David was a friend of Quentin during the last twenty years of his life.

John Watson as Quentin in *Resident Alien* in New Zealand, 2008 (photograph by Max Osborne).

Leon Acord as Quentin in Jeffrey Hartgraves' *Carved in Stone*, 2009 (photograph by Peter Solari).

John Hurt reprising Quentin in *An Englishman in New York,* a film by Leop-ardrama for ITV, 2009.

Quentin was in favor of *The Naked Civil Servant* being done as a musical and was later disappointed when plans for it to be put on Broadway did not come off. So I think he would have been pleased with David's show.

Tea 'N Crisp is a one-man show written by and starring acclaimed Bay Area character actor Richard Louis James. In *Tea 'N Crisp* Richard brings Quentin back to life based on his writings and public appearances, presented in the format of *An Evening with Quentin Crisp*, updated for the twenty-first century. It debuted at the Ashby Theatre, in Berkeley, California, in 2007 and has since played three more times in 2008. It was picked as one of five shows for the Ross Valley Players Festival in the Solo Performances section in February 2009. Richard has many plans for the future of his show.

When John W. Mills was approached in 2003 by the British Art Medal Society he decided to produce a medal based on the earlier bronze sculpture he had done of Quentin wearing his felt fedora. Thus "Quentin Crisp's Fedora" became a British Art Medal.

In 2007 Cherry Red records released a CD of the live studio recording of his 1979 performance of *An Evening with Quentin Crisp*, which was recorded in America. This double CD also contains Morgan Fisher's excellent interview

Phillip Ward and Tom Steele at the Tribeca Film Festival premier of *An Englishman in New York* in 2009 (photograph by Charles Barron, courtesy Phillip Ward).

with Quentin which was done in his room at 129 Beaufort Street, London, in June 1980.

A digitally remastered version of *The Naked Civil Servant* has also been released on DVD. On the same DVD you will also find Denis Mitchell's 1969 documentary as well as Quentin's 1989 interview with Mavis Nicholson. This is a superb DVD for anyone interested in Quentin.

Then of course we have John Hurt reprising his role as Quentin in 2009 in *An Englishman in New York*. With a title taken from the song by Sting, this sequel to *The Naked Civil Servant* tells us what happened to Quentin after the end of that film and follows his move to America in 1981 and his subsequent years there. The movie had its world premiere at the Berlin International Film Festival on 7 February 2009. At the premiere, Hurt said he had at first felt "cagey" about playing Quentin again, but said, "I do identify with Quentin, it's been such a long time I've known him.... And he once said, 'Mr. Hurt is my representative on earth,' so I have a certain papal blessing."[6]

The film has had many showings throughout the world, receiving top reviews everywhere. John Hurt was nominated for a British Academy of Film Television Arts award for his performance. It was shown on British Television on 28 December 2010 and can now be purchased on DVD.

L. Brandon Krall released on DVD her film of Quentin's performance of *An Evening with Quentin Crisp* at the Intar Theatre on 24 January 1999.

In 2009, filmmaker Adrian Goycoolea, Quentin's great-nephew, produced his documentary about Quentin, *Uncle Denis*, which premiered in London and was also screened in New York and San Francisco. It shows how much a part of the family Quentin had become, at least with the next generation. He is shown to have been perfectly happy and relaxed as a regular attendee at marriages, christenings and other family occasions.

As Quentin's executor, Phillip Ward continues to run The Quentin Crisp Archives at www.crisperanto.org. He is also editing Quentin's final book, *The Dusty Answers*. Phillip organizes regular events to promote Quentin's memory.

So it looks like Quentin is in no danger of being forgotten. I hope that as you have read this book you realize why he should not be. Why the world would have been a lesser place had he not lived in it and why the world will lose something special if it ever does forget him. Just consider this statement which my wife made to me several years ago: "If people lived by Quentin's philosophy, perhaps the world would be a better place and the people in it a bit more human."[7] I couldn't put it better or leave you with a more appropriate thought.

APPENDIX 1

Crisperanto: The Philosophy of Quentin Crisp

"He was a true philosopher and the only one who actually lived his own philosophy." — John Hurt, *An Evening for Quentin Crisp*, 2000

Quentin's philosophy is his greatest legacy to the world. His philosophy was based on his own practical experiences of real life and the real world, not on highbrow theories which no human being could possibly adhere to. As proof of this, consider that he actually lived his own philosophy in every aspect of his life.

It is often said that only those on the outside looking in can really see what is going on. Quentin was on the outside of life for most of his first seventy years. From this position he observed other people with a level of intellectual and emotional detachment. "I have to be excluded from what is human so that I may look at humanity with a sense of detachment. It is then that I guess at its motives and what makes it the way it is."[1]

The entire theme of his own one-man show *An Evening with Quentin Crisp* was trying to teach members of his audience how to be happy. By a process of intensive self-study of who you really are, you can achieve a state of total self-awareness. This process involves not just the person's own self-examination, but also consideration of what other people think about you. "The very purpose of existence is to try to reconcile the glowing opinion we hold of ourselves with the terrible things that other people say about us."[2] The application of this knowledge to all aspects of your life will result in the creation of your own unique style. Out of this style will come the understanding of what job you should be doing; where you should live; what clothes you should wear. Once this process is completed it will be an immediate form of communication to everyone you meet. Everyone who meets you will know exactly who you are, and therefore what attitude and approach to you is

169

appropriate; what kind of conversation is suitable. Quentin often said, "No one talks to me about the weather."[3]

The basis of his teaching came from his philosophy, which he encapsulated in his bons mots — witty one-liners (mostly) which at first seem light, throwaway remarks, but under closer examination are anything but. They were his technique of imparting his philosophy to the world in a way that would be easily digestible and easy to remember. They were so cleverly constructed — he had been "polishing" them for decades — that they sink into your mind without you even realizing it. Firstly they make you laugh, and because of this you remember them. When you remember them they almost force or rather coax you to think about what they mean. It is then that you realize they are loaded with meaning. While some can be taken literally at face value, some are actually a double-bluff and even a triple-bluff.

I have met people who know by heart his sayings such as "Never try to keep up with the Joneses,"[4] or "Never clean the place where you live."[5] But they do not know who said them. So we see how far Quentin's philosophy has filtered into the world.

Quentin wanted people to think for themselves: "I believe the human mind is better engaged through imagination than obedience."[6] So I shall not attempt to analyze any of his wisdom, it is for each of you to do so as you read. I shall simply present you with those for which he is most known, as well as some which you may not have heard, but which are worth examining. I have also included a number of longer pieces, which I think you will agree are must-reads.

To paraphrase Guy Kettelhack — you may find yourself laughing out loud, but when you stop and think about it you'll realize what you have just learned.

Enjoy, think and learn.

His Philosophy

Ask yourself if there was to be no praise and if there was to be no blame, who would I be then?[7]

The very purpose of existence is to try to reconcile the glowing opinion we hold of ourselves with the terrible things that other people say about us.[8]

Never desire to be anyone's equal.[9]

If we are to be totally free from blame for our anonymity, we must never say no to anything.[10]

If at first you don't succeed, failure may be your style.[11]

What we can only retain by force we should try to do without.[12]

It's no good running a pig farm badly for 30 years while saying, "Really, I was meant to be a ballet dancer." By then, pigs will be your style.[13]

Fashion is what you adopt when you don't know who you are.[14]

In an expanding universe, time is on the side of the outcast. Those who once inhabited the suburbs of human contempt find that without changing their address they eventually live in the metropolis.[15]

If a problem is stated with sufficient accuracy, the solution has already been formulated.[16]

When we say of somebody else that he is boring, it is ourselves that we criticize because we have not made ourselves into that wide-open vessel into which people can pour their entire life. Nothing is boring except for a lie.[17]

I look neither forward, where there is doubt, nor backward, where there is regret; I look inward and ask myself not if there is anything out in the world that I want and had better grab quickly before nightfall, but whether there is anything inside me that I have not unpacked. I want to be certain that, before I fold my hands and step into my coffin, what little I can do and say and be is completed.[18]

All concealment is wrong. If there were none half the problems of the world would disappear overnight. There would be no snooping and therefore no fixing; there would be no blackmail and therefore no fear in the world other than physical fear. That wouldn't be a bad start.[19]

Art

When people say "What I've got against pictures?" I reply, What have you got against the wall?[20]

Charisma

I would say charisma is the ability to influence without the use of logic.[21]

Co-Habitation

The continued propinquity of another human being cramps the style after a time unless that person is somebody you think you love. Then the burden becomes intolerable at once.[22]

Death

Is death final? "Well, I hope so. Eternal life is something I wouldn't wish on my worst enemy."[23]

Death is the least awful thing that can happen to anyone.[24]

We never grieve for the dead.[25]

Domestic Chores

Never keep up with the Joneses. Drag them down to your level. It's cheaper![26]

There's no real need to do housework. After the first four years the dust doesn't get any worse. It's just a case of not losing your nerve.[27]

Only a fool would make the bed every day.[28]

You only need to do the dishes after you've passed the fish barrier. It works like this — You taste your plate and it says egg so you think, "I could have some bacon." Next morning your plate says bacon so you think, "I could have some fish." But after the fish you have to do the dishes.[29]

Education

Being well informed is but a stone's throw from being boring and stones will be thrown.[30]

All education is a complete waste of time. It's no good cluttering your head with facts about anything other than yourself. All general knowledge can be found in the nearest library.[31]

Family Life

If one is not going to take the necessary precautions to avoid having parents, one must undertake to bring them up.[32]

The trouble with children is that they're not returnable.[33]

If Mr. Vincent Price were to be co-starred with Miss Bette Davis in a story by Mr. Edgar Allan Poe directed by Mr. Roger Corman, it could not fully express the pent-up violence and depravity of a single day in the life of the average family.[34]

To most men a wife and family are things incurred by accident and bravely borne.[35]

Happiness

The essence of happiness is its absoluteness. It is automatically the state of being of those who live in the continuous present all over their bodies. No effort is required to define or even attain happiness but enormous concentration is needed to abandon everything else.[36]

The consuming desire of most human beings is deliberately to plant their whole life in the hands of some other person. I would describe this method of searching for happiness as immature. Development of character consists solely in moving toward self-sufficiency.[37]

Health

Health consists of having the same diseases as one's neighbors.[38]

Human Rights

I don't think anyone has any rights. I think you fall out of your mother's womb, you crawl across open country under fire, you grab at what you want, if you don't get it you go without, and you flop into your grave.[39]

If we all got what we deserved we would starve.[40]

Journalism

It is a skill to give readers what they wish to hear while claiming to present stark, unbiased truth.[41]

Love

Love is the extra effort we put in our dealings with people we do not like.[42]

You must learn not to value love because it is requited. It makes no difference whether your love is returned. If you have love to give, you give it and you give it where it is needed. Once you've got that in your head, the idea of your heart being broken will disappear.[43]

The message that "love" will solve all of our problems is repeated incessantly in contemporary culture — like a philosophical tom-tom. It would be closer to the truth to say that love is a contagious and virulent disease which leaves a victim in a state of near imbecility, paralysis, profound melancholia and sometimes culminates in death.[44]

Manners

To say what we think to our superiors would be inexpedient; to say what we think to our equals would be ill-mannered; and to say what we think to our inferiors is unkind. Good manners occupy the terrain between fear and pity.[45]

The lie is the basic building block of good manners. That may seem mildly shocking to a moralist — but then what isn't?[46]

Manners are a way of getting what you want without appearing to be an absolute swine.[47]

Music

The maximum amount of noise conveying the minimum amount of information.[48]

Music is a mistake. When I was young the world was silent.... But this is no longer the case. Music is everywhere. One cannot help asking of what were you afraid? Why couldn't you bear the sound of the puff-puffs on the station, why did you have to have the music? Why couldn't you bear the sound of the barber's clippers? Why have you reduced all human experience to one experience? The Music. You've taken away all the variety that there used to be in life. And worse than that you've had to give up the speech. There is no point in trying to speak and when you give up the words you give up the thoughts. In the beginning there was the word and the word prompts thought. It's when you realize that there are words like greedy, materialistic, avaricious and so on that you start to find ideas which express these shades of meaning. With the music you can only gibber and twitch.[49]

Politics

Politics are not for people, they are for politicians.[50]

Politics are not an instrument for effecting social change; they are the art of making the inevitable appear to be a matter of wise human choice.[51]

The trouble with politics is it makes children believe that the perpetual violent turmoil of the world is soluble and this means they grow up with this terrible feeling that the world has been mismanaged by their parents. Therefore they either take jobs where they opt out entirely; or have the view that they should all go out to the middle of Biafra, and this to my mind is bad. There are situations which cannot be resolved; there are questions for which there are no answers and if you don't accept this then you will rapidly develop a police mentality. You will search for culprits, you will tear up contradictory evidence and you will push people around until they are in easily labeled and easily controlled blocs. Zealots are totally incapable of any emotion other than rage. It is an unalterable law that people who claim to care about the human race are utterly indifferent to the sufferings of individuals.[52]

Prejudice

It is not the simple statement of facts that ushers in freedom; it is the constant repetition of them that has this liberating effect. Tolerance is the result not of enlightenment, but of boredom.[53]

Relationships

The formula for achieving a successful relationship is simple: you should treat all disasters as if they were trivialities but never treat a triviality as if it were a disaster.[54]

Love is not enough. It must be the foundation, the cornerstone — but not the complete structure. It is much too pliable, too yielding.[55]

It is explained that all relationships require a little give and take. This is untrue. Any partnership demands that we give and give and give and at the last, as we flop into our graves exhausted, we are told that we didn't give enough.[56]

As a test of the closeness of your relationship with the world being loved could never be a patch on being murdered. That's when someone really has risked his life for you.[57]

Religion

If God is the universe which encloses the universe, or if God is the cell inside the cell, or if God is the cause behind the cause, then this I accept absolutely. And if prayer were a way of aligning your body with the forces that flow through the universe, then prayer I accept. But there is a worrying aspect about the idea of God. Like witchcraft or the science of the zodiac or any of these other things, the burden is placed elsewhere. This is what I don't like. You see, to me, you are the heroes of this hour. I do not think the earth was ever meant to be your home. I do not see the sky as a canopy held over your head by cherubs or see the earth as a carpet laid at your feet. You used to live an easy, lying-down life in the sea. But your curiosity and your courage prompted you to lift your head out of the sea and gasp this fierce element in which we live. They are sitting on Mars, with their little green arms folded, saying, "We can be reasonably certain there is no life on Earth because there the atmosphere is oxygen, which is so harsh that it corrupts metal." But you learned to breathe it. Furthermore, you crawled out of the sea, and you walked up and down the beach for centuries until your thighbones were thick enough to walk on land. It was a mistake, but you did it. Once you have this view of your past — not that it was handed to you but that you did it — then your view of the future will change. So you don't have to worry. Don't keep looking into the sky to see what is happening. Embrace the future. All you have to do about the future is what you did about the past. Rely on your curiosity and your courage, and ride through the night.[58]

I cannot believe in a God susceptible to prayer — that's a lot of rubbish. I simply haven't the nerve to imagine a being, a force, a cause which keeps the planets revolving in their orbits is going to stop to give me a bicycle with three speeds.[59]

Any fool can believe in what is self-evident. It takes a genius to believe what is clearly a palpable lie![60]

Sex

Sex suffers from the same malaise as television: there is too much of it, with the result that it repeats itself: halfway through what you had assumed was going to be a new episode, you realize that it's a re-run: you know how it will end. After that, it's difficult to remain interested.[61]

Masturbation is not only an expression of self-regard: it is also the natural emotional outlet of those who, before anything has reared its ugly head, have already accepted as inevitable the wide gulf between their real futures and the expectations of their fantasies.[62]

For flavor, instant sex will never supersede the stuff you have to peel and cook.[63]

I maintain that now that sex is valueless, through repeated depreciations, it is pursued with even greater frenzy; people are doing it more and enjoying it less. If a man has forty orgasms a week what can he expect but death on Sunday.[64]

Sex is the last refuge of the miserable.[65]

Style

You need to cultivate a life-style first for your own benefit — to give you a firm belief in your own identity and to prevent you from importuning others for their approval to make up for your lack of self-esteem.[66]

Style is not the man; it is something better. It is a dizzy dazzling structure that he erects about himself, using as building blocks materials selected from his own character.[67]

Style is the way in which a man can, by taking thought, add to his stature. It is the only way.[68]

Style is a consistent idiom arising spontaneously from the personality but deliberately maintained.[69]

Writing

Books are for writing. Do not read any more books. Everyone can write one little book, and it should be about himself. But if you read books, you will try to write literature, and that is always a mistake. It makes your work like other people's; it means we lose the sound of your voice.[70]

There are three reasons for becoming a writer: the first is that you need the money; the second that you have something to say that you think the world should know; the third is that you can't think what to do with the long winter evenings.[71]

All you have to ask yourself is have you said what you meant to say.[72]

Muddled syntax is the outward and audible sign of a confused mind, and the misuse of grammar the result of illogical thinking.[73]

APPENDIX 2

Tributes

On the following pages you will find a series of personal tributes written by people who knew Quentin, and others whose life he touched. I think they provide special insight into his life — how he was with people, the impact that being with him, even if only for a short time, had on so many. Tributes are from (in alphabetical order by author surname) Penny Arcade, Taylor Black, Richard Gollner, David Leddick, David-Elijah Nahmod, Tom Steele, Phillip Ward and Graham Watson.

Off the Hook at Ninety — Penny Arcade

Meeting Quentin in 1981 when he was 73 years of age and knowing him until his death a few weeks short of his 91st birthday, I saw no reason why he couldn't live to 100. He had a robustness of spirit one generally finds in Mediterranean goat herders. The long days of solitude that stretch into years give an agility to body and mind and a twinkle in the eye, if the person is not driven half mad from human isolation. Quentin was not mad at all. Madness was a quality, which despite his eccentricity, [that] was not part of his emotional or mental palette, although most who saw him in his early years of hennaed hair, rouged lips, and what was considered inappropriately flamboyant dress would have found that hard to believe.

In 1988, in response to a remark made to me by the columnist Michael Musto that I was the only person he had ever heard Quentin have a real conversation with, Quentin replied: "Most people are never with me. They are in my presence. Most people never talk to me." He continued, "They interview me."

In 1996 Quentin called me to ask for a dispensation from having to live to the age of 100, and instead be let off the hook at 90. He had publicly promised me to live to be 100 years old many times. I begged him to reconsider, reminding him of his promises. "You bullied me." he replied. "I said it to please you. You were being selfish." Certainly I was selfish, I overlooked his long list of ailments, much as he did, including the kind of ennui that comes as one nears 90, to all but the very few. I could not imagine the world without Quentin in it and when I told him so, remarking that 90 was a mere two years away, he answered dryly, "I think I can eke it out."

Ten days before he died in 1999, I commented that he might in fact die in Manchester, as a way of talking him out of going on that torturous trip, and with his amused laughter egging me on, I built on the premise that he might actually die on the plane, causing his producer to not only lose the cost of bringing him to England but also depriving him of the income from Quentin's appearances. Quentin had a trickster's heart and an innate orneriness.

He loved the idea of the producer, who had been making a pretty penny off him and underpaying him, getting short shrift. Quentin laughed heartily, "That would be marvelous." However, nothing would change the fact that he was set on dying as soon as possible.

When I would chastise him for not taking his heart medicine he would only reply, "But taking my heart medicine is inconsistent with my desire to die." Later in the conversation on the day he left for Britain, I wailed into the phone "But what will I do when you die?" A moment passed in silence and he replied, "It is very simple Miss Arcade," he puttered on, seemingly unfazed by my sorrow, "I am going. You are staying. I feel sorry for you." An Edwardian dandy, he never completely lost the traces of the middle class that could not contain him no more than he could tolerate its limits. Quentin Crisp saw most of a century with clear and open eyes from his bird seat at the edge of society.

In 1999, on September 26, a few weeks before Quentin died, he and I did a final performance together at the Knitting Factory in New York City. Our last performance together fell oddly on the anniversary of our first public performance on the same date in 1992. Before an admiring crowd, I asked Quentin to comment on aging and he replied, "When you are in your 80s your body just starts to hang on you." I adored stating openly that Quentin would die soon, as the resulting shock and annoyance towards me from other people delighted Quentin so much. "They are very angry with me Quentin because I said that you are very old and soon you will die." "But why should that annoy them?" he asked, turning right and left in his chair and scanning the audience, "It is true." "Because they spend hours at the gym, Quentin, and they think that they will never grow old and that they will never die." In the hush that followed, Quentin pulled himself up in his chair, made eye contact around the room and said disdainfully, "I see. How foolish they are."

If it were not for his health I think Quentin would have stayed on to reach his centennial, as there was nothing wrong with his mind. Quentin was not a sensualist, he ate heartily when he was hungry, and nothing when he was not, and largely ignored the needs of his body. He bathed like a cat, only when necessary, and despite his body crying in pain, he did little to alleviate his physical discomforts, from ingrown toenails to hernias, and later prostate cancer and congestive heart failure. Quentin lived in his mind and he lived for the pursuits of the mind. There was no better companion of any age than Quentin when it came to reading a scene, an event or an individual. He was quick, direct and honest as long as it was not in public and would cause none discomfort. Quentin was intellectually perverse, a contrary like certain American Indians who live their lives doing everything backwards. A natural provocateur, he enjoyed getting everyone in a lather and then benignly looking around in mock surprise at the results.

I believe the rejection and isolation that his appearance caused him in the early part of his life, coupled with the fact that it doomed him in many ways to a very narrow and intellectually stifling and ultimately unfulfilling milieu, was something he never fully recovered from. Those insults came not only from the straight society of his day but also from the closeted gay one. This spurred his desire to be at the center of humanity and not restricted to a gay ghetto.

I think he would have been shocked, truly shocked, by 9/11 because he was America's greatest supporter. He was a true believer in the American Way. This curious adulation was one of the very few things he was naive about and it was at the center of many quarrels between us. While he hated grandiosity in people he adored it in America, which was like a person to him, not just a country. From his vantage point of long years of observation from the sidelines of life, he was largely an unerring reader of the mores and foibles of humanity and society at large, yet he saw America as a good parent, trying to stem the quarrels of unruly children around the world. He died just before the world changed for good but he had seen it coming, the loss of a way of life that had been filled with structure, both good and bad. I wonder what he would have made of Enron and the Iraq War, and the fall of the dollar. I think the chaos would have been unbearable for him. While he had suffered much, beneath his acceptance and humaneness, he had never forgiven a second of it; the chaos that he saw coming in society, once finalized and made concrete, would have made him sad and as someone who had no room for sorrow in life, even his own, I believe it would have been untenable for him. Like most of us, Quentin didn't have a fallback position regarding the end of Western civilization.

Quentin hated the encroaching gentrification of his neighborhood in 1999 and what it has become now would have infuriated him, and he had spent long years removing fury from his emotional menu. Part of his glee in life was to accept the horror of everyday life, but nothing would have prepared him for the real death knell of society. He adored that there was greed, and injustice and corruption in both people and in the world, but he liked a cozy kind of greed, injustice and corruption, the kind that exists in fairy tales and dime store novels. I believe that the ogre of modern free market capitalism, with its outsourcing, homogenization and flagrant thievery at the highest levels of commerce and the government would have shocked him into a position he had spent his life escaping.

Caring. Caring would have been a terrible position for Quentin, who believed as humans we deserve nothing. Quentin believed neither in charity nor kindness for kindness' sake except for the most surface kind of polite societal courtesy. It was this detachment that made him accept everyone and everything that came into his life equally. He for the most part suspended judgment, yet in a strange way he held on to the middle class mores that he was raised with. His life was one boundaried by limited expectations of what people or the world could offer him and with a mind as great as his, his own understanding of the strictures placed on his development by society left him little sympathy for the strictures of others. He offered instead his own life as a kind of path that leads to what he considered the most valuable treasure of all, personal authenticity.

You Don't Have to Win: New Year's Thoughts on Quentin Crisp and the Future of Homosexuality— Taylor Black

As I sit here in the second day of 2011, trying to summon up the proper words of respect and admiration for Mr. Quentin Crisp, my mind keeps returning to a concise and foreboding phrase that he, never one to miss a chance to give his opinion on any matter or leave any question unanswered, gave around this time each year, when asked his opinion on the year to come: "It will all get worse." Like anything he said, this prediction could easily be understood—as pert, negative and even bitchy. However, as easy as these kinds of conclusions about Mr. Crisp are for other human beings to make, they miss the spirit behind his words and his intentions for them—indeed, about the true worth and effect of the life of this overlooked and misunderstood man.

It was almost exactly three years ago to this day that I had my first "encounter" with Quentin Crisp. Sometime before I left New York City to visit my family in North Carolina, I received a film in the mail through one of those online rental companies that have become so popular in the United States. Entitled *Resident Alien*, and advertising on the blurb of the sleeve a brief account of a true iconoclast, of one of the relics of bohemian Manhattan, I packed it in my suitcase and, shamefully, let it sit there until I returned home two weeks later.

After almost sending the thing back, I decided, in one of those annual hangover states that seem only to come after New Year's festivities, to pop it in and give Mr. Crisp a try. Not even fifteen minutes into the film, my entire life was changed. A montage featured two different scenes of him placed on trial, both for his inconvenient views and misunderstood presence on earth. Oscillating back and forth between a scene of him defending himself to a gay rights group in New York City and as a featured guest on one of the more popular (and trashy) talk shows of the day, Quentin responds to a question of whether or not his effeminate and outlandish appearance was a help or a hindrance to the struggle for gay rights and equality with a simple confirmation of what it was his audience was looking for — with a simple "No." It was, however, his continued commentary given in a follow-up interview to this scene in *Resident Alien* that floored me, that made me an immediate and dutiful follower of Quentin Crisp and missionary of what he termed *Crisperanto*: "The worrying thing to me about the gay community is that they are fighting for their rights, and I don't believe anybody has rights. If we all got what we deserved we would starve."

The ultimate usefulness of this comment, much like his New Year's proclamation, is that it is absolutely, staggeringly true. Quentin did not, in his own phrasing, step out of his mother's womb onto dry land in order to say those things about his presence and about the world that it wanted to hear. Born and bred a mistake, Quentin learned to take every step and make every gesture on earth with the full, embodied understanding of himself as totally unique, as completely self-reliant. However, as this montage in *Resident Alien* displays so clearly, as utterly declarative and well rehearsed his statements and mannerisms became over time, he never was — and, I would argue, still has never been — able to meet an audience worthy of his glory and his wisdom.

Of course rights discourses are problematic and fictitious, especially for sexual minorities. If Quentin was trained as and understood properly to be an academic or a philosopher, no one would protest his saying this. The effect of his statement to the skeptical crowd of gay community members is not only to protect himself from their attacks upon him and their attempts to place judgment on his life within a political narrative he knew he was not a part of. His "No" to the question of the convenience of his life and the helpfulness of his words is an answer to all his naysayers — to all those people, whether through homophobic attack or political interpolation, who would like to judge him as anything other than himself, as Quentin Crisp as any more or less than Quentin Crisp. For him, prejudice against an identity or a lifestyle was never something he knew, and indeed never a fight he felt the need to dedicate himself to.

The problem facing Quentin is and has always been his own; the prejudice the world has had against Quentin Crisp has been for being too like himself, too willing to fix what the world always insisted were ontological wounds. What I find so inspiring about Quentin and his life's work is his insistence upon himself, as well as the very humble and imminently useful ways in which he explains how anyone else might follow his lead in their own professions of being and becoming. Here in America, at the rise and fall of yet another year, homosexuals find themselves again in true need of Quentin's words of eternal wisdom. Following a string of suicides by queer youth, both the gay and mainstream press in the States have started a new campaign to convince homosexuals, both young old, that "It Gets Better," [yet] the continued presence of homophobic violence and queer suicides, unfortunately, works against the logic of this admittedly optimistic and well-intentioned campaign to change the sexual climate culture.

The pressure facing these young people upon the tragic decision to end their lives is one that narratives of identity and equality and sexuality only work to encourage; understanding themselves as homosexual-people-to-come, queer suicide victims have decided that this is not a fight they can win. While homosexuals, as a political category or epistemological category, may, over time win through measures of political acceptance or cultural equality, actual, living people who find themselves in situations with which they cannot cope in a way they cannot recognize in any human being around them only need to understand the words that Mr. Crisp came on earth, not only to say, but to embody and display, in his own wicked and wonderful way: that you don't have to win.

Don't Be Anonymous — Richard Gollner

I recall that sometime in the early nineties while talking to Quentin on the phone he mentioned that he'd been invited to address a meeting of Alcoholics Anonymous in Dallas. I did express to him that this particular engagement seemed to me even more full of challenges than his invitations normally were. I think he said something like, "It would be too impolite to refuse, because that would mean that I'm better than they are, and that can't be right."

A month later I was talking to him on the phone again and out of idle curiosity asked him, "How did the gig in Dallas go?" and more specifically, "What did you actually say?" He said, "I said the usual things in the usual way," and "I started the evening by saying to them that of course it's entirely up to you whether you stay or stop being alcoholics, but whatever happens, my recommendation is that you should never ever be anonymous."

Quentin and I— David Leddick

I first met Quentin Crisp in New York in what must have been his first theatre tour. I had read about him and took friends to see him at the Provincetown Playhouse in Greenwich Village, not far from where I lived. I was very taken with his courage and outspokenness. The year had to be about 1979 or 1980.

At that time I was contributing a hundred dollars a month just to help struggling artists. I would provide the support for one year and then select another artist for one year's assistance. It was time to renew this kind of mini-endowment so I called Quentin. It was quite easy. He was listed and I got the number, called and heard that voice who always answered, "Oh, Yes?" Later Quentin told me he thought I was joking but gave me the address and I began sending checks, to which he always replied with a short thank-you note.

I was living in France not long afterward but I continued to send checks once I had seen his apartment. True to his determination to never clean, the curtains hung in tatters, the seat was out of the chair in front of the television, the bed was unmade and the sheets had seen a lot of duty. I thought, "I could spend a little money and fix this place up for him." And then I said to myself, "No, he wouldn't even notice it." He always emerged from that room neat and clean. It was a kind of zen study for him; he completely ignored his surroundings.

Although I saw him regularly for twenty years and the checks never stopped, there would only be small flashes when he would let down his guard. In his eighties I took him to the doctor from time to time because he hated doing this and only would if someone else made the appointment. But I think never being intimate was a part of his great braveness. He had extraordinary courage and part of that depended upon his always being Quentin Crisp. He had adopted a name and a personality and it was his barricade against the world.

My First Hero— David-Elijah Nahmod

Ten years after his passing, it seems like a dream. But no, I was one of the lucky ones. I really knew and worked with Quentin Crisp.

I first heard of him in the mid 1970s, when the Thames TV adaptation of *The Naked Civil Servant* premiered on American television. I was around 20 years old, and still coming to terms with my gay identity—not an easy task, having been raised an Orthodox Jew in Brooklyn, New York.

The first time I saw him was when he was a guest on NBC's late night chat fest, *The Tomorrow Show* with Tom Snyder. Snyder took himself and his show quite seriously—Mr. Crisp was the sole guest for the hour. I heard him speak of how horribly he had been treated as an out gay man in London during the 1930s, 40s and 50s. What he had endured seemed unimaginable. Somehow the occasional taunt that I'd put up with in Brooklyn paled in comparison to his arrests, his trial for "solicitation," and his beatings. Yet his grace, dignity and wit remained intact. All he had lived through and he had no bitterness at all. To me, he embodied the very best that a gay man could be.

Nearly twenty years later, Neil Ira Needleman, an old high school friend, and I decided that it would be fun to be filmmakers, never mind that we had no funding or experience. Neil owned a hand held digital video camera and a microphone. I had enough chutzpah for both of us. We were ready to go.

I wrote a short story called "Aunt Fannie." Neil turned it into a script. He would direct, I would produce and play Jeremy, the lead—never mind that I couldn't act. Now, who would play Aunt Fannie, the ghost of an elderly lesbian who helps her gay nephew Jeremy step out of the closet?

Quentin Crisp, by that time, was in his eighties, and living in an East Village rooming house. He was quite the man about town, and let it be known that he would go to lunch with anyone who was buying. I took him to lunch and asked him to play Aunt Fannie. "I say yes to everything," he said.

So there we where, two geeks with a video camera. A world famous celebrity, who had just appeared in the acclaimed British film *Orlando*, and who had been the subject of a tribute song by no less than Sting ("An Englishman in New York") was our star.

I still couldn't act, but we made the film. True to form, Mr. Crisp was as gracious as gracious could be. And, by the way, we always addressed him as Mr. Crisp. We never even considered calling him Quentin. He did the film for meals.

Solely on the strength of his name, *Aunt Fannie* enjoyed several sold-out screenings at New York's Gay and Lesbian Community Services Center. Several video stores in New York and Los Angeles stocked it on their shelves.

David and Neil had arrived.

Later that same year, Neil wrote a script called *Red Ribbons*. Again I produced. Even though I still couldn't act, I cast myself as Zach, a foul mouthed gay basher—just to show my range as an actor, I said. Amazingly, no one laughed.

At 63 minutes, *Red Ribbons* was a feature. The character of Horace Nightingale III was specifically written for Mr. Crisp.

While *Aunt Fannie* was shot over two days, *Red Ribbons* took several weeks. Mr. Crisp again worked for meals and was the star of our set. This time we had a second celebrity cast member—the famed 1970s porn queen Georgina Spelvin (*The Devil in Miss Jones*), who had read all of Mr. Crisp's books and was a big fan. She couldn't wait to meet him. As I introduced them, she bowed, kissing his hand. "I'm honored to meet you, Your Highness," Georgina said, with a perfectly straight face.

"I rather like her," Mr. Crisp said with a smile. Then he took me aside. "Is she the porn queen?" he asked, indicating the now 58 year old, long retired adult performer.

"That's her!"

"She doesn't look like a porn queen, she looks like one of the ladies who lunch!" proclaimed Mr. Crisp.

The quips kept coming. One day, during a pizza break, a cast member told us about a biography she was reading of the great Hollywood star Bette Davis. The book, we were informed, was all about what a "bitch" Bette had been.

"Typical," I said. "You live your life, and when you're not here anymore, people say terrible things about you."

"Then we must all be careful not to die," Mr. Crisp said, without missing a beat.

Never before, or since, had I known anybody who could come up with so many brilliant off the cuff one liners, one after the other. Yet not once did he ever venture into "bitchy queen" territory. He was a genuine wit, and had no need to hurt people's feelings for a cheap laugh. He was irreverent, outrageous, yet always respectful of the feelings of others.

Because of his (and Spelvin's) fame, Water Bearer Films released *Red*

Ribbons to home video in 1994. Because of their names, it sold reasonably well. I owe much of that to Quentin Crisp.

Until his death in 1999, I would occasionally call him to see how he was doing. I last called him on a Friday — I was in his neighborhood. "Do you need anything?" I asked, knowing that he was now 90 years old and having health problems.

"You're very kind," he said. "But some lesbians have brought me a chocolate cake, so all is well with the world."

Two days later, the *New York Times* reported the death of Quentin Crisp.

To this very day, it amazes me that I knew and worked with such a legendary and iconic figure, and one who had meant so much to me when I first ventured out of the closet.

Sitting here in San Francisco, where I moved in 2003, it all seems like a dream.

On a wall over the very desk where I sit typing this memoir hangs a picture of Quentin Crisp and Georgina Spelvin that I took on set in 1993. Both of them signed the picture for me.

A dream indeed, albeit one that came true for a nice Jewish boy from Brooklyn, New York.

Still Vivid — Tom Steele

Quentin was such a vivid presence that I still can't believe he's gone, after all these years. I once told him that he was in Technicolor and the rest of us were in black and white. But the late James Purdy said it best when he once told me, "Quentin is more *himself* than anyone alive." Quentin would demur, insisting that he has — and had — no choice in these matters. This, in turn, is what most people would define as rare courage.

For in a time and place when most homosexuals were not only closeted, but completely invisible, Quentin accentuated and paraded his effeminacy, if not with what we now call pride, then certainly with invincibility. His openness nearly cost him his life on a number of occasions, and — to say the least — restricted his career options. But his insistence on being completely himself gave him insights that few people of our century ever attained. He also lived ninety healthy years, the happiest of which probably were the last 18 years of his life spent in the East Village, where he chose to rent a dilapidated studio apartment. "And I've never worked, in all that time! Isn't that wonderful?"

Writing is obviously not Quentin's idea of work. He is the author of a number of books; the best known is *The Naked Civil Servant*. When the book was made into a film (for Thames Television) in the early 1970s with John Hurt playing Quentin, he was catapulted to international fame. He began performing a one-man show in London, telling bewildered and enchanted audiences how to have a lifestyle, how to become a virgin, why one must never do housework, have a lover, keep a pet, or try to keep up with the Joneses: "You must drag the Joneses down to your level," he explained, probably thousands of times. The show, which also featured some truly remarkable question-and-answer sessions, attracted the attention of the esteemed director and choreographer Michael Bennett, who first brought Quentin and his show to New York in 1977. It was mutual love at first sight.

Probably the greatest love of Quentin's life was the movies. In his book *How to Go to the Movies* (St. Martin's, 1989), he wrote, "If we go to the movies often enough and in a sufficiently reverent spirit, they will become more absorbing than the outer world, and the problems of reality will cease to burden us."

It was, in fact, movies that brought us together. When I was the editor of *Christopher Street* magazine and the *New York Native*, Quentin's agent called and asked whether we'd be interested in movie reviews from him. I was absolutely thrilled, of course, and a week later Quentin and I went to see *Tootsie*. The rest is gay history. For most of the next 18 years, Quentin reviewed a movie or two every month for *CS*, and in the mid–1980s, the publisher, Chuck Ortleb, suggested that he begin keeping a diary every week in the weekly *Native*. (Some of the reviews and the diaries have been collected in book form, and a new gathering of diaries is being assembled.) We were even in a movie together — Jonathan Nossiter's *Resident Alien*, an engrossing exploration of Quentin's life in New York.

On his 90th birthday, a medium-sized party was thrown (one of many that year), and a few of us were asked to propose toasts to Quentin. I remember telling about the time I said to Quentin, after knowing him for over 16 years, that he looked exactly the same as he did the day we met. Without a beat, he replied, "That's very deliberate."

I continue to wait for the phone to ring and to hear, "Not to worry, it's only me." Every single day, something happens to remind me of him, and I think that wherever he is, it's likely that he has something to do with those little and large reminders.

It is my fervent hope that the new movie about him, *An Englishman in New York*, will generate new interest in his legacy, and that the vast body of his unpublished and out-of-print writing will at long last appear and reappear. I still think Tim Burton should make a film of Quentin's novel *Chog*. He was especially fond of that book. But, as Quentin taught me, one mustn't hope for too much in this life.

Personally, Quentin— Phillip Ward

Quentin Crisp was a friend, a mother, a father, a sister, a brother, and a lover. He was that and more to all who came to know him. Quentin was a special man and meant so much to many people. He was a total being of what it means to be human: be true to one's self. If you breathe it, live it! That is what Quentin Crisp did, he lived his life to the utmost every day and died as he wished: alone. Indeed, he lived his life as he saw fit. Quentin's honesty will be missed in our lives.

For over thirty years now have I known Quentin Crisp — through his writings and on an intimate, personal level. I listened to his wisdom, as he was a mentor and a friend. He listened as well and, with that, I learned how to "be" with calm ease. There is no more fear of being discovered or harassed by threatening forces or other forms of hostility. And with this considered, I am a better human for having known Quentin Crisp. I am honored to have worked with Quentin Crisp, but I am most honored to have been a part of his life and his friend. I thank him for sharing this quiet joy, and for enriching my being. I will miss Quentin every day of my life.

One evening in 1975, my mother and a few siblings were gathered about the living room watching television. Bored with game shows, Mother stood and moved toward the television set to turn the dial. She stopped at the local public television station where a movie had just begun. It was *The Naked Civil Servant*, and "the" Quentin Crisp was introducing the movie with teacup in hand addressing the viewers. Mother left the dial on that station and returned to the sofa to watch the movie. And while watching the film, never did I realize or even imagine the significance or importance Quentin Crisp would be in my life. Never!

My stomach wrenched in fear that others in the room would see the delight in my eyes while watching this man's life unfold on the screen. It was as though he was addressing me directly. It was a directive to be one's self at all cost. "Be" was the answer to life's experience and adventure. Meanwhile my family were all laughing and offering bigoted jokes and anti-homosexual commentary. Little did they know that they were also directing the same sentiments toward me. Mother never switched the channel, though, and we watched the movie to the very end. That night, while lying in bed, I stared at the ceiling and pondered what it all meant; the movie and this gentle man's life had made an immediate impact on me.

After college in 1979, I moved to Manhattan, where I have lived these past thirty-plus years. In February 1986, however, I met the "live and in person" Quentin Crisp. My secretary, Kathy Hurt, met him while standing in line at the East Village post office during her lunch hour and engaged him in conversation. I goaded Kathy to call him, as he was listed in the phone directory, and set up a date for dinner. I would come along! And, consequently, I was overwhelmed by his generosity of spirit and kindness — and with his honesty of heart. And despite his spoken adversity toward love and being loved, Quentin exuded unconditional love to those he trusted and believed in. Because of this and over the years that followed, I enjoyed an intimate and close friendship with Quentin Crisp, and one which I cherish daily.

During the beginning of our friendship, I would often escort Quentin to movies or to restaurants to meet up with fans that had invited him out for dinner. It was at such events that Quentin would become the actor, and the "persona" would take the lead role while entertaining his guests and providing them what they came to hear. He would almost always attend any event which he received invitations to, and particularly art openings at the Leslie/Lohman Gay Art Foundation, where he would often pose for several of their artists, and particularly Patrick Angus, who painted New York's gay underground scene of the 1990s and is profiled in the recent pseudo-biopic *An Englishman in New York* starring John Hurt reprising his role as Quentin Crisp.

Our relationship evolved to where I became pretty much Quentin's personal assistant and attended to many of his needs, especially as he grew older and required help from his friends (even though he insisted he did not believe in friends). I also became his "no" man, the one to pull him away from additional invitations even while at events, mainly because Quentin could never say no to any invitation presented him. We had our own language of codes in which to alert me to quickly whisk him away while he assumed the role of "I go where I am told to go" and in order for him not to have to decline their requests.

In the early 1990s, Quentin lost the capacity to use his left hand due to illness. This prevented him from using his trusty companion: the typewriter. Luckily, "My useless hand!" was not his dominant right hand, and he was able to continue to scratch out his compositions. Mr. Crisp received many offers for articles and reviews, but he needed assistance in providing hard copy. Along with my computer, or the Demon Machine as he liked to call it, and Quentin's clear dictation, I was able to transcribe his voice as quickly as he spoke the words. Thus, I became his "Left-hand Man" and typed and readied his manuscripts for publication over a number of years. This is when I took an active role at being his typist and then editor. He was happy for the comfort my assistance provided him.

Quentin's health began to decline in the winter of 1998-99, while performing on 42nd Street at the Intar Theatre under the direction of John
Glines. This was Mr. Crisp's last run in New York City of his one-man show,
An Evening with Quentin Crisp. It opened on his 90th birthday and closed
on January 31, 1999. During this time, Quentin became ill and probably had
pneumonia, but most definitely the flu. Still, he struggled getting to the theater
on time by taking a bus up Third Avenue and then across 42nd Street to the
theater, despite a taxi allowance given him by the producer. "Money is for
saving, not for spending." He was determined not to fail or to disappoint
Mr. Glines and the theatergoers who paid money to come see him. Quentin
never missed a performance, despite his ill health.

Immediately following the run at the Intar and between all his appearances and lunches and dinners already scheduled in his "Sacred Book" (his
daily planner), we continued our work sessions in providing new material to
be published. Nearing the end of July, though, Quentin began tidying up his
room, creating a small path for one to go from here to there. And anyone
who knows anything about Quentin Crisp, it was unlike him to clean any
part or rearrange anything in his room. He did not do it and did not allow
others to do so either. However, he wanted to prepare his room for the people
who would visit it after his death. By summer's end, Quentin's room met his
approval. It was navigable and tidy. And he was happy that we had arranged
the closet so that all his legal documents and estate papers would be easily
found. He had great concern about such matters, especially his last will and
testament. Quentin wanted all his affairs in order and that is what we had
done.

Also during the early days of 1999, Quentin was approached to tour
England with his one-man show, *An Evening with Quentin Crisp,* which he
agreed to do with Authors on Tour (Charles Lago and Charles "Chip" Snell).
At some point during the days of summer, a concerned friend had unexpect-
edly canceled the tour. And despite the fury raging inside him, Quentin
kept an outward calm repose and immediately set the tour back in motion
and began to focus on his November trip to Manchester. He made a decision
to go, knowing well that his health may even fail him along the way there.
I reminded Quentin that there would be significant stress on his already
weak heart, especially with the two air-pressured flights he would take to
arrive there. He was pleased and felt it might be a "significant death." He
was happy to be going and did not care where he died, whether it be in
England or in New York. "In my present condition, I look forward to being
extinct."

During the last two years of his life, though, Quentin and I worked on the manuscript of his final book, *The Dusty Answers (as I have said before)*. It was recorded on audiotape in his room on East Third Street and at my apartment on Christopher Street. Regularly, I would visit him, bringing him food and supplies, and always delivering his mail from the lobby's counter where the postman deposited mail for the whole building. We would begin our sessions with conversation about our day, and Quentin would open his mail while quickly deciding which ones required his reply.

Quentin would either sit on the side of the bed or stretch out on it, resting comfortably as though he were visiting a psychiatrist's couch. And always with a smile, he would say, "Where shall we begin?" He was excited about doing this new book, but doubted he would be alive to see it printed. It remains unpublished. Quentin was bringing closure to his life and wanted to have the last word on it. He was hurriedly energetic and challenged his failing body daily in order to complete the manuscript for his final memoir.

In July 1999, Quentin finished the "official" recordings for *The Dusty Answers*; however, we continued recording our sessions together. These moments became more an ongoing conversation, or an assessment of the full picture of which was his life. As a friend and editor of *The Dusty Answers*, I was provided an overwhelming sense of respect and responsibility, a period of focus and concentration, and an enormous thank you to Quentin for allowing me to be part of his life.

The night before his departure, Quentin joined my partner, Charles Barron, and me for dinner at Haveli, an Indian restaurant on Second Avenue. Earlier in the evening at his apartment, he seemed agitated for some reason. I was unsure why, though I suspected Quentin was not taking the heart medicine I had delivered to him only a couple days earlier. I wanted to make sure he had all his medicines and toiletries before leaving on his trip to England. As for the heart pills, though, he felt why take them, especially if they were to prolong his life when he only wanted to die. I convinced Quentin that the medicine would not prolong his living but would only make his life more comfortable and less painful until the end.

Charles and I walked Quentin back to his apartment. I sensed this was our last walk together, with him holding onto my arm while slowly walking down Second Avenue toward his building. I escorted him inside, and we quickly spoke before hugging one another farewell. I kissed Quentin on his cheek and said, "Have a safe trip, sweetheart. Hurry back home! I love you, Quentin." And he said, "Thank you. You are very kind. And I love you too! Goodbye." I stood at the bottom of the stairs and watched him climb the first flight, huffing and puffing, with his right hand grasping the railing to help pull himself up the stairs. I remained in the lobby listening to him continue to his floor. His grunts and sighs still sing inside my head remembering him that night.

Intuitively, I felt this was the last time I would see Quentin. He was not coming back alive. A deep pang struck my heart as I left his building. Sorrow enveloped me. Charles and I were quiet on our way home. We sensed the same sadness, the same truth. I called Quentin the following morning wishing him well and much success with the tour, and a wish for him to hurry back home. He was eager to leave, though, especially knowing the possibilities of what the flights might do to his heart. Quentin embraced the chance! His life was in order, with all corners tidied, and the discarded in the trash heap. He was ready and prepared to die, and off to England he went.

Quentin's first evening in England became his last. He and Chip arrived in Manchester safely and enjoyed an evening visiting with his hostess before heading off to his room for sleep. On the morning of November 21, 1999, Chip found Quentin lying on his bed lifeless and with nitro pills clutched in his hand. He had died in style by having a heart attack during the night. And Quentin died alone, which was one of his greatest desires.

Following Quentin's passing, I created The Quentin Crisp Archives on the Web from the personal effects that he left me in his will. It is QCA's mission "to preserve and maintain the manuscripts, letters, recordings, artwork by and about, and various artifacts and ephemera related to the life and legend of Quentin Crisp, and to promote his philosophy of individuality, self-acceptance, and tolerance."

Quentin provided us, the world at large, gay and straight, a simple philosophy of happiness and being. He was an atheist, yet his Buddhistic and existentialistic instructions offer an insight into the man he was while providing an insight into who and what we are to ourselves and to others. I encourage everyone to read Quentin Crisp's works, to hear him on recordings, and to visit his official Web site at crisperanto.org. Quentin's philosophy will have some sort of impact on you, whether you invite it or not.

From *The Dusty Answers*, Quentin writes: "I have kept my optimism going so far by coming to America. But now my optimism is dwindling and I long for death, which most people would consider was pessimistic, though I do not think so. I shall like being dead. At least I shall enjoy dying. When I'm dead, of course, I shall have no opinions about anything.... And I can't afford to believe in life after death. The nicest thing you can say about life is that it will end. The idea of falling out of your mother's womb with the words, 'Here again!' is too much for me to bear.... I'm not afraid of dying. So, a heart attack would do fine. That would be dying in style."

How Quentin Crisp Can Save Your Life— Graham Watson

He once wrote that he wanted to die in battle. While the bomber-haunted London skies were being strobed by searchlights, Quentin Crisp was trying to enlist in the British Army. He had one aim: to embrace a "glorious and convenient death." Despite there being any number of secretly-gay men fighting on both sides all over Europe, the military recruiters who examined him recognized his dyed hair and long fingernails as the banners of a different kind of campaign. He was bawled out, exempted from military service, to be officially — and notoriously — declared a sexual pervert. Unvanquished and undaunted, he returned to the streets of London, where he was fighting a war of his own.

By 1940 his personal propaganda was scandalous. The lipstick had become bloody and savage, the hair fierier, the eyes smokier. He spread his fingers when he paraded around to make sure everyone could see his gold lacquered nails. At that time such displays would have been outrageous on a woman. On a man, it provoked violent contempt. People jeered, threw stones and often physically attacked him. But this was Quentin Crisp's call to arms against sexual conventions, his volley at ignorant suburban propriety, his charge against everything straight and narrow. A lesser man would have surrendered. But every street battle brought him back in brighter colors. "My way of going on is a protest, and the beating up is a counter-protest. It is people's way of saying that they don't accept the way that I am," he explained to documentary maker Denis Mitchell.

Crisp is often described as the last Edwardian dandy, a powdered fop in velvet and rouge. But turning make-up into war paint and clothes into weapons of social rebellion made him a punk forty years before punk.

Although he adored the superficial currency of image, his appearance was emblematic of the transformation he was certain all of humanity could — and should — affect for themselves. The clothes and the make-up (and the assumed name) were his way of rocketing beyond the bounds of an identity created by society. His transformation was a gauntlet thrown at the feet of the multitudes who had accepted the world's opinion of them. He refused to be an amalgam of other people's interpretations, and projected the self he thought would have blossomed without the corrosive influence of era and class. We must overcome our inhibitions and reservations to give voice to the self that informs our every action because, he believed, happiness springs from an uncompromisingly truthful interaction with the world. By disregarding society's opinions we would lose the desire for concealment, and without concealment there could be no fear of threats, blame or deception. His view that selves were for authoring, not for interpreting, mirrors his commandment that books were only to be written, never read.

In his later years he had the air of an all-knowing zen mystic — with wisecracks — a Dalai Lama of the hooligan world, fielding questions about love, death and the meaning of life from the telephone in his New York bedsit, steadfastly refusing to conceal his telephone number — in case, he joked, God should be brave enough to answer him back one day.

By the time I had a telephone conversation with him, just after the Christmas of 1998, he was godly, tottering around the Lower East Side of Manhattan where he had exiled himself in the early 80s. I remembered his description of dealing with a stream of anonymous abusive calls — he invited threatening callers to come round "next Tuesday" — so I decided to buck the trend: I gave him an anonymous praise call. I didn't want him to perform, I didn't want a sound bite, I only wanted to pass on my love and appreciation.

I got his listed number from International Directory enquiries. ("There's a Quentin Crisp on East Third Street!" the operator said incredulously, as though surprised he existed at all.) I called it and amazingly, Quentin Crisp answered. Faced with an intelligence that was responsible for shaping so much of mine, I could've been speechless, but I was prepared. It was like calling Mount Sinai and have Moses pick up. I told him that I'd called to heap praise on his name. "Ohhhh, that'sss nnnice," he drawled. "You are a miracle!" I blurted. And for a second he sounded taken aback before he replied, "Oh. Well. That's very kind of you. Thhhank yoooou."

I asked about his recent 90th birthday on Christmas Day. As my birthday is the day before, I told him I knew what it was like to be upstaged by Jesus. And he laughed! He was one of the 20th Century's greatest wits, and he actually laughed at my joke. He asked me a little about myself, I told him, and asked if he had any advice for someone my age. He growled into my ear: "Discover who you are. And be it. Like *mad*."

I thanked him, let him go, and then jumped round the room for about five minutes before I phoned everybody to tell them. Less than a year later he was dead. Ten years later I applied to English Heritage to commemorate him at his London address for forty years, 129 Beaufort Street, with a blue plaque. After a few months of deliberation they gently declined, saying they could not be certain he had lasting historical influence, and advised me to reapply in ten years' time, when their policy will allow him to be reconsidered. The building will wait, and so shall I. But let their doubt be an incentive to those who love him. Write to his publishers and demand that his books are reissued. Then buy them, read them and give them.

"We must work away at the unlovable chiefly," he once said. "We must use our love. If it's going to be any use at all it must make a world in which everyone is equally beautiful, equally desirable, equally loveable. That's the only work we can do with it."

He was a declaration of war on hypocrisy and inequality. He intended to raise the level of tolerance so the less brave could stand in his wake.

We did, we still do.

APPENDIX 3

Quentin's Family Tree

Quentin seldom mentioned his family, and usually when he did it was often not in complimentary terms, especially with regards to his most immediate family, his parents and siblings. However, he was part of an extended family and especially with the next generations he was a welcome and loved member. One of his nieces was named after him (Denise Pratt) and one of his great-great-nephews was also named after him (Ian Quentin Crawford).

He was a regular guest at family occasions such as christenings, marriages and birthdays, especially after his move to America. Take a look at his great-nephew Adrian Goycoolea's film *Uncle Denis* for an insight into his interaction with his family.

I felt it appropriate to have a go at putting together his family tree. For this I owe a big thank you to Quentin's three nieces, Frances Ramsay, Elaine Pratt-Goycoolea and Denise Pratt-Renner, his great-nephew Adrian Goycoolea and Adrian's sister Michèle Elaine Goycoolea Crawford.

Over Christmas 2010 and New Year's 2011 (when I rather suspect they might have had better things to do) they put up with my repeated communications with graciousness and patience and filled in the pieces for me.

My thanks to you all.

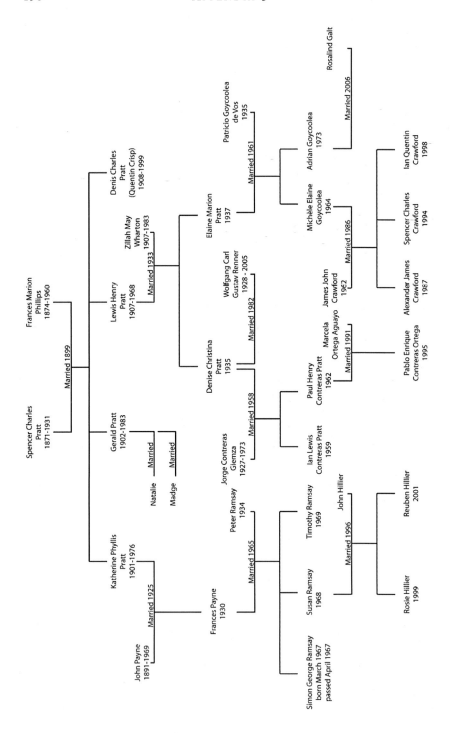

Chapter Notes

Preface

1. Quentin Crisp, *How to Become a Virgin* (Fontana, 1981), 114.
2. Ibid., 114.

Chapter 1

1. Quentin Crisp, *The Naked Civil Servant* (Duckworth, 1977), 8.
2. Ibid., 9.
3. Ibid., 16.
4. Ibid., 15.
5. Ibid., 16
6. Ibid., 8.
7. Ibid., 8.
8. Quentin Crisp, *Resident Alien* (Alyson Books, 1997), 54.
9. Phyllis Pratt, quoted by Andrew Barrow, *Quentin and Philip: A Double Portrait* (Pan, 2004), 27.
10. Crisp, *Resident Alien*, 214.
11. Crisp, *The Naked Civil Servant*, 15.
12. Ibid., 11.
13. Ibid., 202.
14. Ibid., 39.
15. Ibid., 12.
16. Quentin Crisp, quoted by Barrow, *Quentin and Phillip*, 29.
17. Ibid., 29.
18. Ibid., 29.
19. Ibid., 29.
20. Crisp, *The Naked Civil Servant*, 25.
21. Quentin Crisp, *An Evening with Quentin Crisp*, 1975–1999.
22. Ibid.
23. Crisp, *The Naked Civil Servant*, 15.
24. Quentin Crisp, quoted by Barrow, *Quentin and Phillip*, 26.
25. Crisp, *The Naked Civil Servant*, 9.
26. Ibid., 9.

27. Ibid., 10.
28. Ibid., 13.
29. Ibid., 13.
30. Ibid., 17.

Chapter 2

1. Quentin Crisp, *The Naked Civil Servant* (Duckworth, 1977), 17.
2. Ibid., 17.
3. Ibid., 17.
4. Ibid., 17.
5. Ibid., 17.
6. Ibid., 19.
7. Ibid., 19.
8. Quentin Crisp, *Resident Alien* (Alyson Books, 1997), 26.
9. Crisp, *The Naked Civil Servant*, 20.
10. Ibid., 20.

Chapter 3

1. Quentin Crisp, quoted by Andrew Barrow, *Quentin and Philip: A Double Portrait* (Pan, 2004), 44.
2. Ibid., 60.
3. Quentin Crisp, *The Naked Civil Servant* (Duckworth, 1977), 25.
4. Ibid., 24.
5. Ibid., 24.
6. Ibid., 26.
7. Ibid., 26.
8. Ibid., 26.
9. Ibid., 26.
10. Ibid., 26.
11. Ibid., 26.
12. Ibid., 26.
13. Ibid., 24.
14. Crisp, quoted by Barrow, *Quentin and Phillip*, 64.

15. Ibid., 64.
16. Crisp, *The Naked Civil Servant*, 29.
17. Ibid., 31.
18. Ibid., 35.
19. Quentin Crisp, *An Evening with Quentin Crisp*, 1975–1999.
20. Ibid.
21. Crisp, *The Naked Civil Servant*, 36.
22. Crisp, quoted by Barrow, *Quentin and Phillip*, 66.

Chapter 4

1. Quentin Crisp, *The Naked Civil Servant* (Duckworth, 1977), 35.
2. Quentin Crisp, quoted by Andrew Barrow, *Quentin and Philip: A Double Portrait* (Pan, 2004), 182.
3. Quentin Crisp, *An Evening with Quentin Crisp*, 1975–1999.
4. Crisp, *The Naked Civil Servant*, 35.
5. Ibid., 39.
6. Ibid., 40.
7. Ibid., 40.

Chapter 5

1. Quentin Crisp, quoted by Andrew Barrow, *Quentin and Philip: A Double Portrait* (Pan, 2004), 55.
2. Quentin Crisp, *An Evening with Quentin Crisp*, 1975–1999.
3. Quentin Crisp, *The Naked Civil Servant* (Duckworth, 1977), 47.
4. Ibid., 48.
5. Ibid., 48.
6. Ibid., 49.
7. Ibid., 50.
8. Ibid., 52.
9. Ibid., 52.
10. Ibid., 53.

Chapter 6

1. Quentin Crisp, quoted by Andrew Barrow, *Quentin and Philip: A Double Portrait* (Pan, 2004), 140.
2. Phillip O'Connor, quoted by Barrow, *Quentin and Philip: A Double Portrait*, 91.
3. Barrow, *Quentin and Phillip*, 90.
4. Guy Kettelhack, "The Enigma of Denis Pratt," *The Quentin Crisp Archives*, www.crisperanto.org.
5. Quentin Crisp, *The Naked Civil Servant* (Duckworth, 1977), 57.
6. Ibid., 73.

7. Ibid., 74.
8. Ibid., 73.
9. Ibid., 84.
10. Ibid., 84.
11. Ibid., 86.
12. Quentin Crisp, A.F. Stuart, *Lettering for Brush and Pen* (Frederick Warne, 1969), 3.
13. Crisp, *The Naked Civil Servant*, 94.
14. Ibid., 99.
15. Ibid., 91.
16. Ibid., 92.
17. Ibid., 93.

Chapter 7

1. Quentin Crisp, *The Naked Civil Servant* (Duckworth, 1977), 198.
2. Quentin Crisp, quoted by Andrew Barrow, *Quentin and Philip: A Double Portrait* (Pan, 2004), 104.
3. Crisp, *The Naked Civil Servant*, 103.
4. Ibid., 104.
5. Quentin Crisp, *Colour in Display* (Blandford Press, 1938), 7.
6. Crisp, *The Naked Civil Servant*, 105.

Chapter 8

1. Quentin Crisp, *The Naked Civil Servant* (Duckworth, 1977) 116.
2. Ibid., 152.
3. Quentin Crisp, quoted by Andrew Barrow, *Quentin and Philip: A Double Portrait* (Pan, 2004), 140.
4. Crisp, *The Naked Civil Servant*, 107.
5. Ibid., 107.
6. Quentin Crisp, *An Evening with Quentin Crisp*, 1975–1999.
7. Crisp, quoted by Barrow, *Quentin and Philip: A Double Portrait* (Pan, 2004), 135.
8. Estelle Murison, quoted by Barrow, *Quentin and Phillip*, 137.
9. Crisp, *The Naked Civil Servant*, 153–154.

Chapter 9

1. Quentin Crisp, *The Naked Civil Servant* (Duckworth, 1977), 128.
2. Ibid., 130.
3. Ibid., 131.
4. Ibid., 131.
5. Ibid., 132.
6. Ibid., 134.
7. Ibid., 138.

8. Ibid., 138.
9. Quentin Crisp, quoted by Andrew Barrow *Quentin and Philip: A Double Portrait* (Pan, 2004), 147.
10. Barrow, *Quentin and Phillip*, 147.
11. Quentin Crisp, *The Naked Civil Servant* (Duckworth, 1977), 160.
12. Crisp, quoted by Andrew Barrow, *Quentin and Phillip*, 148.
13. Maria Gabriele Steiner, quoted by Andrew Barrow, *Quentin and Phillip*, 148.
14. Crisp, *The Naked Civil Servant*, 156.
15. Ibid., 157, 158.
16. Ibid., 157.
17. Ibid., 157.
18. Ibid., 158.
19. Ibid., 159.
20. Ibid., 165.
21. Ibid., 165.
22. Ibid., 167.
23. Ibid., 169.
24. Ibid., 123.
25. George Melly, *The Stately Homo*, edited by Paul Bailey (Bantam Press, 2000), 64.
26. Ibid., 65.

Chapter 10

1. Quentin Crisp, *The Naked Civil Servant* (Duckworth, 1977), 173.
2. Ibid., 173.
3. Anne Valery, *The Stately Homo*, edited by Paul Bailey (Bantam Press, 2000), 49.
4. Crisp, *The Naked Civil Servant*, 173.
5. Quentin Crisp, quoted by Andrew Barrow, *Quentin and Philip: A Double Portrait* (Pan, 2004), 188.
6. Bernard Kops, quoted by Barrow, *Quentin and Phillip*, 189.
7. John Haggarty, quoted by Barrow, *Quentin and Phillip*, 192.
8. Ibid., 193.
9. Crisp, quoted by Barrow, *Quentin and Phillip*, 197.
10. John W. Mills, personal communication with the author, 2009.
11. Ibid.
12. Ibid.
13. Ibid.
14. Crisp, *The Naked Civil Servant*, 202.
15. Ibid., 203.
16. Ibid., 202.
17. Ibid., 202.
18. Ibid., 203.
19. Ibid., 202.

Chapter 11

1. John Haggarty, quoted by Andrew Barrow, *Quentin and Philip: A Double Portrait* (Pan, 2004), 199.
2. Bobbie Battersby, quoted by Barrow, *Quentin and Philip: A Double Portrait* (Pan, 2004), 199.
3. Quentin Crisp, *The Naked Civil Servant* (Duckworth, 1977), 174.
4. Roland Camberton, from his novel *Scamp*, 1950, quoted by Barrow, *Quentin and Phillip*, 185.
5. Crisp, *The Naked Civil Servant*, 175.
6. James Kirkup, *The Stately Homo*, edited by Paul Bailey (Bantam Press, 2000), 98.
7. Quentin Crisp, "The Declining Nude," *Little Reviews Anthology*, edited by Denys Val Baker (Methuen, 1949), 53.
8. Ibid., 54.
9. Crisp, *The Naked Civil Servant*, 180.
10. Ibid., 179.
11. Ibid., 179.
12. Ibid., 180.
13. Ibid., 181.
14. Ibid., 182.
15. Ibid., 182.
16. Ibid., 182.

Chapter 12

1. Quentin Crisp, *The Naked Civil Servant* (Duckworth, 1977), 176.
2. Ibid., 176, 177.
3. Ibid., 177.
4. Ibid., 178.
5. Ibid., 177.
6. Ibid., 184.
7. Ibid., 184.
8. Ibid., 185.
9. Ibid., 185.
10. Quentin Crisp, quoted by Andrew Barrow, *Quentin and Philip: A Double Portrait* (Pan, 2004), 207.
11. Quentin Crisp, *World in Action: Quentin Crisp*, directed by Denis Mitchell, Granada Television, 1969.
12. Crisp, *The Naked Civil Servant*, 143.
13. Ibid., 143.
14. Ibid., 144.
15. Ibid., 145.
16. Veronica Nugent, quoted by Harold Pinter, *The Stately Homo*, edited by Paul Bailey (Bantam Press, 2000), 84.
17. Hilda Lumley, quoted by Barrow, *Quentin and Phillip*, 205.

18. Crisp, quoted by Barrow, *Quentin and Phillip*, 205.
19. Crisp, *The Naked Civil Servant*, 146.
20. Ibid., 146.
21. Ibid., 144.
22. Ibid., 144.
23. Ibid., 191.
24. Ibid., 186, 187.
25. Ibid., 205.
26. Ibid., 205.
27. Ibid., 205.
28. Ibid., 206.
29. Ibid., 213, 214.

Chapter 13

1. Andrew Barrow, *Quentin and Philip: A Double Portrait* (Pan, 2004), 186.
2. Quentin Crisp, *The Naked Civil Servant* (Duckworth, 1977), 108.
3. Quentin Crisp, quoted by Barrow, *Quentin and Phillip*, 242.
4. Quentin Crisp, *How to Become a Virgin* (Fontana, 1981), 16.
5. Ibid., 16.
6. Ibid., 17.
7. Barrow, *Quentin and Phillip*, 293.
8. Crisp, *The Naked Civil Servant*, 7.
9. Ibid., 217.
10. Crisp, *How to Become a Virgin*.
11. Ibid., 84.
12. Ibid., 23.
13. Ibid., 24.
14. Ibid., 25.
15. Ibid., 26.
16. Ibid., 29.
17. Ibid., 27.
18. Ibid., 27.
19. Ibid., 28.
20. Ibid., 29.
21. John W. Mills, personal communication to the author, 2009.
22. Ibid.
23. Quentin Crisp, *How to Become a Virgin*, 33.
24. Ibid., 34.
25. Ibid., 34.
26. Quentin Crisp, *World in Action: Quentin Crisp*, directed by Denis Mitchell, Granada Television, 1969.
27. Ibid.
28. Maurice Wiggin, quoted by Barrow, *Quentin and Phillip*, 314.
29. Crisp, quoted by Barrow, *Quentin and Phillip*, 384.

Chapter 14

1. Jack Gold, quoted by Andrew Barrow, *Quentin and Philip: A Double Portrait* (Pan, 2004), 386.
2. Quentin Crisp, *How to Become a Virgin* (Fontana, 1981), 74.
3. John Hurt, quoted by Barrow, *Quentin and Phillip*, 387.
4. Crisp, *How to Become a Virgin*, 63.
5. Richard Gollner, personal communication to the author, 2010.
6. Ibid.
7. Crisp, *How to Become a Virgin*, 31.
8. Quentin Crisp, *How to Have a Lifestyle* (Cecil Woolf, 1975), 3.
9. John Hurt, quoted by Crisp, *How to Become a Virgin*, 71, 72.
10. John Hurt, quoted by Barrow, *Quentin and Phillip*, 387.
11. Crisp, *How to Become a Virgin*, 71.
12. Ibid., 72.
13. *The Naked Civil Servant* (film), 1975, introduction by Quentin Crisp.
14. Crisp, *How to Become a Virgin*, 114.
15. Ibid., 69.
16. Barrow, *Quentin and Phillip*.
17. Crisp, *How to Become a Virgin*, 67.
18. Crisp, quoted by Barrow, *Quentin and Phillip*, 388.
19. Crisp, *How to Become a Virgin*, 75.
20. Ibid., 75.
21. Nancy Banks Smith, quoted by Crisp, *How to Become a Virgin*, 81.
22. Clive James, quoted by Crisp, *How to Become a Virgin*, 81.
23. Crisp, *How to Become a Virgin*, 25.
24. Quentin Crisp, *An Evening with Quentin Crisp*, 1975–1999.
25. Ibid.
26. Ibid.
27. John Osborne, quoted by Crisp, *How to Become a Virgin*, 74.
28. Crisp, *How to Become a Virgin*, 85.
29. Ibid., 85.
30. Ibid., 89.
31. Ibid., 90.
32. Ibid., 97, 98.
33. Anne Valery, *The Stately Homo*, edited by Paul Bailey (Bantam Press, 2000), 53.
34. Crisp, *How to Become a Virgin*, 101.
35. Ibid., 102.
36. Ibid., 103.
37. John W. Mills, personal communication to the author, 2009.
38. Ibid.

39. Ibid.
40. Ibid.

Chapter 15

1. Back cover of VHS tape of *Hamlet*, Dangerous to Know Productions, 1994.
2. Ibid.
3. Ibid.
4. John W. Mills, personal communication with the author, 2009.
5. Ibid.
6. Ibid.
7. Quentin Crisp, quoted by Andrew Barrow, *Quentin and Philip: A Double Portrait* (Pan, 2004), 401.
8. Quentin Crisp, *How to Become a Virgin* (Fontana, 1981), 127.
9. Ibid., 133.
10. Ibid., 151, 152.
11. Ibid., 152.
12. Richard Gollner, personal communication to the author, 2010.
13. Ibid.
14. Crisp, *How to Become a Virgin*, 114.
15. Barrow, *Quentin and Phillip*, 419.
16. Crisp, quoted by Barrow, *Quentin and Phillip*, 419.
17. Quentin Crisp, "The Dusty Answers," edited by Phillip Ward, unpublished.
18. Elaine Stritch, quoted by Crisp, *How to Become a Virgin*, 119.
19. Harold Pinter, quoted by Barrow, *Quentin and Phillip*, 421.
20. Crisp, *How to Become a Virgin*, p. 137.
21. Ibid., 141, 142.
22. Ibid., 141.
23. Ibid., 141.
24. Ibid., 142.
25. David Hartnell, personal communication to the author, 2009.
26. Ibid.
27. Ibid.
28. Ibid.
29. Crisp, *How to Become a Virgin*, 143.
30. Ibid., 145.
31. Richard Gollner, personal communication to the author, 2010.
32. Guy Kettelhack, personal communication to the author, 2009.
33. Richard Gollner, personal communication to the author, 2010.
34. Bette Midler, quoted by Crisp, *How to Become a Virgin*, 161.
35. Crisp, *How to Become a Virgin*, 148.

36. Ibid., 149.
37. Ibid., 175.
38. Ibid., 168.
39. Ibid., 172.
40. Quentin Crisp, *Resident Alien* (Alyson Books, 1997), 7.
41. Quentin Crisp, *An Evening with Quentin Crisp*, 1975–1999.
42. Mrs. Elkins, quoted by Crisp, *How to Become a Virgin*, 188.
43. David Leddick, personal communication to the author, 2008.
44. Jeffrey Bernard, quoted by Barrow, *Quentin and Phillip*, 426, 427.
45. Back cover of *Chog* (Methuen Paperbacks, 1979).
46. Morgan Fisher, personal communication to the author, 2009.
47. Ibid.
48. Quentin Crisp, Morgan Fisher's 1980 interview, Cherry Red Records, 2007.
49. Crisp, quoted by Barrow, *Quentin and Phillip*, 427.
50. Quentin Crisp and Donald Carroll, *Doing it with Style* (Franklin Watts, 1981), 3.
51. Donald Carroll, introduction to *Resident Alien*, 2.
52. Ibid., 2.
53. Ibid., 2, 3.
54. Quentin Crisp, *An Evening with Quentin Crisp*, 1975–1999.
55. Crisp, *How to Become a Virgin*, 192.
56. Crisp, *The Naked Civil Servant*, 190.
57. Richard Gollner, personal communication to the author, 2010.

Chapter 16

1. Quentin Crisp, quoted by Andrew Barrow. *Quentin and Philip: A Double Portrait* (Pan, 2004), 429.
2. Donald Carroll, introduction to *Resident Alien* (Alyson Books, 1997), 1.
3. Crisp, *Resident Alien*, 7.
4. Ibid., 27.
5. Ibid., 27.
6. Ibid., 25
7. David Leddick, personal communication to the author.
8. Eric Bentley, *The Quentin Crisp Archives*, www.crisperanto.org.
9. Ibid.
10. Crisp, *Resident Alien*, 11.
11. Ibid., 12.
12. Guy Kettelhack, "My Mentor, Mr. Crisp," *Middlebury Magazine* (January 2001).

13. Richard Gollner, personal communication to the author, 2010.
14. Guy Kettelhack, *The Wit and Wisdom of Quentin Crisp* (Alyson Books, 1998), 11, 12.
15. Tom Steele, *The Stately Homo*, edited by Paul Bailey (Bantam Press, 2000), 184.
16. Ibid., 185.
17. Crisp, *Resident Alien*, 40.
18. Crisp, quoted by Barrow, *Quentin and Phillip*, 450.
19. Ibid., 450.
20. Quentin Crisp, *Mavis Catches up with Quentin Crisp*, interview with Mavis Nicholson, Thames Television, 1989.
21. Crisp, *Resident Alien*, 9.
22. Ibid., 9.
23. Quentin Crisp, *Wogan*, British Broadcasting Corporation, 1986.
24. Ibid.
25. Crisp, quoted by Michele Goycoolea Crawford, *The Stately Homo*, 228.
26. Donald Carroll, quoted by Barrow, *Quentin and Phillip*, 453.
27. Crisp, *Resident Alien*, 17.
28. Ibid., 17.
29. Quentin Crisp, *Manners From Heaven* (Harper and Row, 1984), back cover.
30. Crisp, quoted by Barrow, *Quentin and Phillip*, 453.
31. Barrow, *Quentin and Phillip*, 454.
32. Ibid., 381.
33. Crisp, quoted by Barrow, *Quentin and Phillip*, 455.
34. Phillip Ward, personal communication to author, 2009.
35. Ibid.
36. Quentin Crisp, *How to Go to the Movies* (St. Martin's Press, 1988), page 197.
37. Crisp, *Resident Alien*, 222.
38. Crisp, quoted by Barrow, *Quentin and Phillip*, 456.
39. Phillip Ward, personal communication to the author, 2009.
40. Crisp, *How to Go to the Movies*, 3, 4.
41. Quentin Crisp, *Quentin Crisp's Book of Quotations* (Macmillan, 1989), back cover.
42. Crisp, *Mavis Catches up with Quentin Crisp*, interview with Mavis Nicholson, Thames Television, 1989.
43. Ibid.
44. Ibid.
45. Crisp, quoted by Andrew Barrow, *Quentin and Phillip*, 459.
46. Quentin Crisp, *An Evening with Quentin Crisp*, 1975–1999.

Chapter 17

1. Quentin Crisp, *The Naked Civil Servant* (Duckworth, 1977), 202.
2. Quentin Crisp, *An Evening with Quentin Crisp*, 1975–1999.
3. Quentin Crisp, quoted by Andrew Barrow, *Quentin and Philip: A Double Portrait* (Pan, 2004), 460.
4. Ibid., 460.
5. Quentin Crisp, *Resident Alien* (Alyson Books, 1997), 30.
6. Ibid., 54.
7. Penny Arcade, personal communication to the author.
8. Ibid.
9. Crisp, *Resident Alien*, 90.
10. Ibid., 90.
11. Ibid., 96.
12. Ibid., 97, 98.
13. Ibid., 97.
14. Ibid., 116, 117.
15. Ibid., 134.
16. Ibid., 183.
17. Ibid., 59.
18. Ibid., 68.
19. Ibid., 68.
20. Ibid., 68.
21. Ibid., 68.
22. Ibid., 99.
23. Crisp, *An Evening with Quentin Crisp*, 1975–1999.
24. Crisp, *Resident Alien*, 76.
25. Ibid., 77.
26. Sally Potter, *The Stately Homo*, edited by Paul Bailey (Bantam Press, 2000), 210.
27. Ibid., 210.
28. Ibid., 212.
29. Ibid., 211–213.
30. Crisp, *Resident Alien*, 121.
31. Ibid., 121.
32. Ibid., 122.
33. Ibid., 122.
34. Ibid., 121.
35. Crisp, *An Evening with Quentin Crisp*, 1975–1999.
36. Crisp, *Resident Alien*, 147.
37. Ibid., 147.
38. Ibid., 167.
39. Ibid., 122.
40. Crisp, *The Naked Civil Servant*, 109.
41. Crisp, *Resident Alien*, 166.
42. Ibid., 166.
43. Ibid., 171.
44. Ibid., 171.
45. Ibid., 14.

46. Quentin Crisp, quoted by David-Elijah Nahmod, personal communication to the author.
47. David-Elijah Nahmod, personal communication to the author.
48. Ibid.
49. Crisp, *Resident Alien*, 191.
50. Ibid., 191.
51. Quentin Crisp, *The Alternative Queen's Speech*, a Panoptic Production for Channel 4, 1993.
52. Ibid.
53. Ibid.
54. Ibid.
55. Ibid.
56. Ibid.
57. Crisp, *Resident Alien*, 192, 193.
58. Ibid., 193.
59. Ibid., 194.
60. Ibid., 194.
61. Quentin Crisp, *The Devine Mr. Crisp*, directed by Neil Ira Needleman, 1994.
62. Quentin Crisp, *Resident Alien*, 195.
63. Penny Arcade, personal communication to the author.
64. Ibid.
65. Ibid.
66. Quentin Crisp, afterword to omnibus edition, *The Naked Civil Servant, How to Become a Virgin, Resident Alien* (Quality Paperback Book Club, 2000), 633.
67. Phillip Ward, personal communication to the author.
68. Georgina Spelvin, personal communication to the author.
69. Neil Ira Needleman, personal communication to the author.
70. Ibid.
71. Ibid.
72. Crisp, *Resident Alien*, 211.
73. Ibid., 208.
74. Ibid., 208.
75. Ibid., 209.
76. Ibid., 210.
77. Crisp, quoted by Barrow, *Quentin and Phillip*, 466.

Chapter 18

1. Phillip Ward, personal communication to the author.
2. Ibid.
3. Sara Moore, personal communication to the author.
4. Ibid.
5. Ibid.

6. Ibid.
7. Ibid.
8. Ibid.
9. Penny Arcade, personal communication to the author.
10. Donald Carroll, introduction to *Resident Alien* (Alyson Books, 1997), 3.
11. Ibid., 4.
12. Crisp, *Resident Alien*, 5.
13. Ibid., 5.
14. Ibid., 18.
15. David Whitworth, personal communication to the author.
16. Michael Andersen-Andrade, personal communication to the author.
17. Quentin Crisp, quoted by Andrew Barrow, *Quentin and Philip: A Double Portrait* (Pan, 2004), 517.
18. Crisp, *Resident Alien*, 6.
19. Quentin Crisp, quoted by Penny Arcade, personal communication to the author.
20. Quentin Crisp, quoted by Guy Kettelhack, "My Mentor, Mr. Crisp," *Middlebury Magazine* (January 2001).
21. Ibid.
22. Kettelhack, "My Mentor, Mr. Crisp."
23. Crisp, quoted by Barrow, *Quentin and Phillip*, 420.
24. Ibid., 65.
25. Ibid., 63.
26. Quentin Crisp, *Love in Tow*, Reve Entertainment and Filmwerk Media, Lisa France, director, 1999.
27. Neil Ira Needleman, personal communication to the author.
28. Ibid.
29. Ibid.
30. Barrow, *Quentin and Phillip*, 4.
31. Crisp, *Resident Alien*, 6.
32. Phillip Ward, personal communication to the author.

Chapter 19

1. L. Brandon Krall, personal communication to the author, 2010.
2. L. Brandon Krall, http://www.essential-quentinCrisp.com.
3. L. Brandon Krall, personal communication to the author, 2010.
4. Quentin Crisp, quoted by Andrew Barrow, *Quentin and Philip: A Double Portrait* (Pan, 2004), 517.
5. Quentin Crisp, afterword to omnibus edition, *The Naked Civil Servant, How to Be-*

come a Virgin, Resident Alien (Quality Paperback Book Club, 2000), 633.

6. Quentin Crisp, *The Significant Death of Quentin Crisp*, produced by Tim Fountain, Channel 4, 2002.

7. Crisp, quoted by Barrow, *Quentin and Phillip*, 518.

8. Ibid., 518.

9. Ibid., 517.

10. Phillip Ward, personal communication to the author, 2009.

11. Ibid.

12. Tim Fountain, *Quentin Crisp* (Absolute Press, 2002), 14.

13. June Lang, personal communication to the author, 2007.

14. Ibid.

15. Penny Arcade, personal communication to the author, 2010.

16. Crisp, quoted by Barrow, *Quentin and Phillip*, 521.

17. June Lang, personal communication to the author, 2007.

18. Tom Steele, personal communication to the author, 2008.

19. Phillip Ward, personal communication to the author, 2009.

20. Simon Hattenstone, *The Stately Homo*, edited by Paul Bailey (Bantam Press, 2000), 235.

21. Crisp, Quoted by Barrow, *Quentin and Phillip*, 521.

22. Ibid., 516.

23. Barrow, *Quentin and Phillip*, 516.

24. Crisp, *The Naked Civil Servant*, 213.

25. Phillip Ward, personal communication to the author, 2009.

26. Barrow, *Quentin and Phillip*, 520.

27. Ibid., 521.

28. Phillip Ward, personal communication to the author, 2009.

29. Quentin Crisp, quoted by Barrow, *Quentin and Phillip*, 522.

30. Crisp, *The Independent*, interview by David Osborne, 18 November 1999.

31. Richard Gollner, personal communication to the author, 2010.

32. David-Elijah Nahmod, personal communication to the author, 2009.

33. Phillip Ward, personal communication to the author, 2009.

34. Ibid.

35. Ibid.

36. Penny Arcade, personal communication to the author, 2009.

37. Emma Ferguson, *The Significant Death of Quentin Crisp*, produced by Tim Fountain, Channel 4, 2002.

38. Ibid.

39. Ibid.

40. Emma Ferguson, quoted by Tim Fountain, *Quentin Crisp* (Absolute Press, 2002), 168.

41. Phillip Ward, personal communication to the author, 2009.

42. Ibid.

43. Ibid.

44. Patrick Newley, quoted by Andrew Barrow, *Quentin and Phillip*, 525.

45. Ryan Levitt, quoted by Barrow, *Quentin and Phillip*, 524.

46. June Lang, personal communication to the author, 2007.

47. Quentin Crisp, *An Evening with Quentin Crisp*. 1975–1999.

48. Quentin Crisp, *Mavis Catches up with Quentin Crisp*, interview with Mavis Nicholson, Thames Television, 1989.

49. John Hurt, quoted by Barrow, *Quentin and Phillip*, 524.

50. Phillip Ward, personal communication to the author, 2009.

51. Miguel Adrover, personal communication to the author, 2009.

52. Phillip Ward, personal communication to the author, 2009.

53. Francis Ramsey, *An Evening for Quentin Crisp*, 2000.

54. Eric Bentley, *An Evening for Quentin Crisp*, 2000.

55. Penny Arcade, *An Evening for Quentin Crisp*, 2000.

56. John Hurt, *An Evening for Quentin Crisp*, 2000.

57. Quentin Crisp, afterword to omnibus edition, *The Naked Civil Servant, How to Become a Virgin, Resident Alien* (Quality Paperback Book Club, 2000), 635.

58. Quentin Crisp, *The Naked Civil Servant* (Duckworth, 1977), 217.

59. Quentin Crisp, "The Dusty Answers," edited by Phillip Ward, unpublished.

60. Sara Moore, personal communication to the author, 2009.

61. Ronald Harwood, *The Stately Homo*, edited by Paul Bailey (Bantam Press, 2000), 81.

Afterword

1. Quentin Crisp, *Mavis Catches up with Quentin Crisp*, interview with Mavis Nicholson, Thames Television, 1989.

2. Quentin Crisp, quoted by Louis Co-laianni, personal communication to the author, 2009.
3. Quentin Crisp, quoted by Andrew Barrow, *Quentin and Philip: A Double Portrait* (Pan, 2004), 522.
4. Crisp, quoted by Barrow, *Quentin and Phillip*, 517.
5. Leon Acord, personal communication to the author.
6. John Hurt, Berlin International Film Festival, 2009.
7. Karen Curlett Kelly, personal communication to the author.

Appendix 1

1. Quentin Crisp, afterword to omnibus edition, *The Naked Civil Servant, How to Become a Virgin, Resident Alien.* (Quality Paperback Book Club, 2000), 635.
2. Quentin Crisp, *An Evening with Quentin Crisp*, 1975–1999.
3. Ibid.
4. Ibid.
5. Ibid.
6. Ibid.
7. Ibid.
8. Ibid.
9. Ibid.
10. Quentin Crisp, *The Naked Civil Servant* (Duckworth, 1977).
11. Quentin Crisp, *An Evening with Quentin Crisp*, 1975–1999.
12. Quentin Crisp, quoted by Andrew Barrow, *Quentin and Philip: A Double Portrait* (Pan, 2004), 449.
13. Crisp, *An Evening with Quentin Crisp*, 1975–1999.
14. Ibid.
15. Crisp, *The Naked Civil Servant*, 8.
16. Quentin Crisp, *An Evening with Quentin Crisp*, 1975–1999.
17. Ibid.
18. Quentin Crisp, *Resident Alien* (Alyson Books, 1997), 99.
19. Quentin Crisp, *An Evening with Quentin Crisp*, 1975–1999.
20. Crisp, *Resident Alien*, 217.
21. Crisp, *An Evening with Quentin Crisp*, 1975–1999.
22. Ibid.
23. Ibid.
24. Crisp, *Resident Alien*, 124.
25. Crisp, *An Evening with Quentin Crisp*, 1975–1999.
26. Crisp, *World In Action: Quentin Crisp*, directed by Denis Mitchell, Granada Television, 1969.
27. Ibid.
28. Crisp, *The Naked Civil Servant*, 107.
29. Ibid.
30. Ibid.
31. Ibid.
32. Crisp, *The Naked Civil Servant*, 25.
33. Ibid., 8.
34. Crisp, *An Evening with Quentin Crisp*, 1975–1999.
35. Ibid.
36. Crisp, *The Naked Civil Servant*, 54.
37. Crisp, *An Evening with Quentin Crisp*, 1975–1999.
38. Crisp, *The Naked Civil Servant*, 148.
39. Crisp, *An Evening with Quentin Crisp*, 1975–1999.
40. Ibid.
41. Ibid.
42. Ibid.
43. Ibid.
44. Ibid.
45. Quentin Crisp, *Manners From Heaven* (Harper and Row, 1984), back cover.
46. Ibid.
47. Crisp, *An Evening with Quentin Crisp*, 1975–1999.
48. Crisp, *The Naked Civil Servant*, 200.
49. Crisp, *An Evening with Quentin Crisp*, 1975–1999.
50. Ibid.
51. Ibid.
52. Ibid.
53. Crisp, *The Naked Civil Servant*, 208, 209.
54. Crisp, *An Evening with Quentin Crisp*, 1975–1999.
55. Ibid.
56. Ibid.
57. Ibid.
58. Ibid.
59. Ibid.
60. Crisp, *World In Action: Quentin Crisp*, Directed by Denis Mitchell, Granada Television, 1969.
61. Crisp, *Resident Alien* (Alyson Books, 1997), 54.
62. Crisp, *The Naked Civil Servant*, 20.
63. Crisp, *An Evening with Quentin Crisp*, 1975–1999.
64. Ibid.
65. Crisp, *The Naked Civil Servant*, 53.
66. Crisp, *An Evening with Quentin Crisp*, 1975–1999.

67. Crisp, *How to Have a Lifestyle* (Cecil Woolf, 1975), 3.
68. Ibid., 3.
69. Ibid., 15.
70. Quentin Crisp, *The Wit and Wisdom of Quentin Crisp*, edited by Guy Kettelhack (Alyson Books, 1998), 160.

71. Crisp, *The Naked Civil Servant*, 181.
72. Crisp, *An Evening with Quentin Crisp*, 1975–1999.
73. Crisp, *Resident Alien*, 77.

Quentin's Books

"Quentin's great legacy is in his writing. Everyone can have a personal relationship with Quentin through his writing and I encourage you if you haven't read him to read him." — Penny Arcade, *An Evening for Quentin Crisp*, 2000

Lettering for Brush and Pen
A.F. Stuart and Quentin Crisp.
Blandford Press Ltd. 1936

Colour in Display
Quentin Crisp
Blandford Press Ltd. 1938

All This and Bevin Too
Quentin Crisp (With illustrations by
    Mervyn Peake)
Ivan Nicholson & Watson. 1943

Little Reviews Anthology
Various authors including Quentin Crisp.
    Edited by Denys Val Baker.
Methuen. 1949

The Naked Civil Servant
Quentin Crisp
Jonathan Cape. 1968.

How to Have a Lifestyle
Quentin Crisp
Cecil Woolf. 1975

Love Made Easy
Quentin Crisp
Gerald Duckworth and Co. 1977

Chog: A Gothic Fable
Quentin Crisp
Methuen. 1979

How to Become a Virgin
Quentin Crisp
Fontana. 1981

Doing It with Style
Quentin Crisp and Donald Carroll
Franklin Watts. 1981

The Wit and Wisdom of Quentin Crisp
Compiled and edited by Guy Kettelhack
Harper & Row. 1984

Manners from Heaven
Quentin Crisp
Harper & Row. 1984

How to Go to the Movies
Quentin Crisp
St. Martin's. 1988

Quentin Crisp's Book of Quotations
Quentin Crisp
Macmillan. 1989

Resident Alien
Quentin Crisp
HarperCollins. 1996

Books about Quentin

Bailey, Paul, ed. and comp. *The Stately Homo: A Celebration of the Life of Quentin Crisp*. Bantam Press, 2000.

Baker, Denys Val, ed. *Little Reviews Anthology*. Methuen, 1949.

Barrow, Andrew. *Quentin and Philip: A Double Portrait*. Macmillan, 2002.

Fountain, Tim. *Quentin Crisp*. Absolute Press, 2002.

Kettelhack, Guy, ed. and comp. *The Wit and Wisdom of Quentin Crisp*. Harper and Row, 1984.

Web Sites

Crisperanto: The Quentin Crisp Archives. www.crisperanto.org/index1.html.

Quentin Crisp Info: Dedicated to the Memory of Quentin Crisp. www.quentincrisp.info.

Index

Numbers in **bold italics** indicate pages with photographs.